Anthropology and Sexual Morality

Anthropology and Sexual Morality

A THEORETICAL INVESTIGATION

Carles Salazar

Berghahn Books
New York • Oxford

First published in 2006 by
Berghahn Books
www.berghahnbooks.com

Library of Congress Cataloging-in-Publication Data
Salazar, Carles.
Anthropology and sexual morality : a theoretical investigation /
Carles Salazar.
p. cm.
Includes index.
ISBN 1-84545-091-4 (alk. paper) -- ISBN 1-84545-092-2 (pbk.)
1. Ethnology--Papua New Guinea. 2. Ethnology--Ireland. 3. Sex
customs--Papua New Guinea. 4. Sex customs--Ireland. 5. Sexual
ethics--Papua New Guinea. 6. Sexual ethics--Ireland. 7. Papua New
Guinea--Social life and customs. 8. Ireland--Social life and customs.
I Title.

GN671.NSS25 2005
306.7'09953--dc22

2005043630

British Library Cataloguing in Publication Data
A catalogue record for this book is available from the British Library
Printed in the United States on acid-free paper

ISBN 1-84545-091-4 hardback

'When will we be open to the conviction that the definitive being of the world is neither soul nor matter, nor a determinate thing, but a perspective? God is the perspective and the hierarchy: Satan's sin was an error of perspective.'

José Ortega y Gasset

A la memòria del meu pare,
Joan Salazar i Garcia (1930–2001)

CONTENTS

ACKNOWLEDGEMENTS

All anthropologists are in debt to whom we used to call our informants. After knowing them for so many years, I cannot think of them other than as my friends from the west of Ireland. Their participation in this book is more indirect than in other of my works, but I still wish to thank them for being so patient and for teaching me so much about themselves and about life. There are also other friends from Ireland who should be mentioned here. With a research grant from the Catalan government, I spent three months of 2002 at the University of Maynooth. I am very thankful to Séamas Ó Síochiáin and to the staff of the Anthropology Department for all their help and assistance during my stay.

The following people read earlier drafts of the manuscript: Joan Bestard, Joan Frigolé, Heonik Kwon, Àngel Martínez, Enric Porqueres, Octavi Rofes and Ignasi Terradas. I am most grateful to all those who were so kind as to share their insights with me, and I remain solely responsible for mistakes and misrepresentations which may have persisted. I obtained invaluable assistance from Frances Littikhuizen, who helped me to clarify my ideas and make the book more readable. I am also grateful for the constructive comments made by an anonymous reader and, specifically, for the encouragement I have received from the publisher, Marion Berghahn, who always had confidence in this somewhat unconventional project.

Parts of chapters 6 and 9 have been published in the journal *History and Anthropology*. Permission to print is thankfully acknowledged.

And, finally, a simple thank-you cannot possibly convey my indebtedness to Núria. Her love and her constant emotional and intellectual support have kept me going for so long, I just cannot imagine what life would be like without her.

INTRODUCTION

How can the study of sexual morality be approached from an anthropological perspective? What can social anthropologists say about sexual morality that cannot be said by other social and human scientists? These are two-edged questions about an area of knowledge and about how knowledge is produced and this book is an attempt to answer these questions. I wish to develop some theoretical ideas concerning the nature of anthropological knowledge and to explore the way in which those ideas can shed light on the study of sexual morality from a specific point of view. I propose to analyse a dialectical relationship of sorts between sexual morality as an area of social-scientific knowledge and social anthropology as the means to produce that knowledge. My analysis will be constructed around a particular ethnographic study based on fieldwork done in a rural community in the west of Ireland. However, I not only wish to clarify research on sexual morality in the west of Ireland from an anthropological perspective; I also hope to throw into relief the specific contribution of an anthropological approach to the study of human behaviour.

The reader may wonder why we should emphasise the importance of a particular approach to the study of sexual morality. Should we not rather try to analyse human experience in itself, irrespective of the theoretical tools we choose for that purpose? I could answer this question in two different ways. First, I could say that I have decided to proceed in this manner simply because I was interested in researching into the nature of anthropological knowledge. Secondly, and perhaps more decisively, I believe that subjects chosen for research in the social sciences are, to a great extent at least, the product of the social-scientific disciplines that are meant to analyse them. In fact, I maintain that any kind of empirical research in the social sciences throws as much light on the particular academic discipline within which that research is being done as on the subject of research itself. In this book, I only wish to make explicit that which usually remains implicit in more empirically oriented approaches.

Precisely because of my concern with academic disciplines, I view with special interest the need to establish the limitations of knowledge, in this case, to define what can be said and what cannot be said about sexual morality from a specifically anthropological perspective. Social scientists very often suffer from a theoretical disease, which could be called cognitive imperialism. Nothing human should be foreign to us, however it presents itself. Historians, sociologists, anthropologists, psychologists, and even political scientists and political economists claim time and time again that all human phenomena can be caught in their analytical nets. The results are frequently confusing and disorientating. I do not think that everything or anything human can be studied by social anthropologists. On the contrary, only in so far as we can define the limits of what constitutes a specifically anthropological approach, or a specifically anthropological subject of research, will some form of valuable knowledge eventually emerge.

But what is specific to the anthropological approach? I will begin by looking at human sexuality as a subject of research. It may seem that the study of human sexuality from an anthropological perspective is just a narrow disciplinary whim. In fact the reverse is true. Although the origins of anthropology were marked by 'concerns and debates over the topic', as Davis and Whitten pointed out, contemporary anthropologists have generally moved away from it, and hence sexuality remains a rarely studied aspect of human experience (Davis and Whitten 1987: 69; cf. Vance 1991). I would even venture to say that the study of human sexuality has become interdisciplinary almost by definition, since none of the established academic disciplines in the field of social and human sciences – perhaps with the exception of Freudian psychoanalysis – can claim it as their own. This might have to do with human sexuality's characteristically ambiguous ontological status; it is neither strictly biological nor strictly cultural but seemingly both at the same time. (I will have more to say more about this in the following chapters.) But the problems involved in studying human sexuality do not end there. In fact, this is where the specifically anthropological problems begin.

However we may decide to categorise the interrelationships between biological and cultural aspects when defining human sexuality, there is no doubt that the social anthropology of sexuality deals essentially, if not exclusively, with its cultural aspect. Unfortunately, once we have decided that we will leave the biological aspect to natural scientists, we soon realise that a strictly cultural analysis of human sexuality does not seem to make the outline of our subject of research any clearer. 'Indeed, part of the research problem for anthropologists examining sex in non-Western societies', Kulick contends, 'is first of all deciding whether it even exists as a culturally salient domain' (1995: 7). In other words, in addition to being mystified by the biological-cum-cultural essence of the sexual, as soon as we decide to concentrate exclusively on the cultural dimension, this seems to dissolve itself as merely an ethnocentric projection of middle-class Western values and obsessions. 'If ... we look to anthropology for answers to questions about sexuality, it can indeed show us that sexuality, at least in kinship-based societies, is not a "thing in itself"' (Caplan 1987: 17).

One might wonder at this stage why in a book that attempts to be an essay on general anthropological knowledge I have decided to start from such an ambivalent, elusive and problematic topic. How can something which is not a 'thing in itself' provide the basis for anything close to a solid argument? Would it not have been better to depart from firmer anthropological grounds such as those provided by kinship theory or the interpretation of ritual symbolism? It might. But this is precisely the reason why I have chosen so indefinite a point of departure: 'all discourses about sexuality are inherently discourses about something else; sexuality, rather than serving as a constant thread that unifies the totality of human experience, is the ultimate dependent variable, requiring explanation more often than it provides explanation' (Simon 1996: xvii). Taking everything that has been said so far into consideration, I would argue that the social anthropology of sexuality, because it is nearly always the social anthropology of something else, offers a most apposite theme for an essay whose purpose is to look at different aspects of anthropological thought and research. In sexuality, 'as we peel off each layer (economics, politics, families, etc.), we may think that we are approaching the kernel, but we eventually discover that the whole is the only "essence". Sexuality cannot be abstracted from its surrounding social layers' (Ross and Rapp 1981: 54). It is the layers that surround a non-existing kernel that I will be looking at in the following pages.

As Ortner and Whitehead feared concerning their book on sexual meanings, the reader might end up wondering 'where is the sex' (Ortner and Whitehead 1981: 24–25). This question can hardly be pertinent to the present essay, if for somewhat different reasons. My concern is not with the erotic but with the institutions and regulations that surround human sexuality in a particular context. Thus some might call the anthropological view of human sexuality I hope to develop a 'deconstructive analysis', a gradual peeling off of several social and cultural layers with no intention of approaching the essence. It is the nature of anthropological knowledge I am concerned with, and this is what will constitute the central target of my investigation. Be that as it may, I must rush to add that sexuality in this essay is not a mere rhetorical device to talk about the presumably more substantial topics of economics, politics and the like. As was once said about the anthropology of kinship, sexuality in this book is not a mere idiom; in the end I hope to have said something substantive about the cultural construction, or deconstruction, of human sexuality.

Now the institutions and regulations that surround human sexuality are what I call 'sexual morality'. Seemingly, but only apparently, we have made the purpose of our investigation a bit more concrete, because in actual fact sexual morality is as much an elusive and ambivalent research object as human sexual behaviour. The sexual morality I am interested in does not consist of a set of explicit rules. On the contrary, much of what will be analysed in this book under this concept can only be indirectly inferred from the existence of other institutions whose manifest concern does not seem to be the regulation of human sexual behaviour as such. Thus sexual morality is largely an analytical construct. Let me insist on this point: I am not saying that the people we will meet in the ensuing chapters do not have any moral values that rule their sexual life, I am simply arguing that those moral values do not normally present themselves as an explicitly sexual morality. The issue is then: why do we have to interpret as sexual morality what does not present itself as such? This is the key question that will enable us to identify the characteristics of a specifically anthropological approach.

I have said before that, perhaps with the exception of psychoanalysis, none of the human sciences can claim human sexuality as their specific research object. Practically the same could be said as regards sexual morality. It is necessary to say a few words concerning the way in which I have decided to engage with Freudian psychoanalysis in this essay. There are two aspects in particular of Freud's work that I wish to highlight. First, there is Freud's commitment to scientific research. At a time when so many and so virulent attacks against the alleged scientific status of anthropology, and even the social sciences on the whole, are being levelled, it is certainly refreshing to probe into the intellectual project of a man who felt science as a vocation, even as a moral principle and duty. Next, I am similarly intrigued and fascinated by Freud's capacity to combine the physicality of human biology, of the biological study of the human body, with a hermeneutical analysis of the human subject in what is meant to be a general theory of human behaviour. Despite all the criticisms that this unseemly articulation has received from several quarters, I believe there is something unique in it that deserves careful consideration.

My admiration for Freud's work is not paralleled by a commitment to any of the branches of the so-called psychological or psychoanalytical anthropology. Specific examples of psychologically oriented ethnographies will be critically assessed in this essay. Furthermore, I believe that the anthropological perspective on human sexuality and sexual morality I espouse is, in many respects, at the antipodes of psychoanalysis and of Freud's thought. It is not the affinity but the contrast that I wish to emphasise. And it is precisely through this contrast that I hope to clarify the contours of my own approach.

The notion of contrast plays a very prominent role in what follows. Not only with psychoanalysis, for the concatenation of several contrasts, dichotomies, binary oppositions perhaps, provides the rhetorical tools I need to unfold my theoretical propositions. A cursory view of these contrasts will serve as a presentation of the structure of this book. The first is an ethnographic one. All the ethnographic and historical information I use in my analysis comes, directly or indirectly, from fieldwork done in a rural parish of western Ireland. But the book begins with a presentation of Gilbert Herdt's studies of ritualised homosexual behaviour in Papua New Guinea. The ethnographic contrast is multi-stranded. Melanesian societies are perhaps the most culturally distant societies we can find from the rural communities of the west of Ireland. Furthermore, the sexual behaviour analysed in Herdt's ethnography, ritual fellatio, is in all appearances a sexual practice radically alien to the sexual customs of

my Irish informants. And, finally, Herdt's specific interest in the
ethnography of the erotic appears also fairly distant from my
concern with sexual morality. Cultural distance is a precondition of
anthropological knowledge, even though, as I will argue in this essay,
it cannot be taken for granted. Cultural distance is not an absolute
category but is relative (obviously enough, it seems to me) to the
subjects who participate in the ethnographic encounter and to the
specific object of the anthropological research. Now underlying all
the patent dissimilarities between the culture of sexuality analysed in
Herdt's work and my ethnography of sexual morality in an Irish rural
Catholic community there is an interesting, if highly polemical,
common thread. Both societies have been defined, by Herdt in one
case and by several social scientists and commentators in the other,
as 'repressive' societies as regards their sexual mores. They both
seem to constitute the perfect apt illustrations of Freud's theory of
sexual morality. That is the reason why in chapter 1 I have decided
to use Herdt's work on ritualised homosexuality in Papua New
Guinea as an introduction to Freud's thought. Thus we go from
ethnographic contrast to theoretical contrast.

As I have pointed out, in this book Freudian psychoanalysis will
be recurrently used as a foil to my own approach. In chapter 2 there
is a short presentation of the part of Freud's theory specifically
relevant to my argument: the role that he attributed to 'cultural
constrains' in the configuration of adult sexuality in what he
understood as a 'civilised' society. A similar move is undertaken in
chapter 3, this time in relation to the other author whose theories I
also wish to discuss: Michel Foucault. The bearing of Foucault's
work on my analysis is different from Freud's. Foucault deliberately
erected his theory on human sexuality as the polar opposite to
Freud's perspective – what he termed 'the repressive hypothesis'.
Thus it comes as no surprise that my affinities in this respect run
closer to the Foucauldian approach, specifically in what concerns
the historical understanding of the Western sexual theories and
moral ideologies he proposed. Be that as it may, I make no attempt
at introducing the whole of Foucault's theoretical and philosophical
project. My purpose is merely to situate his *History of Sexuality*
within the context of what to my mind constitutes his methodology
for the analysis of cultural and historical formations. I will use some
of Foucault's insights to interpret my own material and to articulate
several parts of my argument. This is particularly clear in chapter 8,

where I discuss the relationship between culture and power, and in chapter 9, which posits a systematisation of the history of Irish sexual morality into what I term 'disciplinary regimes'. As will become apparent throughout this essay, however, there are also important aspects of Foucault's perspective which I do not follow. This is partially expounded in chapters 3 and 11.

My aim with this presentation of Freud's and Foucault's thought is to delimit the theoretical space within which my analysis of sexual morality in rural Ireland will proceed. It is the contrast between these two approaches to the study of human sexuality that I wish to emphasise rather than their theoretical legitimacy in itself. But there are more theoretical contrasts in the following chapters. In part II, I undertake the analysis of my Irish material, which begins in chapter 4 with a discussion of the traditional way in which the history of Irish sexual morality has been interpreted. These traditional arguments can be properly defined as 'functionalist' or 'structural-functionalist' arguments in the anthropological sense of these words. I wish to underline the merits and the limitations of this theoretical paradigm or paradigms in anthropology, and critique it in the chapter that follows. My aim is to show that the emergence of a particular sexual morality and ideology in Ireland cannot be reduced to its social and economic conditions of possibility, which is what the functionalist arguments claim to be able to demonstrate. To clarify my point, I introduce in chapter 6 an assessment of the incidence of so-called 'cultural factors' in explaining Irish demographic history. We can see in this analysis an attempt at delimiting the culture concept this time by reference to another conceptual dichotomy, that between structure and event. Culture originates in certain social and economic conditions but its interpretation cannot be reduced to those social and economic conditions, in the same way as culture is the product of a historical process without being in itself 'historical'.

The complex relationship between culture and history, another way of talking about the structure/event opposition, is explored from two complementary angles. Up to chapter 6 the discussion focuses on the ways in which culture can be said to explain history, to explain the production of particular events. In chapter 7, I consider the opposite, namely, how history can account for the constitution of a cultural form. The key question in all this discussion is the question of power, the power we attribute to cultural forms to mould human behaviour. What is the power of culture to determine the production of particular actions, what does it mean to say that culture 'explains' this or that act, this or that event? Chapter 8 deals with the theoretical analysis of power from what I define as an anthropological perspective. Finally, in chapter 9 the history of sexual morality in Ireland is reinterpreted in the light of that theoretical analysis. Chapter 9 concludes the examination of the Irish case-study; further references to this material will crop up here and there in the chapters that follow, but my concern is from then onwards to proceed on a more abstract level.

Part III has the nature of anthropological knowledge as its main theme. Several theoretical points or theoretical problems that have emerged in the former account will be reconsidered and re-argued, taking into account that it is the subject-matter of anthropology, the anthropological perspective on human affairs, that I wish to examine. Thus part III begins in chapter 10 with a 'clarification' of the culture concept. I say clarification because I do not intend to put forward any new formulation of this controversial concept. In a way, the whole book can be considered as a protracted reflection on the culture concept – to my mind, that is what an anthropological perspective amounts to. Clarification means simply the identification of the key elements that should be taken into account while thinking about culture in anthropological terms. Culture is a bit like language, I argue in that chapter, it tells us how to say things but it does not tell us what to say. But, again, it is the contrasts that I wish to highlight – together with the analogies. The difference between culture and language lies in the concept of intersubjectivity, to be discussed in chapter 11. Intersubjectivity is inherent to the culture concept as it is to anthropological knowledge. And intersubjectivity leads us to the problem of subjectification and to the last concept to be discussed in the concluding chapter of this essay: the concept of interpretation. In this way, my critique of the psychoanalytic approach is somehow resumed. As far as the study of human sexuality is concerned, interpretation in both psychoanalysis and anthropology seems to be interested in uncovering some sort of sexual meaning, or sexual 'truth', behind non-sexual appearances. But there is an important difference between the two perspectives that turns the anthropological project into the theoretical opposite of psychoanalysis. I hope to be able to convey clearly the sense of this crucial difference.

This is an essay on interpretative social science specifically concerned with drawing the limits of its object of knowledge. The theoretical field that makes interpretation possible in social anthropology will be constituted by means of a non-essentialist, 'perspectivist' concept of culture. What looks like culture from one point of view is no longer culture from another point of view. But it is precisely in this shifting viewpoint that anthropological knowledge originates.

A last point related to my Irish material should receive brief notice now. There is both first-hand and second-hand information, historical and ethnographic. All historical information has been obtained from secondary sources, whereas a substantial part of the ethnography comes from the fieldwork I have been doing in a rural Catholic parish of western Ireland since 1990. My informants are mainly middle-aged men and women, most of them married, in their forties and fifties, sometimes older. The majority of men are middle-sized, full-time or part-time farmers and factory workers; most of the women are housewives, helping their husbands on the farm and a few of them with off-farm jobs. Primary education is widespread amongst both men and women, and a few women but fewer men have gone to secondary school. The community lies on good farm land, even though for the last ten years several families have been giving up farming altogether. Those with off-farm jobs normally commute to the nearest town, only ten miles away. Tourism is practically non-existent. The reader can consult my monograph (Salazar 1996) for further data on this community.

In keeping with ethnographic research, I make no claims to any general applicability of my findings beyond the people I met. Even though I do not think that my data are in any way unique, nothing of what I will say, particularly in the more ethnographic chapters, is meant to be by any means representative of Irish society, not even of the rural society of western Ireland. Ethnography is valid as long as it is meaningful, not as long as it is typical or has general applicability. It is true, on the other hand, that to interpret and to complement my ethnographic material I will use historical and demographic information that presumably represents the whole of Ireland. But this should not be taken as a proof, let me stress this point, that the ethnography that this information complements or helps to interpret is similarly representative of the whole Irish society. Ireland is a complex society in a double sense. First, as is the case in the majority of modern nation-states, Ireland is a heterogeneous conglomerate of ways of life, many of them with very little in common apart from sharing some politically bounded territory. Secondly, again, as in the majority of modern complex societies, Irish society has been studied from the viewpoint of a host of different academic fields in the social sciences, each one providing its own image out of its own particular set of data. The research tools of social anthropology are utterly inappropriate to producing general statements concerning such a vast and complex unit, not only because of its inherent size and complexity, but also because such statements would be meaningless in the face of the more quantitative and statistically informed facts that can be supplied by other disciplines.

At any rate, in this book I have very little interest in delivering general 'truths' concerning the Irish or any other national groups, even though I believe that much of what I will say in my ethnography will resonate with those who are familiar with Irish rural society and several other rural societies in Europe. But the main objective of this book is theoretical and can be formulated in the following way, in very simple terms: what do we mean when we say that the culture concept is needed to understand human behaviour? This may be a burning issue, perhaps, for contemporary social sciences but, without a doubt, it is the most elementary and perennial question for social anthropology. What follows is an invitation to look at and to think about a particular human phenomenon in a certain way. I would like to introduce my essay as an invitation to social anthropology, to the practice of anthropological research and, eventually, to anthropological thought. I firmly believe that social anthropology is a 'mode of thought', a distinctive way of reflecting upon human experience. Nothing better than a concrete investigation can show the way in which this mode of thought proceeds.

PART I

Approaches to Human Sexuality

CHAPTER 1

Sex in the Highlands of Papua New Guinea

Let me begin by taking the reader on a short journey to the highlands of Papua New Guinea. I believe that anyone interested in the cultural construction of sexuality will find in Gilbert Herdt's research on ritualised homosexual behaviour in Menalesia a unique point of departure (Herdt 1984a, b, 1993, 1994, 1999a, b). Exoticism and radical alterity combine with excellent ethnographic detail in the description of a form of sexual life that could not be more at odds with Western beliefs and attitudes. Herdt did his ethnography among the Sambia, a pseudonym for a New Guinean community of the eastern highlands. As has been observed in some other Melanesian societies, the Sambia practise a form of ritualised homosexual behaviour that consists in the fellatio of men and older youths by young boys during initiation. The Sambia believe that through oral insemination boys get the strength and power (*jerungdu*) that turns them into men, warriors, capable of engaging in the warfare activities that were very common not so long ago. Semen is thus a highly prized resource that men should administer with the utmost care. They obtain this treasured good from their elders and they should hand it over to the younger boys so that they can all share of its miraculous power. Women are also entitled to a portion of men's semen, which they will acquire from their husbands first by oral insemination and eventually through vaginal copulation. With men's semen women can become pregnant and feed their offspring with their breast milk, which is believed to be a sort of semen by-product.

The most elementary and simple description of the Sambia system of beliefs would lead us to conclude that their sexual practices have very little in common with sexuality as is ordinarily understood in the West. In point of fact, one could even rightfully wonder to what extent fellatio among the Sambia is, properly speaking, a sexual act. In all appearances, we are confronted with a form of behaviour semantically closer to our notions of feeding or nourishing, for instance, than anything remotely related to sexual love and erotism. If we define Sambia fellatio as a form of sexual or erotic behaviour, are we not unduly projecting our own notion of sexuality onto a way of life that has nothing, or very little, to do with it? How can we cover with the same term – sexuality – behaviours, attitudes and beliefs that are so overtly dissimilar? Could not this be taken as a proof that sexuality, from a cross-cultural point of view at least, is not a 'thing in itself'? It is no more than a mere biological given with no inherent cultural significance, a biological given that our sex-ridden culture has essentialised into a supreme value, so that we can morally evaluate alien societies according to their degree of sexual 'freedom' or sexual 'repression', for instance. In other words, this is just another instance of Western cognitive imperialism, so characteristic of erstwhile anthropological theories and current non-anthropological views of non-Western societies. But modern anthropology, with its relativistic conceptual weaponry, can help us rid ourselves of our deeply embedded ethnocentric prejudices: what is sexual for us, the relativistic anthropologist will resolutely show us, is non-sexual for them, what is 'effeminate' for us is masculine for them, etc.

But all this, interestingly enough, differs quite sharply from Herdt's own interpretation. It would have been 'too easy', he disparagingly asserts, to put forward such an ordinary relativistic view and conclude that Sambia behaviour is somehow unique (Herdt and Stoller 1990: 361–62). Far from it: one of the key points in Herdt's argument is to demonstrate that Sambia ritualised homosexuality is, first of all, a sexual behaviour, that is, a form of behaviour that has to be understood, to some extent at least, with the same concepts as we understand our own sexuality. So there is nothing 'unique' in it. Thus his main concern is to show that, despite Sambia discourse about the nourishing qualities of semen, the reasons for which they practisce oral insemination are definitely erotic; that is, Sambia fellatio is a homoerotic activity.

In homoerotic activity, men offer boys the normative goal that semen 'grows' them. But from the donor's standpoint, although initiates' growth does provide vicarious (because of homosexual promiscuity) long-term confirmation of the fellated's manhood, a fellator's growth is not of direct importance to a bachelor's personhood [the fellated]. Rather, homoerotic play takes precedence as the fellated's motive; the boy's growth is a latent social function of the bachelor's behavior (and is, I think, largely a rationalization on the men's part). (Herdt 1984b: 183)

Hence the Sambia belief that men have to feed boys with their semen in order to make them grow is just a secondary rationalisation, a kind of ideological screen that hides the real homoerotic meaning of this behaviour. Now the question this poses is, if this is really erotism, what is the purpose of the ideological screening? Why is it that the Sambia do not openly recognise the erotic nature of their homosexual behaviour? Herdt resorts to an interesting blend of political economy and psychoanalysis to make Sambia behaviour intelligible to Western minds. His politico-economic approach provides us with a picture of Sambia society in which semen appears as the key strategic resource. The control of semen transactions thus becomes becomes the mechanism by which adult men, the owners of this crucial 'commodity', exercise their power over the rest of the society. What the whole circulation of semen, between men and boys and between men and women, sustains is a rigid and severe male power structure. In other societies the key strategic resources may be material goods, means of production, weapons, women, whatever; among the Sambia, it is semen. Commodity fetishism in capitalism would correspond to a sort of 'semen fetishism' among the Sambia, which would have produced a genuine form of false consciousness: the belief in semen's superlative nourishing qualities. I refer the reader to Herdt's excellent paper on semen transactions in Sambia culture (1984b) for details of his well-constructed argument. And yet he does not seem to be fully satisfied with his own of politico-economic explanation: 'this view does not explain ritualized homosexuality among the Sambia; it merely elucidates the phenomenon in broader terms. For to seek causes, not just of the sociocultural system of values, but of individual acts of homosexual behavior, we should have to examine its individual subjectivity and development context, according them an analytic role I have here ignored' (Herdt 1984b: 204).

A more psychoanalytic-oriented approach may complement or make up for the limitations of political economy. But before going into it let us try to find out what makes Herdt so unhappy with political economy. Why is 'to seek causes of the sociocultural system' not enough to provide a satisfactory explanation for Sambia sexual customs? Obviously, I can only speculate regarding Herdt's internal motives for choosing this particular approach over another. Whatever his motives, I suspect there is some theoretical input here. Herdt is probably not fully comfortable with political economy because from this point of view Sambia fellatio entirely loses its sexual meaning; that is, its sexual meaning becomes totally irrelevant for explanatory purposes. It all boils down to a power system. It makes little difference if this system compels individuals to a form of behaviour that greatly resembles sexual behaviour, because ultimately it is the power tricks that we are interested in. We are aiming at the inner substance of power, not its external form. Hence the form this power assumes, in this or that particular society, recedes endlessly into a background of contingent, accidental or historical information. One could substitute the word 'culture' for the 'contingent, accidental and historical' and we have a faithful portrait of a mode of thought in social anthropology quite fashionable in certain quarters, especially a few years ago. This is a mode of thought in which social anthropology becomes the younger sister of a master discipline, and the aim of social anthropology is to show how the dreadful things that the master discipline has painfully and courageously denounced in our own society happen as well in so many distant places.

I shall have to say more about power, power and culture, in a later chapter, but now let us move on to the psychoanalytic side of Herdt's approach. He is not fully happy with the politico-economic interpretation of Sambia sexual conduct and insinuates the need for a different kind of explanation, for in that interpretation the sexual nature of Sambia behaviour becomes somehow secondary to the main argument, and Herdt wants to give the sexual and the erotic a prominent role. But, alas, this sexual nature is just barely apparent. In their external discourse, the Sambia insist on the need to feed young boys with semen in order to grow them into adult men. There must be a way of digging up sexual desire out of these layers of ideological debris, and this is the sort of job for which psychoanalysis is particularly handy. So much so that Herdt decided to work with the help of a professional psychiatrist–psychoanalyst, Robert J. Stoller, in order better to be able to extricate the hidden and, seemingly, deeply repressed sexual meanings of Sambia culture. The result was a collection of 'clinical' interviews with several Sambia men, and one woman, published under the title of *Intimate Communications* (Herdt and Stoller 1990). I call them 'clinical' interviews because this is what Herdt himself explicitly calls his ethnographic method: 'clinical ethnography'.

Clinical ethnography is not the result of psychoanalysing informants. Herdt is adamant that his method should not be confused with plain psychoanalytic practice. The analyst is primarily concerned with the patient's private feelings and practices, whereas the ethnographer 'is concerned mainly to use these as a way to better understand what shapes cultural institutions and public behavior' (Herdt and Stoller 1990: 378). But there is something which places Herdt's clinical ethnography very close indeed to ordinary psychoanalysis: both are interested, specifically interested, in uncovering some form of hidden truth.[1] To this effect, both share a common perspective that originates in what Ricoeur called the 'hermeneutics of suspicion' (Ricoeur 1970: 32–36). Appearances are deceptive, their truth lies elsewhere. Thus, while reflecting on the differences between traditional (non-clinical) ethnographers and psychoanalysts, Herdt observes: 'where the ethnographer is satisfied – with appearance, with the outward form of the behavior – the trained clinician (when competent) is not' (Herdt and Stoller 1990: 338). This is what traditional ethnographers should learn from trained clinicians in order to turn their conventional unsophisticated research into clinical ethnographies. 'The mystery of the world is the relationship between the visible and the invisible, of cultural disguises and underlying subjectivity. And of that we anthropologists have much to learn' (Herdt 1994: 63). Furthermore, Herdt understands that this confusion between appearances and reality is particularly characteristic of much contemporary cultural analysis and what he terms 'socio-centric social sciences' (Herdt and Stoller 1990: 24). They all fall victims of deceptive looks, of external fashion, and they all believe to be the case what only appears to be the case.

As Ricoeur points out, this hermeneutics of suspicion is not an exclusive invention of Freudian psychoanalysis but it is also shared by the two other 'masters of suspicion' of modern Western thought:

Marx and Nietzsche. Indeed, we can go so far as to say that some form of 'suspicion' is common to all scientific research. Nothing could be more agreed upon than the definition of science as an ongoing quest to go beyond the appearances. Hence, it is not so much this hermeneutics of suspicion that makes Herdt's proposal akin to psychoanalysis, but rather the location of the hidden truth to be uncovered and the means by which this uncovering takes place. In his view, what the 'cultural disguises' hide is the 'underlying subjectivity'; it is this underlying subjectivity that will provide the ultimate reality for the all too apparent cultural constructs. Notice that Herdt had already uncovered a somewhat hidden truth with his politico-economic interpretation of Sambia ritualised homosexuality: the power structure that sustains men's domination of Sambia society. He could have been just as pleased by showing that behind Sambia semen ideology – the 'cultural disguises' – lies a system of power, domination, exploitation, etc., as a conventional Marxist argument would call it. But he was not fully satisfied with it because that did not 'explain ritualised homosexuality among the Sambia'. Stated otherwise, it was too apparent a truth, not hidden enough, while the real thing must lie somewhere deeper; hence the need to resort to subjectivity.

Herdt's notion of subjectivity is not the same as Freud's concept of the unconscious. He is very much aware of the gross simplifications that the uncritical use of the psychoanalytic method has given rise to among psychologically oriented anthropologists in the past (Herdt and Stoller 1990: 362–63). Herdt claims that his concept of subjectivity does not stem from the individual's psyche but is part of a culture and, therefore, should be part and parcel of the anthropologist's object of analysis. Yet it seems that anthropology is unable to reach this portion of a culture (only) through its conventional method: thick description based upon deep participant observation. It is by means of 'clinical interviews' that we can produce an ethnography of subjectivity.

But what is a 'clinical interview'? Interviews are a commonly accepted research technique in anthropology, particularly when they are complemented by, or rather subordinated to, the information obtained through participant observation. In this, the clinical interviews carried out by Herdt and Stoller certainly appear very 'anthropological'. But there is something that, in my view, makes them differ substantially from customary ethnographic interviews.

This is precisely the fact that they have a very clear aim: to make explicit the interviewee's erotic feelings in a context in which sex talk is conspicuously absent from everyday interaction. This is the 'hidden truth' of Herdt's concept of subjectivity, the hidden truth that the examination of the individual subjectivity of homosexual behaviour is meant to disclose.

Our next step will be to find out why the sexual and the erotic happen to be a 'hidden truth' in Sambia society. Herdt's views are based on the assumption that erotism is a human universal. 'Do ethnographers need a Freud', he asks himself rhetorically, 'to tell them children and adults have erotic lives and that erotism drives and shapes culture and experience besides New York and Kiriwina?' (Herdt and Stoller 1990: 419 n.14). Once we accept that erotism must exist in all kinds of societies, we ought to explain why in some societies it is culturally explicit – an 'open' truth – while in others it lies deeply buried in individual subjectivity under a myriad of cultural cloaks. Clearly, my earlier allusion to the founder of psychoanalysis is not in vain. What happens in societies like the Sambia where sex and the erotic do not seem to be culturally salient is that they are repressive societies: 'I argue against Foucault that the repressive hypothesis is an historical fact in Sambia and that its power stems from a psycho-social process of social control mechanisms and individual repression in people's lives' (Herdt 1993: 194).

Repression and its counterpart – 'resistance' – become powerful explanatory tools in Herdt's argument. Repression exists in Sambia society and this accounts for the fact that sex talk is absent in everyday interaction. It also explains why people are often reluctant to talk about their erotic feelings: they 'resist' (see Herdt and Stoller 1990: 288–89, 291–92). Now repression, in Freudian theory, does not lead to the suppression of sexual desire but to its storage in the unconscious and its eventual manifestation either in neurotic symptoms or in a sublimated form. This is what has been rightly called the 'hydraulic' theory of sexuality: if you press it here it must come out somewhere else. Herdt understands that the very rigid sexual hierarchy and sexual segregation, the strong taboos that surround anything that has to do with sexuality and the erotic and, specifically, the secret character of men's homosexual activities all validate the conclusion that Sambia society is a repressive society. Hence his very explicit criticism of Foucault's theory about the repressive hypothesis. For Herdt, the repressive hypothesis is not a mere hypothesis, it is a fact, a plain and undeniable fact, in Sambia society.

But, if sexual desire is so severely repressed among the Sambia, what are the 'neurotic symptoms' or the sublimated forms into which it has been converted? Herdt never states explicitly and openly that ritualised homosexuality should be so defined, but he comes very close to it. While referring to Melanesian societies in general he makes the following comment: 'Sexual segregation must be counted as a key contributing factor to the institutionalization of homosexuality. When residential segregation is added to sexual restrictiveness and socio-economic polarity, homosexual activity as an acceptable sexual outlet seems likely' (Herdt 1984a: 69). From here comes Herdt's insistence on the separation between homosexual behaviour and homosexual identity (Herdt 1994: 319): the Sambia behave homosexually but they are not homosexuals, they behave in this way because they have no other choice due to the repressive nature of their society. He even suggests that, were it not for this repression, ritual homosexuality would probably disappear (Herdt 1984b: 206).[2] This is simply a logical consequence of the preceding argument: given the explanatory power for ritual homosexuality that Herdt has conferred upon repression, the disappearance of this latter can only lead to the disappearance of the former. But not only is homosexual behaviour the result of repression. Somewhat unexpectedly, Herdt comes up with the radical conclusion that even Sambia male adult heterosexual practices are also a consequence of the particular repressive nature of Sambia society: 'It is only because of sexual antagonism – social regulation – that Sambia males are normatively able to perform as competent heterosexual adults, within the rigid parameters of their gender hierarchy' (1993: 204). This is a bit like saying that, once the dam doors have been opened, the force of the falling water should be explained as a consequence of the very fact that it had been enclosed.

I shall try to expound the underlying conception of human sexuality that supports Herdt's ethnographic researches. We have seen how repression, resistance and a 'clinical' ethnographic methodology are the main characteristics of his approach. Repression is the main constituent of Sambia society and accounts for all the apparent characteristics of its (male) inhabitants' sexual conduct, both homosexual and heterosexual. Resistance is an immediate consequence of repression, it is what explains Sambia sex-avoiding attitude: because they are repressed, they resist sex and thus they avoid sex talk. Finally, clinical ethnography is the method by which resistance may be successfully vanquished and the repressed erotic motivation of Sambia behaviour can be disclosed; namely, it is the method by which we can eventually reach the hidden sexual 'truth' of Sambia society. For Herdt, sexual desire is an ever-present and almighty force, an energy of sorts that exists in all human societies and that 'drives and shapes culture and experience' everywhere. I am deliberately using the hazy words 'force' and 'energy' because this very obscurity as to the actual nature of sexuality is inherent to in this argument. The only clear conclusion to be drawn is that sexuality, due to its universal presence, must be, or must have its origins in, something pre-cultural or simply non-cultural. In order to gain some further insight, it will be helpful to dwell briefly upon the theoretical roots of this type of analysis.

Notes

1. In his later writings, Herdt has been mildly self-critical regarding his earlier psychoanalytic perspective (Herdt 1999a: 7, 12), but he still insists on the cross-cultural nature of the erotic, and this is precisely the reason why he finds cultural relativism unacceptable.
2. The same argument was put forward by Freud in order to account for the increase of 'homosexual means of gratification' in contemporary and, in his view, highly repressed, societies: 'in addition to all those who are homosexuals in virtue of their organization, or who become so in their childhood, there must be reckoned the great number of those in whom, in their maturer years, a blocking of the main stream of their libido has caused a widening in the side-channel of homosexuality' (1959: 200–201). In a similar vein, Malinowski (2001: 74–75) understands that it is precisely the absence of sexual repression in the Trobriands that explainsed the rarity of homosexual practices.

CHAPTER 2

Freud and the Repressive Hypothesis

'You must not forget', Freud warned us in the first delivery of his 'Introductory Lectures on Psycho-Analysis', 'that at the moment we are not in possession of any generally recognized criterion of the sexual nature of a process' (Freud 1963: 320). This was written between 1916 and 1917, more than ten years after the publication of his celebrated 'Three Essays on the Theory of Sexuality'. Freud always believed that the real nature of sexuality would some day be discovered. For him it was very clear that sexuality, like any other human phenomenon, had an objective existence that would become apparent to scientists sooner or later. The real nature of sexuality is to be found in the complex biochemical processes in which sexual desire originates. Nothing of that was known at the time, but this did not deter Freud from carrying out his research, since he was positively sure that, once the mystery of human sexuality had been unveiled, all his theories would be finally and irrefutably confirmed. Obviously, it never occurred to him that his own approach to the study of sexuality might ultimately be responsible for the existence of the very object he so eagerly wished to be discovered.

Now whether sexuality exists 'out there' or is just an external projection of our own mental constructs is not merely an old philosophical riddle. A great deal of what I shall argue in this essay hinges on the way we approach the duality between sex as a biological given and sex as a cultural form. What I wish to do in the following pages is to undertake an 'ethnographic' enquiry into Freud's thought, similar to what I have just done with Herdt's.

I want to account for Freud's belief system regarding sexuality in the same way as any ordinary anthropologist attempts to make sense of his or her informants' beliefs and behaviour, in the same way Herdt himself tried to uncover Sambia sexual theories, but, to my mind, with an important difference. Unlike the Sambia, Freud had a very explicit view on human sexuality. My aim is to show how both Herdt's and Freud's perspectives amount to a particular conception of human sexuality and, consequently, of the role played by culture in its final concretisation. In other words, they amount to a particular conception of what culture is all about in its relation to one of its more impervious limits: the biological nature of human beings.

Allow me to introduce a short excursus in order to expand a bit on this notion of limits. It might come as a surprise to contend that sexuality sets up the limits of culture, for it is normally assumed that it works the other way round. The central point of my thesis is to defend precisely this apparent inconsistency. I will argue extensively against the Freudian notion of an inborn and limitless, polymorphously perverse, sexual desire progressively shaped by culturally induced repressions. My point will be that, whatever usefulness this notion might have from a psychoanalytical perspective, it is anthropologically unsound. A critique of the Freudian thesis, however, does not lead naturally to its very opposite. In what way can it be said that sexuality places a limit on the idea of culture? It is hardly questionable that social anthropology needs a 'limited' concept of culture. This is so because, from an ontological point of view, culture definitely appears as a limitless notion. If under this concept we see a system of meanings that makes the world intelligible for us, we can barely imagine anything falling outside it. As the commonplace Wittgensteinian paraphrase would have it: 'The limits of my culture are the limits of my world.' But this is, I insist, an ontological, pre-scientific, notion. It is pre-scientific because what is reputed to be a science of culture cannot, for obvious reasons, take the world as its object of knowledge. So we must draw some limits if we wish to make the concept of culture epistemologically operative. But how can we do that? The problem for anthropology is that those limits do not exist in a definitive and immobile way. Each ethnographic object has its own cultural limits, so to speak. Thus the idea that sexuality can in any way set a limit on culture is actually as theoretically arbitrary as any other idea. But this is just the sort of arbitrariness I am planning to develop.

The arbitrary is not equivalent to the absurd. There are reasons that might justify why sexuality is particularly appropriate when considering the limits of culture. Western ethnoscience, like Freudian psychoanalysis, clearly views sexual desire as originating in the biological constitution of human beings. This means that any approach to sexuality from the point of view of social anthropology has to come to terms with the idea that its object is endlessly overstepping the limits of its own knowledgeability. Stated otherwise, a cultural analysis of sexuality must draw the limits of its epistemological object very explicitly precisely because that object is not ontologically present as an exclusively cultural object. Take, for instance, as a counter-example, the social anthropology of art. There is no need to explicitly draw the limits of art as a cultural object of knowledge because there is no way we can think of art as anything other than a cultural object. The ontological and epistemological limits of art happily coincide. This is precisely not the case with sexuality. The paradox, or apparent paradox, is that, in a cultural analysis of sexuality, by drawing the limits of its object – sexuality as a cultural object of knowledge – it is culture, not sexuality or sex as a non-cultural given, that becomes delimited. This is the way in which I hope to invert the Freudian dictum. In social anthropology it seems to work in the opposite direction: it is not culture that must draw the limits of sexuality but it is sexuality, because of its extracultural origin, that sets up the limits of culture.

In what follows I will focus my attention only on one particular aspect of Freud's theory: the role attributed to culture in the constitution of human sexuality. Interestingly, and significantly, despite being so uncertain as to the nature of human sexuality, Freud is known as one of the founders of what Foucault (1978: 51ff.) called *scientia sexualis*. But Freud's uncertainties were not meant to be dissipated by his own research. He clearly understood that, even though psychoanalysis could throw some light upon the biology of the sexual life of human beings, it was the biologist's job to undertake this kind of research and carry it out to its end. This is what gives Freud's intellectual project a characteristically ambiguous and indefinite foundation. His whole approach to human conduct is based upon his belief in the existence of biological entities called 'instincts', whose real nature was a total mystery to him: 'The theory of the instincts is so to say our mythology. Instincts are mythical entities, magnificent in their indefiniteness. In our work we cannot for a moment disregard them, yet we are never sure that we are seeing them clearly' (Freud 1964: 95). In the meantime, he had no doubts concerning the objective existence of a sexual instinct: 'the fact of the existence of sexual needs in human beings and animals is expressed in biology by the assumption of a "sexual instinct", on the analogy of the instinct of nutrition, that is of hunger' (Freud 1953: 135). Freud called this sexual instinct 'libido'.

What is the purpose of the libido? To make possible the reproduction of the species appears to be an obvious answer. But this is precisely one of the 'confusions' Freud wished very decisively to dispel with his research. Children's sexuality, one of Freud's most genuine discoveries, could not be considered as such were we to make this ingenuous equation between sexuality and reproduction. Hence, the field of sexuality without a doubt surpasses that of mere reproduction, and yet reproduction plays a crucial role in Freud's conceptualisation of sexuality. Not all sexuality has the reproductive function as its *raison d'être*, only 'normal' sexuality does. In this way he managed to include clearly non-reproductive practices within his concept of sexuality and at the same time grant reproduction a prominent position in his conceptual scheme. There is certainly non-reproductive sexual activity: the 'perverse' sexual activity, of which children's activity constitutes an outstanding instance. Thus Freud can happily conclude that 'the abandonment of the reproductive function is the common feature of all perversions' (Freud 1963: 316). Perversion is equated, in Freud's thought, to that sexual practice that by losing its final reproductive aim has become an end in itself. In Marcuse's words: 'The perversions express rebellion against the subjugation of sexuality under the order of procreation, and against the institutions which guarantee this order... Against a society which employs sexuality as means for a useful end, the perversions uphold sexuality as an end in itself' (1987: 49–50).

Now, despite placing the perverse at the margins of normal sexuality, the analysis of sexual perversions does not occupy a marginal space in Freud's theory of sexuality. Far from it: the first of the 'Three Essays' is explicitly devoted to that topic, and thus it sets the tune for the ensuing two essays. But why is the perverse so important in Freud's approach? To some extent, it could be argued that it was because of the therapeutic overall aim of Freud's theory that the analysis of the perverse, namely, the pathological, enjoyed this paramount position. But this is only a partial truth. Freud's objective in his 'Three Essays' is not merely a theory of sexual pathologies but a theory of normal human sexuality, in which, undoubtedly, an understanding of sexual perversions turns out to be crucial. But this is precisely the question we should attempt to answer: why did Freud allot so much importance to the deviant? The second essay can give us the clue.

In the second essay, Freud addresses the question of infantile sexuality. Against the prudish and patronising atmosphere of his time, he boldly asserted that children, very young children at that, had sexual desires. They had a sexual life of their own and therefore the sexual instinct should be considered as an innate disposition of human beings. At the same time, Freud made it very clear that children's sexuality was very different from that of an adult human being. Children had a sexual life but of a perverse kind. Worse yet, children's sexuality was 'polymorphously perverse' (Freud 1953: 191). There is no wonder that Freud's views caused so much havoc among the bourgeois Victorian hypocrites of the time. Not only do children have sexual desires but they have polymorphously perverse sexual desires. Plainly, this means that we are all native-born perverts and, therefore, the sort of explanation we need to provide in order to account for the emergence of adult normal sexuality has to be, let me stress this, an evolutive explanation: how do we manage to pass from an innate perverse disposition into a normal one? That is the reason why Freud's analysis of human sexuality had to start with an account of sexual perversions. We are all sexual perverts right from our cradle, so an explanation of normal sexuality must tell us why and how we stopped being so as we grew into adults.

Following the above-mentioned hydraulic metaphor, Freud understood that in the course of the individual's psychosexual development early perverse dispositions would be inhibited thanks to the emergence of 'dams' that would channel the individual's libidinal energy into the appropriate path. When these dams worked properly, the initial polymorphously perverse disposition could only survive into adulthood in an atrophied way. For instance, copulation being the normal aim of adult sexuality, Freud observed that there were all sorts of other activities, such as watching, touching, kissing, etc., that could only be defined as sexual and yet were only indirectly related to copulation. These were the 'preliminary sexual aims' (Freud 1953: 149–50). Now, when there is an overvaluation of any of these preliminaries so that they become ends in themselves, ultimate ends so to say, we have a particular kind of sexual perversion that Freud called 'deviation in respect of the sexual aim'. When no such overvaluation takes place, the preliminary sexual aims, so characteristic of normal sexual adulthood, can be seen as atrophied forms of archaic libidinal manifestations. Hence, the difference between normal and deviant sexuality seems to be a matter of relative stress. In a footnote added in 1920 to the second of his 'Three Essays', Freud remarked: 'The differences separating the normal from the abnormal can lie only in the relative strength of the individual components of the sexual instinct and in the use to which they are put in the course of development' (1953: 205).

Similarly, there are other kinds of sexual perversion that Freud called 'deviations in respect of the sexual object', of which homosexuality (inversion) constituted a prominent example. Again, the child's polymorphously perverse disposition makes no initial distinction between homosexual and heterosexual desires. It all depends on where the 'dam' is going to be built. In a footnote added in 1915 we read:

> psychoanalysis considers that a choice of an object independently of its sex – freedom to range equally over male and female objects – as it is found in childhood, in primitive states of society and early periods of history, is the original basis from which, as a result of restriction in one direction or the other, both the normal and the inverted types develop. (Freud 1953: 145–46)

Notice Freud's deliberate use of evolutive language and his generally recognised parallelism between childhood and 'primitive states of society', such that the abnormal, the perverse, is invariably equated with the primeval stages of development, which is precisely when the dams have not yet been built and thus libidinal energy flows in a totally unrestricted fashion. The conclusion to be drawn, as to the origins of normal adult sexuality, seems to leave no room for doubt: 'It is an easy conclusion that normal sexuality has emerged out of something that was in existence before it, by weeding out certain features of that material as unserviceable and collecting together the rest in order to subordinate them to a new aim, that of reproduction' (Freud 1963: 322). Very little is known about the nature of this 'something', and psychoanalysis can tell us very little since it belongs to the biologist's epistemological province, as we saw earlier. But what about the dams? What is the nature of those dams, which happen to be so decisive in the formation of a proper adult sexual personality? In the conclusions to the first essay Freud wrote: 'Our study of the perversions has shown us that the sexual instinct has to struggle against certain mental forces which act as resistances, and of which shame and disgust are the most prominent. It is permissible to suppose that these forces play a part in restraining that instinct within the limits that are regarded as normal.' And in a footnote written in 1915, he added:

> On the other hand, these forces which act like dams upon sexual development – disgust, shame and morality – must also be regarded as historical precipitates of the external inhibitions to which the sexual instinct has been subjected during the psychogenesis of the human race. We can observe the way in which in the development of individuals, they arise at the appropriate moment, as though spontaneously, when upbringing and external influence give the signal. (Freud 1953: 162)

What does Freud mean by 'historical precipitates'? The beginning of the second essay is somewhat confusing in this respect. He discusses the nature of the sexual inhibitions that take over in the period of latency and are responsible for the systematic sublimation of libidinal energy until puberty. Freud clearly states that these inhibitions are 'organically determined' and 'education' only plays a secondary role (1953: 177–78). This does not seem to match with the notion of 'historical precipitates' added ten years later – unless Freud understood that the initial 'mental forces' that restrict sexual instinct within the limits of the normal were of a different nature from the inhibitions that precipitate the period of latency. To make things worse, in the third essay Freud assumed a seemingly Lamarckian view of biological inheritance when he defined the incest taboo as an 'essentially cultural demand made by society' that, according to another 1915 footnote, 'has no doubt already become established in many persons by organic inheritance' (1953: 225).

Apparently, the differences between the 'historical', the 'cultural' and the 'organic' were not very clear-cut in Freud's thought, or at least he did not understand those differences in the same way as we understand them now. Apart from the fact that we can distinguish in his writings a gradual but uneven move from a rather crude biologistic view of human nature towards a more culturally informed perspective, despite his ambiguities and inconsistencies concerning the differences between the organic and the cultural, Freud unhesitatingly concluded his 'Three Essays' with the assertion that there was an 'inverse relation holding between civilization and the free development of sexuality' (1953: 242). Following an overtly evolutionist conception of culture, Freud believed that human societies could be sorted out according to their degree of 'civilisation', in such a way that the more civilised were invariably the more sexually repressed. He put forward this theory in a paper published in 1908 (1959) and he further developed it in his later works, especially in 'Civilization and its Discontents', where he explicitly argued that 'The tendency on the part of civilization to restrict sexual life is no less clear than its other tendency to expand the cultural unit' (Freud 1961: 104). Freud understood that civilisation and sexual desire were antagonistic not only because without the repression of the most elementary sexual drive (incestuous desire) the most elementary form of social life (the family) could not exist, but also because civilisation, in its progress, required from the individual huge amounts of psychical power that could only be obtained through the sublimation of libidinal energy. Thus Western civilisation, the most developed form of civilisation, must correspond to the highest degree of sexual repression.

Freud's views on sexuality, particularly his theory on the antagonism between human sexuality and culture, are neither unique nor original. Their value lies rather in the high degree of systematisation they achieved in his theoretical project. Nevertheless, the idea that sexuality not only lies at the margins of culture, but that culture itself originates as a form of response to natural sexual drives, a response that necessarily involves repression, is undoubtedly pervasive in Western thought (see Lacqueur 1990: 203). As a matter of fact, it constitutes one of the founding pillars of anthropological theorising. There is no need to be reminded here of how much anthropological analysis has been devoted to the understanding of the incest taboo, the first form of sexual 'repression' that marks the signal transition from nature to culture, the structural origin of human society.

To mention just one of the most explicit instances, consider Morgan's conjectural theory of the history of family forms, which can be taken as a synecdoche for the history of civilisation. Morgan maintained that the starting-point of the history of humankind, the zero degree of civilisation, corresponded to the period of 'promiscuous intercourse', 'the lowest conceivable stage of barbarism in which mankind could be found' (Morgan 1868: 472). In contrast, the monogamous family was equated to the highest degree of evolution. In between, there were a series of intermediate stages wherein individuals' sexual access to each other was somehow progressively more restrictive – though in a rather irregular fashion. Morgan's theory is particularly apposite to the present discussion because, not only did he take unrestricted sexuality as the hallmark of savagery, he also understood that the moral evolution of humankind, represented in the imagined historical succession of different family forms, resulted from the limitation of sexual bonding. Yet as in later authors – e.g. Lévi-Strauss (1969) – sexual repression loses theoretical importance in his explanatory model. Neither Morgan nor Lévi-Strauss gave much importance to the fact that their respective theories of marriage had their logical origin in a form of sexual prohibition, the prohibition of promiscuity for one and the prohibition of incest for the other, simply because they had other theoretical interests in mind.

In this respect, Freud's approach is emphatically different. He viewed unrestricted sexuality as the antagonistic pole of human social life and he wanted to explain human social life precisely in those terms. Freud, Morgan and Lévi-Strauss, despite their differing theoretical approaches and interests, all agreed upon a very fundamental tenet: human sexuality impinges very clearly on human forms of social organisation and, at the same time, it has a no less clear extracultural origin. If culture begins by the negation of sexuality, sexuality must, *ex hypothesi*, be outside culture. The point I wish to stress is that this understanding of human sexuality has been a commonplace – implicit or explicit – in several specifically anthropological studies regarding human sexuality (see Bolin and Whelehan 1999). In these studies, sex is normally considered as a human universal due to its biological, namely pre-cultural, nature. What an anthropological perspective does is to show how different societies give different meanings to this common biological denominator. Sex is the never-changing natural fact that, because of its cross-cultural social relevance, provides a kind of universal yardstick that enables us to measure human societies according to their degree of restrictiveness, permissiveness, etc.[1]

Note

1. The allusion to Morgan and to Lévi-Strauss was not made at random, because this is very similar to the role that in traditional anthropological thought we have attributed to kinship, for instance. Not so long ago, especially in the heyday of structural-functionalism, the study of kinship systems enjoyed a privileged position in anthropological curricula. The reason for this was precisely the belief in the pre-cultural nature of kinship bonds (see Gellner 1957). This pre-cultural nature turned kinship into a sort of universal screen against which the cultural particularities of specific modes of social organisation could be made visible. It would be theoretically interesting to work further on this comparison between kinship and sex as anthropological tools for cross-cultural intelligibility, but this is a line of argument I will not pursue for the time being.

CHAPTER 3

Foucault: Sex as Culture

Is there another way of looking at human sex and sexuality? In anthropology, the need for cross-cultural intelligibility does not necessarily lead to the search for human universals. And I should say that my own personal way of looking at the anthropological project has little to do with this 'craving for generality'. As regards theories on human sexuality, we can take Foucault's perspective as the most radical critique of Freud's sexual theory. Later on I shall try to show how Freud's and Foucault's views can be said to share common ground. But first let us focus on their very patent differences. We have seen that for Freud and for all those who follow his approach sex becomes the universal biological drive that can only be repressed in order for civilisation to unfold. With Foucault that biological drive is replaced by a historically constructed power mechanism. Sex is no longer the universal biological instinct endlessly repressed by historically specific forms of power but is its most genuine manifestation in a particular society, bourgeois society. Sex does not emerge from biology; it is a historical product, the product of a specific cultural discourse that we call sexuality. This is how Foucault described the making of the first volume of his *History of Sexuality*:

> There were several successive drafts. To start with, sex was taken as a pre-given datum, and sexuality figured as a sort of simultaneously discursive and institutional formation which came to graft itself on to sex, to overlay it and perhaps finally to obscure it. That was the first line of approach. Then I showed some people the manuscript and came to realise that it wasn't very satisfactory. Then I turned the whole thing upside down. That was only a game, because I wasn't sure … . But I said to myself, basically, couldn't it be that sex – which seems to be an instance having its own laws

and constraints, on the basis of which the masculine and feminine sexes are defined – be something which on the contrary is *produced* by the apparatus of sexuality? What the discourse of sexuality was initially applied to wasn't sex but the body, the sexual organs, pleasures, kinship relations, interpersonal relations, and so forth. (Foucault 1980: 210)

If sexuality does not originate in sex but the other way around, where does sexuality come from? In the previous section I have submitted Freud's writings on sexuality to a sort of ethnographic interrogation. I will use a different approach to Foucault's thought. I confess that my theoretical sympathies run closer to his perspective – so perhaps the 'cultural distance' to be bridged by a metaphoric ethnographic enquiry is too short here. By no means do I consider this research as an application of Foucault's theories to a particular case or a particular society. That would be pretentious and, in fact, of little theoretical use. I have been inspired by Foucault's ideas so maybe my only purpose in what follows is to convey to the reader what this inspiration consists of.

As with Freud's, I approach Foucault's work with a very specific agenda. I am interested neither in Foucault's social and political theory nor in his broader philosophical project. I merely wish to comment on the way in which his conception of sexuality foregrounds some specifically anthropological concerns. Foucault's understanding of human sexuality is, anthropologically speaking, relativistic. He sees sexuality above all as a historically constituted discourse characteristic of a particular social formation. Foucault makes sexuality particular by making it historical. And, by making it historical, we could add, he turns it into a cultural construct. We could not be more at odds with Freud's perspective: universal biological drives have no role to play in Foucault's views on human sexuality, not even as a sort of negative pre-cultural background against which the positivity of cultural repression could be thrown into relief. Sexuality is in itself a culturally arbitrary human phenomenon in such a way that its very arbitrariness is the key to its understanding. But what does it mean to understand sexuality as a culturally arbitrary phenomenon? To repeat: where does sexuality come from?

Foucault's theory of discursive formations, as set out in his *Archaeology of Knowledge* (1972), provides the key to his analytical approach. In a series of negative propositions, he tells us what discourse analysis should not be based on. A discourse has an object, but the analysis of discourse should not be seen as a consequence of the prior existence of its object: 'The unity of discourses on madness would not be based upon the existence of the object "madness", or the constitution of a single horizon of objectivity' (Foucault 1972: 32). Sexuality as a discourse has an object in sexuality as a practice, but we should not consider the practice of sexuality as the origin of the discourse of sexuality. It could not be otherwise if we start out from the assumption that sexuality is a historical product. Were we to take sexual behaviour as the origin of sexual discourse, this latter could not be taken as a historical product since all human beings at all historical periods have had sexual behaviour. It is because we began to speak about sexual behaviour and sexual practices, because Western societies began to speak about sexuality at a specific point in their history, that sexuality as an object was eventually constituted.

Would that mean that the origin of discourse is in the speaking subject? Western psychiatrists, physicians, artists, philosophers, theologians have all been talking about sexuality for centuries. If the origins of their discourse do not lie in the object they have been talking about, should not we see instead in these very subjects the ultimate source of their statements? Certainly not. 'I do not refer the various ennunciative modalities to the unity of the subject' (Foucault 1972: 54). Neither the psychological nor the transcendental subject should be posited as the constituting agencies of discourse. Furthermore, Foucault equally discards words and propositions as the unities of discourse analysis. Words are the linguists' concern but it is clear for him that a discourse is not the same as a language. Concepts and propositions, on the other hand, are taken up in logical analysis, whereas discourse analysis focuses on what Foucault calls the 'pre-conceptual' (1972: 62).

A discourse is a set of rules for the production of statements. It is in this set of rules that discourse analysis should ground itself, precisely because 'it would be the interplay of rules that make possible the appearance of objects during a given period of time' (Foucault 1972: 32–33). The interesting thing to note about Foucault's proposal is that sexuality from this perspective appears first and foremost as a mode of thought. It is a mode of thought that constitutes its own object and not the other way around. And it is out of this constitutive capacity that discourse manifests its power, that discourse manifests itself as power.

The question of power is crucial in Foucault's intellectual project. Power in sexual discourse can never result in repression because sexuality as an object is not external to sexuality as a discourse. Freud could only see sexual morality as repressive because for him desire had a reality of its own: because there is such a thing as a sexual instinct prior to any moral regulation, we can understand morality as repressive of the pre-existing sexual instinct. Inversely, in Foucauldian terms, if no sexual instinct can be said to exist prior to its constitution by a particular discourse, there is nothing for this discourse to repress for the simple reason that there is nothing outside it:

> We must cease once and for all to describe the effects of power in negative terms: it 'excludes', it 'represses', it 'censors', it 'abstracts', it 'masks', it 'conceals'. In fact, power produces; it produces reality; it produces domains of objects and rituals of truth. The individual and the knowledge that may be gained of him belong to this production. (Foucault 1977: 194)

There are interesting and somewhat disturbing political consequences to be derived from Foucault's concept of power. If power constitutes its own object it is hard to see how anyone can fight against it, how anyone can place themselves outside it. In chapter 8 I will deal extensively with the question of power from what I take to be an anthropological viewpoint, and many of the ideas that I shall develop are closely associated with Foucault's insights. But now I wish to remark on a very particular aspect of Foucault's power concept: its historicity. The power that does not repress but constitutes is a historically particular form of power, what Foucault calls the power of 'normalisation' (1977: 183–84). In *Discipline and Punish* Foucault contends that this is the form of power characteristic of modernity. We can see how it works in schools, in the army, in hospitals, in factories, etc. Its aim is the internalisation of a particular form of behaviour, the embodiment of a certain rule, so that it is based on rewards rather than on punishment, in such a way that discipline must become the 'normal' mode of conduct: normalising power is disciplinary power, not punitive power. Bentham's panopticon provides us with an exquisite and well-known instance: the individual 'inscribes in himself the power relation in which he simultaneously plays both roles; he becomes the principle of his own subjection' (Foucault 1977: 202–3).

The emergence of sexuality as a historical object is intimately linked with the development of this normalising power form characteristic of modernity. In the first volume of his *History of Sexuality* (1978: 108 ff.) Foucault draws an important distinction between what he calls the 'deployment of alliance' and the 'deployment of sexuality', a distinction that can be said roughly to correspond with two fundamental periods in Western history. The deployment of alliance held sway in the pre-modern period, wherein sexuality was not an object in itself but part of a wider complex of marriage and kinship relationships. At that time, it could be argued that people had sexual behaviour and sexual pleasures but they did not have 'sex': sexual behaviour was not culturally singled out and differentiated from other human activities. The gradual, and never complete, replacement of deployment of alliance by the deployment of sexuality has had two especially productive moments. The first begins in the Middle Ages with the Christian techniques of confession and examination of conscience. These were the first mechanisms to make sexuality explicit, to create a discourse on sexuality fully under the control of the Church, a discourse exclusively moralistic and dominated by the notion of sin. The second moment was the beginning of the nineteenth century, when sex starts to free itself from the ecclesiastical institution and becomes an object of medical interest, it is the advent of the 'medical technologies of sex' (Foucault 1978: 119). The second moment inaugurates the building of bourgeois hegemony and is linked with the changing notions of power we have already seen. Power as the right of seizure, the right to kill, the 'power of death' is replaced by the 'power of life', what Foucault calls 'bio-power' (pp. 135–45). Sexuality can be considered from this perspective as perhaps the most refined mechanism of bourgeois bio-power.

Despite Foucault's initial and pervasive stress on the association of sexuality with bourgeois hegemony – 'the bourgeoisie's "blood" was its sex' (1978: 124) – there is no doubt that for him the roots of this sexual bio-power lie in a cultural complex apparently so distant from modernity as Christianity (see Black 1997: 44–45). Thus in the second and third volumes of his *History of Sexuality* (1985, 1986) Foucault paves the way for an understanding of the emergence of Christian sexual discourse by drawing an instructive contrast with the precedents of Christian thought: Greek classic and Hellenistic philosophy. It is not very clear how his former 'deployment of alliance' period, as set up in the first volume, fits in with this seemingly new periodisation. Whatever the case, it is out of this comparison between Greek ideas and Christian doctrine that Foucault identifies the main characteristics of sexuality's historical constitution. Interestingly, he does not focus his analysis on particular definitions of sexual behaviour as such, but rather on the moral principles that are supposed to regulate it. Cultural definitions of sexuality are clearly, from Foucault's point of view, moral philosophies.

What kind of moral philosophies? The key distinction upon which Foucault unfolds his analysis is that between what he calls 'ethics-oriented' and 'code-oriented' moralities. Whereas in the first the stress is laid upon forms of subjectivisation – self-reflection, self-knowledge, self-examination (i.e. 'practices of the self') – in the second the stress lies on obedience to a certain code or norm. In Greek and Graeco-Roman antiquity the predominant morality was an ethics-oriented morality, that is 'much more oriented towards practices of the self and the question of *askesis* [training] than towards codifications of conducts and the strict definition of what is permitted and what is forbidden' (Foucault 1985: 30). Foucault remarks that Christian morality has both of these elements, though the code-oriented morality would predominate until the Reformation. From here Foucault tries to identify the defining characteristic of the value system that will regulate sexual conduct in each moral philosophy. For the Greeks Foucault coins the expression 'aesthetics of existence':

> And what I mean by this is a way of life whose moral value did not depend either on one's being in conformity with a code of behaviour, or on an effort of purification, but on certain formal principles in the use of pleasures, in the way one distributed them, in the limits one observed, in the hierarchy one respected. (1985: 89)

It is important to point out that this concept does not refer exclusively to a set of values specifically devised to rule upon sexual conducts. It refers to a whole way of being in which sexual behaviour is included alongside an array of human activities but by no means isolated or differentiated from other such activities. As its name suggests, it is the whole human existence that we are concerned with here. This will provide a sharp contrast with Christian morality. The main principle of Christian morality will no longer be the all-encompassing aesthetics of existence but will become another of Foucault's famous and vivid concepts: the hermeneutics of desire. The general and undifferentiated character of Greek moral philosophy gives rise to a moral doctrine which will focus clearly on a particular kind of human conduct for its regulation. It is no longer general human existence that interests us but a specific parcel of this existence: desire. Desire must be discovered, exposed, articulated and sanctioned:

> Subjection was to take the form not of a *savoir-faire*, but of a recognition of the law and an obedience to pastoral authority. Here the ethical subject was to be characterised not so much by the perfect rule of the self by the self in the exercise of a virile type of activity, as by self-renunciation and a purity whose model was to be sought in virginity. This being the case, one can understand the significance that was attached, in Christian morality, to two opposite yet complementary practices: a codification of sexual acts that would become more and more specific, and the development of a hermeneutics of desire together with procedures of self-decipherment. (Foucault 1985: 92)

There are two central interrelated ideas in Foucault's interpretation of Christian sexual doctrine. On the one hand, sexual practices are identified and differentiated from any other human activity; they become a specific object of moral discourse by being first of all uncovered and left in the open for all to see, so to say. In several parts of his work Foucault underscores the Greek 'discretion' as regards the explicit references to sexual activity. Even in Hellenistic and Roman moral philosophy, despite their clear continuities with later Christian principles, the question of sex remained quite often 'in the shadows'. 'Opposing this Greek discretion, there will be the meticulous attentiveness of the Christian pastoral ministry, starting in the Middle Ages' (Foucault 1986: 165). Secondly, disclosure of sexual objects brought about by the hermeneutics of desire goes hand in hand with the code-oriented character of Christian sexual morality. Foucault argues that moral principles did not change that much from classical Greece to the Christian period, what did change was their ethical form. For instance, to commit adultery was wrong both for the Greeks and for Christians, but for different reasons. In Greek, and to a lesser extent in Hellenistic, philosophy it was an aesthetic question, it was the need to lead a 'beautiful life' that made adultery an 'ugly' act and thus immoral. 'Even in its most detailed texts on the life of the couple, such as those of Plutarch, what is proposed is not a regulation that would draw a division between permitted and forbidden acts. It is instead a mode of being, a style of relations' (Foucault 1986: 184). For Christians, it was different. It was a juridical question that concerned everybody – and not just the minority of virtuous people who chose to lead a beautiful existence (Foucault 1983b: 240–41). This juridical, code-oriented, element would clearly demarcate Christian sexual morality from any other kind of moral philosophy that preceded it.

My point in bringing in Freud's and Foucault's theories on human sexuality is to emphasise the important theoretical consequences to be derived from seeing the origins of sexuality either as a pre-cultural object or as a cultural construct. Whereas for Freud sexuality is always equal to itself in whatever form of society we happen to be looking at, for Foucault sexuality as such can only be said to exist in one form of society at a particular historical period. But, as soon as we leave this particular historical period, as soon as we get away from the discourses of theologians, physicians, psychiatrists, policy makers, etc., that produced sexuality – and sex – as an object of knowledge, what do we find? A biological 'pre-given datum'?

Perhaps the first thing we should try to do is to separate the ontological claims of both Freud's and Foucault's theories from the epistemological consequences that can be derived from their perspectives. In this sense, as I have indicated, my approach is more akin to Foucault's but only in so far as I am interested in a particular cultural and historically constituted manifestation of sexuality: sexual morality in Ireland. Nevertheless, I cannot share the ontological corollaries that he seems to draw from his historico-cultural point of departure: the negation of sex as a biological given. Whatever the reasons that Foucault had for reaching so drastic a conclusion, I do not think that a cultural analysis of sexuality should start by negating the existence of biological sex because, as has been argued above, in this particular case biology sets the limits of culture, and culture should have limits if we wish to turn it into the object of a scientific enquiry – and not the springboard for a broad philosophical investigation concerning the way in which objects of knowledge are constituted (something very legitimate in itself, needless to say, but not my aim in this essay). Now the fact that biology sets the limits of culture or that biological sex sets the limits of the culture of sexuality (whatever this happens to be) does not mean that the latter can only be explained, or understood, as a necessary consequence of those biological limits: 'Biology conditions and limits what is possible. But it does not cause the patterns of sexual life' (Weeks 2003: 18).[1] There is a very fundamental principle of cultural analysis that should be recalled now, that of the arbitrary nature of the linguistic sign. As signifieds are arbitrarily related to their signifiers or linguistic signs are arbitrarily related to their nonlinguistic referents, cultural forms are only arbitrarily related to their non-cultural objects. The fact that we can only apprehend those non-cultural objects through cultural forms does not mean that those objects do not exist irrespective of the cultural form by which they are apprehended. Besides, as I shall try to demonstrate at the close of this essay, the very possibility of understanding cultural forms as such presupposes the existence, or the belief in the existence, of non-cultural objects.

After this clarification, there is one further point in Foucault's approach that I wish to emphasise. Let me put it this way: in all sexual behaviour we come across the commensurate and the incommensurate parts. Say that Freud was interested in the first whereas Foucault was interested in second. This means that the Foucauldian understanding of this sexual behaviour and beliefs might lead us to cultural domains that are not specifically sexual domains, that is, domains that do not have the regulation of sexual behaviour as their principal aim and therefore they culturally transform sexual behaviour – the sexual behaviour they regulate – into something else (i.e. 'sexually' incommensurate). To borrow popular Derridean terminology, the analysis of the cultural construction of sexuality could lead quite naturally to its cultural deconstruction. This is precisely what Foucault did in his analysis of sexuality in Greek and Hellenistic philosophy. Perhaps deconstructing sexuality is all a cultural analysis can hope for.

In what follows, however, my concern will be less with any deconstructivist purpose than with intermingling theoretical debates in anthropology with an exploration of sexual morality in a historically and culturally specific context. We shall see that the approach we can elicit from an anthropological perspective, i.e. the perspective originating in the development of anthropological thought (or in one of its developments), is in its own way unique. This is how I hope to attain my double objective, to show how the discipline of social anthropology can furnish a particular view on sexual morality and, conversely, how an analysis of sexual morality can help us understand the nature of anthropological knowledge.

Note

1. 'The physiology of orgasm and penile erection no more explains a culture's sexual schema than the auditory range of the human ear explains its music' (Vance 1991: 879).

PART II

Power, Meaning and Social Structure: an Irish Case-Study

CHAPTER 4

Irish Sexual Morality and Family Systems

This and the following chapters present the historical and ethnographic material on sexual morality in rural Ireland that will substantiate my theoretical investigation. In fact, it is the conventional structural-functional approach to that material that I wish to critically assess in this presentation. By showing the contradictions and inconsistencies of that conventional approach, as well as its merits, my purpose is to create a theoretical empty space of sorts, a space that will only be filled up as the analysis proceeds. This theoretical empty space is what has been variously defined as the product of the 'cultural factor' in the explanation of human behaviour, i.e. that type of conduct, irrational by definition, that cannot be accounted for by any other means than by appealing to a notoriously vague concept of culture. But my purpose is now to render that empty space visible, to explore the social and economic conditions of the irrational.

I will use a Freudian notion as my starting-point. We have seen that in Freud's thought culture appears as the negation of sexuality, as if the only thing that culture could do with sexuality were to repress it. From this perspective, what a hypothetical Freudian social anthropology of sexuality should do is the ethnographic documentation of the human repressive experience, of the different ways in which particular societies carry out their specific forms of cultural repression against the universal biological sexual instincts. But this sexual repression apparently inherent in culture can manifest itself in two different ways. Either culture represses sexuality because that is what culture is all about (this would be the most strictly Freudian interpretation) or it represses sexuality as somewhat of a by-product, so to speak, of a power system with other specific objectives. This distinction is crucial, though for reasons that are here of no immediate interest to us. It is crucial because, from the first point of view, which I believe corresponds more genuinely to Freud's approach, there is no way we can think of a human society without sexual repression precisely because that is what human society is all about. Or, if we take seriously Freud's definition of sexual inhibitions as 'organically determined', maybe that is what human nature is all about. On the other hand, if we adopt the second interpretation, in which repression emerges as the collateral output of a system whose rationale lies elsewhere, the existence of a 'non-repressive culture' becomes, theoretically at least, possible. We shall consider now this left-wing 'mild' Freudianism.

Let us reconsider Herdt's politico-economic interpretation of Sambia semen transactions (1984b). In Sambia social structure we find a severe male power system with a characteristic ideological discourse. The objective logic of this power system is to uphold the privileged status of adult men by means of the specific form of false consciousness derived from semen fetishism. As a result, sexual repression might appear rather inevitable but it is certainly contingent upon the first and foremost sense of Sambia social structure: male domination. The ethnography of Sambia society becomes thus not the ethnography of a particular form of sexual repression but the ethnography of a power system, of a male power system that happens to be sexually repressive. As I have said, strictly speaking, this should not be seen as a Freudian interpretation of Sambia society since sexual repression appears as a secondary effect of a social structure with another, a different, main purpose. What Sambia society is all about is not sexual repression, or the repression of heterosexual desires, but masculine domination, for which sexual repression is definitely instrumental. Now this is the opening idea with which I would like to begin this chapter. My point of departure comes very close to Herdt's politico-economic approach, even though there are also substantial differences between our respective analytical developments, which hopefully will show up as my argument unfolds.

My point of departure is the concept of social structure, the fundamental building-block, without a doubt, in the theoretical edifice of British sociological anthropology. In a way, I believe we can say about this concept what Gellner (1973: 90) said as regards functionalism in anthropology: its merits as a method are as great as its defects as a doctrine. Social structure as a concept has always been poorly defined. Radcliffe-Brown (1952: 190) understood it as the complex network of social relations actually existing between the individuals of a particular society; he defined social relations as some form of 'adjustment' of the interests of two or more individual organisms (1952: 199). Nothing is said about the reasons that might compel these individual organisms to adjust their interests: whether this is the result of some common agreement or it is because they are pushed towards this adjustment by an external force (see Lévi-Strauss 1963: 302ff; Leach 1974: 4–5). In my view, this is a very fundamental distinction because it refers to two radically separate phenomena. Be that as it may, it is not my intention here to furnish a definitive concept, or even a clearer one.[1]

It could be argued that the definition of social structure partakes of the same theoretical problems that some years ago Rodney Needham saw with the definition of kinship – which, incidentally, British social anthropologists normally used as quasi-synonymous with social structure. Needham maintained that the term 'kinship' was, following Wittgenstein, an 'odd-job' word; that is, a word that only gives us trouble when we assume that it must have some specific function (Needham 1971: 5, see Wittgenstein 1969: 44). There is little point in looking for exactly what the concept of social structure refers to or should refer to, or what its 'specific function' is. It is a useful concept, nevertheless, perhaps because we do not know exactly what it means. But the question is why has this theoretically nebulous idea been so methodologically useful for British and for social anthropologists in general? How is it that Radcliffe-Brown regarded its study 'as being in a very important sense the most fundamental part of the science [of social anthropology]?' (1952: 190). His answer is very clear and straightforward: 'the social phenomena we observe in any human society are not the immediate result of the nature of individual human beings, but are the result of the social structure by which they are united' (1952: 190–91).

Rituals, beliefs, anything that can be labelled as 'irrational' are the phenomena that constitute the anthropologist's object of analysis; the social structure is the means that enables us to make this object intelligible. With this Radcliffe-Brown was not merely formulating a sort of programmatic statement. He was not simply saying what he thought social anthropologists should ideally do, but he was defining what his colleagues were actually doing and, most importantly, what they would be doing in the future, at least for a good few years. In 1967, when structural-functionalism was giving the first signs of momentous stagnation, Jarvie (1967: 190) could still say that the concept of social structure 'in various disguises, and somewhat elaborately worked out, is the base on which much of present social anthropology rests'.

In what follows we shall see how this time-honoured concept can help us with our particular ethnographic puzzle: Irish sexuality. But first let me enter a caveat. The way I will be using the concept of social structure differs from the structural-functional tradition in two important respects. On the one hand, 'my' social structure is inherently a historical product, for I feel we cannot reach any ethnographic understanding of a social fact in a historically conscious society without taking a markedly historical perspective. This question will be fully developed later. On the other hand, also contrary to another of Radcliffe-Brown's explicit views, my concept of social structure is by no means opposed to the concept of culture (Radcliffe-Brown 1952: 189; cf. Leach 1974: 16–17). I firmly believe that the detailed study of a social structure constitutes a necessary step for a cultural analysis of any particular form of life. In fact, much of this was already somewhat implicit in many structural-functional accounts. I will say more about the relations between history and culture in the production of anthropological knowledge in the following chapters.

Now for the 'puzzle' of Irish sexuality: what sort of 'irrationality' do we have to confront in an analysis of Irish sexuality? Ethnographers and social historians who have looked at sexual attitudes in rural Ireland invariably agree on the prevalence of a distinctively strict code of sexual behaviour. Nowhere could Freud have found a better instance of a civilised society with highly repressed sexual desire. Irish traditional society has been portrayed as a conspicuous example of the repressive sexuality characteristic of pre-modern or Victorian times. Some authors may dissent as to the temporal depth that should be attributed to such a stern chaste morality. Was it concomitant with the post-Famine arrangements that framed the social structure of Irish rural society from the second half of the nineteenth century, or can its origins be traced back somewhat earlier and thus be disconnected from the social effects of the potato crisis of the 1840s? Whatever the case, the existence of a distinctive sexual ideology is beyond doubt. An astonishingly low level of illegitimacy, widely corroborated by demographers and historians, coupled with a no less astonishingly low marriage rate, is commonly seen as documentary proof of the widespread acceptance of a sexually inhibitive culture that lasted, at least, up to the mid twentieth century. According to Irish demographer Brendan M. Walsh (1985: 132), 'so prevalent was the lack of enthusiasm for marriage and sexual activity in general that Ireland at mid-century may well provide an example of what Malthus called "a decay of the passion between the sexes", a phenomenon that he thought was rare in view of the evidence that "this natural propensity exists in undiminished vigour" throughout the world'.

This view has been endorsed by several well-known ethnographies of rural Ireland. Consider Scheper-Hughes's (2001: 195) observations in a rural parish of the south-west: 'Marriage in rural Ireland is, I suggest, inhibited by anomie, expressed in lack of sexual vitality; familistic loyalties that exaggerate latent brother–sister incestuous inclinations; an emotional climate fearful of intimacy and mistrustful of love; and an excessive preoccupation with sexual purity and pollution.' John Messenger defined the community where he did his research in the early 1960s as 'one of the most sexually naive of the world's societies'(1971: 14–15), and he characterised the average marriageable man in his late twenties and thirties as 'usually repressed to an unbelievable degree'(1969: 68–69). Elliot Leyton (1975: 21) saw the men of his village 'as locked in a constant struggle between their spirituality and the base forces of sexuality; and those who publicly allow their sexuality to conquer them must suffer'. Arensberg and Kimball (2001: 195) observed that 'the country people yield to no one in the strictness of their sexual morality'. Hugh Brody (1973: 180) remarked that in his community 'sexual relationships – from small flirtations to copulation – are rare indeed among today's younger parishioners'. Examples could be indefinitely multiplied (see Inglis 1998b: 23–49).

There are several elements in these conventional definitions of Irish sexuality that deserve careful examination: (a) the ever-present 'repression' as which Messenger and Scheper-Hughes explicitly characterised the sexual culture of their informants; (b) the idea of 'sexual purity and pollution'; (c) the notions of 'sexual inhibition' and 'sexual ignorance' and a 'strict' sexual morality. But first I am interested in looking at the historical and structural roots of such a peculiar attitude, or set of attitudes, to sex so pervasive in Irish society.

In the history of Irish anthropology we have a good example of the merits of the Radcliffe-Brownian structural-functionalism in the work of, interestingly, two American anthropologists: Conrad M. Arensberg and Solon T. Kimball (Arensberg 1937; Arensberg and Kimball 2001 [1940, 1968]). In their 1940 book, they devoted a whole chapter to the analysis of Irish sexuality under the significant title of 'Familism and Sex'. Arensberg and Kimball saw in the family organisation of western Irish farmers the key structural element that enabled them to account for their whole culture. Sexual behaviour and beliefs figured prominently in this culture. We shall focus our attention on the 'social structure' that in their view seems to be responsible for the peculiarities of Irish sexuality. This is a form of family organisation that later came to be called the 'stem family'. I will call it the stem family system (SFS) because, for Arensberg and Kimball, it was not only a particular way of organising family relationships (specifically, a form of post-marital residence, which is actually what the concept of stem family refers to) but a whole social system – an entire form of life – that went with it.

Arensberg and Kimball's study has been recurrently criticised for being 'ahistorical'. 'Moored as it is to a functionalist view of society and culture, it invites such criticism. Indeed, the Ireland of Arensberg and Kimball often seems to float in a timeless void, isolated from the perturbations of modern history' (Birdwell-Pheasant 1992: 205). This is not exactly true, since they were perfectly aware that the SFS depicted in their monographs had not always been the predominant form of social organisation in the Irish countryside (see Arensberg 1937: 109; Arensberg and Kimball 2001: 105). Granted the awareness of the SFS historical nature, the absence in their writings of a broad historical perspective that would account for its constitutive process was somewhat compensated by a debate that took place some years later among Irish scholars known as the 'stem family debate' (Gibbon 1973; Gibbon and Curtin 1978, 1983; Fitzpatrick 1983; Varley 1983; Harris 1988). From these discussions, which were mainly devoted to finding out an economic rationality for the SFS, I would like to take up one point: the emergence of the SFS in Ireland as a result of the post-Famine adjustments of the second half of the nineteenth century – a thesis originally put forward by the Irish social historian Kenneth H. Connell (1968). This will enable me to draw a contrast between the pre-Famine and the post-Famine social structures of rural Ireland, from which, I believe, interesting clues can be obtained for interpreting the history of Irish sexuality.

For those who are not familiar with Irish history, I must say that 'the Famine' refers to the dreadful effects of a potato blight that affected the Irish countryside in the late 1840s. The importance of the Famine as a watershed in Irish history is the object of hot debate among Irish historians, which should not detain us here. My point will be, and I believe that very few would actually disagree, that throughout the nineteenth century important structural changes came about in Irish rural society from which its modern social structure emerged, a social structure that lasted for much of the twentieth century. The mode of production that prevailed in what is known as pre-Famine Ireland, roughly up to the first half of the nineteenth century, was a characteristically dual agrarian economy of big absentee landlords and small cottiers. It was a dual agrarian economy not only because of this polarisation of its social classes, but also to the extent that its main outputs were, on the one hand, a surplus production of grain used to pay the landlords' rents, grain exported to England to feed its growing industrial proletariat, and, on the other, a subsistence production of potatoes to feed the Irish peasantry.[2] Under these conditions, since the potato harvest was so important for the subsistence of the majority of the population, the potato blight could only have an absolutely devastating effect on the Irish countryside.

Potatoes have the virtue of having highly nutritious qualities while needing very little land for growing. Thus, as Adam Smith perceptively noted in *The Wealth of Nations*, they can be suitably compared with rice, specifically in that both crops allow for high population densities (Ross 1986: 204). In a potato subsistence economy it could rightly be said that, in all appearances, land is not a scarce resource, since land parcels can be seemingly almost endlessly subdivided without substantial loss to their productive capacity. From here all the main features of pre-Famine social structure seem to follow quite easily: unproblematic access to land leads to an early and similarly unproblematic marriage, large nuclear families and subsequent subdivision of land tenure to make room for more nuclear families. It all gave rise to the population explosion that Ireland experienced in the eighteenth and first half of the nineteenth century: from around three million inhabitants in 1725 up to more than eight million in 1841 (Ross 1986: 208). 'Subdivision, earlier marriage, larger families, more subdivision; clearly there was a vicious circle: landlord, economist, and State emphasized its peril; but the peasantry, until disaster was imminent, knew more of its pleasure of unrestricted marriage and a large family' (Connell 1968: 115). It is unclear, however, whether this suicidal development should be pinned down to the peasants' 'irrationality', as Connell seems to suggest, or whether it was rather the result of the landlords' pressure on their tenants to subdivide their holdings so that the aggregate rent could increase without diminishing the acreage devoted to cereal (Ross 1986: 207). In any case, this system seems inevitably doomed to end in a Malthusian subsistence crisis, and this is what the potato disaster amounted to: a crisis triggered off by a surplus of population over extant resources.

Although Malthus has been recurrently criticised for disregarding the social constraints that lead to overpopulation (Harris and Ross 1987: 125–38; see also Mokyr 1980), behind his model of subsistence crisis there are certain assumptions concerning the prevailing pattern of sexual and marital relationships that he himself did not fail to notice – in the 1803 edition of his *Essay on the Principle of Population* (Macfarlane 1986: 33 ff.). Our interest here is not with the 'causes' of the Famine as such but with the pattern of marital and sexual relationships that has been conventionally associated with pre-Famine Ireland. This pattern constitutes an almost inverse image of the SFS. 'In the two or three generations following the 1780s peasant children, by and large, married whom they pleased when they pleased' (Connell 1968: 114–15). Again, historians busy themselves trying to dismiss too sharp a dichotomy between pre- and post-Famine marriage customs and sexual mores (see Connolly 1985, 2001: 173–207). Perhaps what we should be looking at here is not so much the actual patterns of behaviour that prevailed at one particular time, but rather the way in which that behaviour was remembered, and thus reconstructed, in the social memory of the following generations, especially after the occurrence of a particularly disastrous event, such as the Famine, which is very likely to dichotomise the temporal sequence into two morally contradictory sides. In this, Kenneth Connell has made, to my mind, a decidedly revealing observation: '[the peasant] hardly dissociated the disasters of the Famine from the marriage customary in his class – for early marriage, laxly "arranged", perhaps romantic, had plausibly aggravated both the growth of population and its dependence on the potato' (1968: 158).

Early and romantic marriage and a high fertility rate seemed to have led to an unprecedented population growth, which inevitably ended up in a catastrophic subsistence crisis, all supported by a dual economy of potato/cereal production that fed into a social system made up of a small and powerful landowning class versus a huge and powerless class of tenant farmers. The potato blight certainly undermined one of the bases of this nicely articulated system. In addition, a set of economic measures delivered the final and deadly blow. These were the abolition of the Cattle Acts, which permitted the livestock trade from Ireland to Britain, the cancellation of the Corn Laws, which enabled the import of cheap continental grain into Britain, and, last but not least, the Land Acts, which by the turn of the century gradually transformed the tenant farmers who had survived the disasters of the Famine (and the subsequent massive emigration) into peasant proprietors. These measures effected a radical transformation of the social landscape of rural Ireland. Commercial stockbreeding based on extensive land use was substituted for the old cereal/potato system and, more or less at the same time, a population of small and middle-sized landowning farmers replaced the erstwhile classes of big absentee landlords and their wretched cottiers. The social and economic foundations of the SFS had finally been laid down.

I have brought in all this historical information because I believe that important aspects of the moral and ideological context in which the SFS thrived are contingent upon this historical narrative. If it is true, as several authors have contended, that the SFS originated in these post-Famine adjustments, the deep social significance of the SFS can only be grasped if we are fully acquainted with the sort of reality that it was meant to 'adjust'. We have seen that the previous family model, with its corresponding patterns of sexual, marital and inheritance behaviour, met quite nicely the requirements of its socio-economic structural context. In a way it could even be argued that it was its functional adequacy that eventually led to its destruction. My concern is not so much with the historical causes of the demise of the pre-Famine social structure, but with the contrast between this family model–land tenure–productive system complex and the subsequent complex that was substituted for it. Taking into consideration the new structural conditions that progressively prevailed in the Irish countryside in the second half of the nineteenth century, the functional adequacy of the SFS is no less conspicuous.

Given the ecological context of the Irish countryside, stockbreeding is very likely to involve a relatively extensive land use, which differs sharply from the intensive use of potato growers (Salazar 1996: 95). In other words, land becomes a scarce resource and, consequently, the endless subdivision of land holdings so characteristic of the previous mode of production can no longer take place. Furthermore, farmers are progressively becoming the legal owners of the land they work, which means, among other things, that they can certainly freely dispose of their estates but they can no longer obtain land-tenure rights from rent-thirsty landlords so as to provide their recently married children with means of subsistence. Marriage and population growth must, therefore, be severely controlled. To this effect we need two things, for which the SFS seems to be quintessentially suited. First, we need an inheritance system that leaves the family land holding undivided as it passes down from generation to generation: an impartible inheritance system in which only one child, one son given the prevailing patrilineal bias, receives the full ownership of the family land. Secondly, we need a marriage ideology that discourages inheriting sons from marrying too early or following their own wishes, since in that case they are very likely to see their inheriting expectations severely hampered, and which also discourages non-inheriting sons from marrying at all, since they have very little chance of acquiring any land on which to settle down and support themselves together with their families. Daughters, who are systematically disinherited from land-ownership in this patrilineal model, might stand a better chance of finding a marriage partner if they manage to accumulate the appropriate dowry. But taking into account that it is mainly, if not exclusively, heirs that they can be matched to, the surplus population of the non-inheriting, and thus non-marrying, sons will have its counterpart in another surplus population of non-marrying daughters. Emigration, needless to say, provides the escape valve for them all. Let us follow Kenneth Connell (1968: 116) in his forceful description:

> Boys, needing land to marry, could no longer marry as they wished on plots pared from their fathers' land or won from the bog; they must, instead, put off their marrying until, by gift or inheritance, they acquired intact their family farm. One boy, usually the eldest, was thus established; one sister married the heir to a neighbouring farm. The rest of the family, chafing, as the Famine receded, at so inequitable an arrangement, might have pressed once more for a share of the land and a chance to settle at home; but family loyalty was stronger than brotherly jealously – family loyalty supported, then overlain, by the pull of emigration, until today the peasant as likely as not envies his emigrant brother.

Everything looks as if the SFS in Ireland functioned as the 'preventive check' that according to Malthus would avoid the disastrous consequences of excessive population growth (Connell 1957: 85; Guinnane 1997: 13). But, given that the 'passion between the sexes', which is what eventually produces population growth, is one of the strongest imperatives of human nature, how on earth can a system work in which the majority of the population are prevented from marrying and thus from satisfying their burning sexual drives, and those who are lucky enough to get married, apart from doing so according to their parents' wishes and not to their own desires, have still to wait a good few years in full chastity until the right time, inheritance, comes? A sexually repressive ideology seems to be inexorable.[3]

> It would be naïve to think that the urge to marry early, so common among the Irish of the previous generations, was suddenly and easily transformed into an urge not to marry. The successful acceptance of postponed marriage and permanent celibacy were dependent on the new discipline and sexual morality which were brought to bear on the body externally through surveillance and schooling, and internally through the creation of shame and guilt about sex. (Inglis 1998a: 166)

We could rightly conclude that the control of sex had the material strength of an almost economic imperative for the SFS, of the same order as the control of land transfers or the control of the agricultural cycle. At this point it definitely looks as if the magic of the social structure fully played its marvellous trick. We began by identifying an unintelligible phenomenon, Irish sexual puritanism, the 'puzzle of Irish sexuality', for which no immediately apparent explanation was available. We followed with a close analysis of the social structure wherein our ethnographic puzzle thrived. The results are clear: the Irish strict code of sexual morality is no longer unintelligible, it is a functional requirement of a specific set of social relations.

I believe that there is a great deal of sense in what we have been looking at so far. There are some major problems, however, with this explanatory model that deserve close examination – perhaps even more directly related to the merits of the structural-functionalist method. On the one hand, my portrait of Irish rural social structure is quite simplistic and incomplete in a rather important respect. On the other, the connections I have drawn between the characters of this social structure and its functional requirements contain certain underlying assumptions that should be made explicit. In my defence, I must say that this is not entirely my fault since this is a conventional type of analysis that appears in the most reputed ethnographic and historical researches.

Notes

1. With Jarvie, I consider that

   As to what social structure *is*, a great deal too much ink has already been expended on this. Suggestions have been: the relations of persons to persons; the relations of persons to institutions; the relations of institutions to institutions; or various combinations of these. Detail of the tortuous arguments need not concern us here. I prefer to say simply that 'social structure' is a metaphor to describe the mechanical relations between entities in the social order. Its 'reality' is of importance only to the positivists. (Jarvie 1967: 192)

2. A much more nuanced portrait of pre-Famine Ireland can be seen in O'Neill (1984).

3. The question of population growth and the peculiarities of Irish demographic history will be explored in chapter 6. But now let me dispel an apparent inconsistency. There is something at first sight paradoxical in the attempt at controlling population growth through a restrictive code of sexual behaviour. In Ireland, a restrictive sexual morality went hand in hand with the highest marital fertility rates in Europe. 'It seems paradoxical', R. Kennedy observes, 'that the Irish should be the best example of population control through marriage practices and at the same time the worst example of population control through acceptance of a small completed family size' (1973a: 13). Can we interpret this as a failure of the intended policy? According to Tom Inglis, 'In nineteenth century Ireland, control of sexual activity was achieved by limiting marriage. The flaw in this social mechanism was that those who did get married had large families' (1998b: 169). But was it really a 'flaw'? I think that the paradox is more apparent than real. The high Irish marital fertility rate was not a failure of the post-

Famine adjustments. Post-Famine demographic ideology was not the crude Malthusianism implied in the need to prevent an excessive population growth. The 'purpose', if such an expression could be used, of post-Famine adjustments was not merely to limit population growth, but rather to limit the increase in the number of families living on the land. This is the demographic rationale of the SFS: to prevent the multiplication of family units living on a limited amount of land at each generational replacement. But the system also has other more problematic effects. The price to be paid for the limitation of family units is, quite obviously, the fall in nuptiality. Celibacy increases, both permanent celibacy for those excluded from land rights and also a prolonged temporary celibacy for those lucky enough to inherit the family land (or to marry into a particular landholding, as the case may be) but, in all likelihood, not before the retirement of the older generation.

CHAPTER 5

Functionalist Dilemmas

It is worth having a closer look at the reasons that presumably account for the need for sexual repression in post-Famine Ireland: first, the economic significance that marriage acquired in the structural conditions arising from the post-Famine adjustments; secondly, the need to keep both bachelors' and spinsters' sexual activity at bay.

Let us begin with the first reason: the economic significance of marriage. In the SFS, marriage is the key factor in the reproduction of the social structure – remember that this is a society of small landowners, thus the marriage process has to be conducted under the severe imperatives of economic rationality, which leave little room for the free expression of love, romanticism or sexual desire. Hence, the matchmaking practices so brilliantly portrayed in Arensberg and Kimball's ethnography (Arensberg 1937: 72–76; Arensberg and Kimball 2001: 103–17; see also Connell 1962). 'Marriage, at least since 1850, has been a matter largely of family economics. Neither romantic nor erotic ideas were regarded as any vital part of the traditional society's life – they were the province of the corrupt, debauched, magical, strange' (Brody 1973: 179). A rural society in which social reproduction was so crucially dependent on marriage arrangements, especially those concerned with access to land-ownership and dowry payments, does not seem to allow for romanticism and sexual love in the constitution of the marital bond. Implicit in all this reasoning is the notion that if sexual love is not constitutive of the marriage bond it somehow becomes culturally redundant and must therefore be 'repressed' or, at least, inhibited or annulled.[1]

I think that with this argument too much is taken for granted concerning the nature of sexual desire and its social regulation. It is assumed that sexuality can only exist within marriage; but there is no need to carry out any exhaustive ethnographic survey to realise that marriage and sexuality are not synonymous. Consider, for instance, Malinowski's classical account of sexual life among the Trobriand islanders (1929). People marry for love, Malinowski was keen to point out, not because of love. The desirability of marriage lies above all in the social status it confers upon both husbands and wives. And yet this socio-political theory of marriage appears within the context of a remarkably uninhibited sexual culture. Thus, the fact that in Ireland marriage was not about sex, but economics, should not necessarily lead to repressed sexual attitudes manifested in the 'lack of sexual vitality' and 'lack of enthusiasm for sexual activity'. I believe that a theory of marriage that defines marriage as a nodal point of intricate political alliances and economic strategies (i.e. something that has nothing or very little to do with sexual love) might certainly coexist with a more or less liberal or non-repressive sexuality, and the fact that it does not cannot be accounted for by that particular characterisation of marriage. In other words, unless we take marriage as coterminous with sexual activity, the desexualisation of marriage should not necessarily result in the desexualisation of society.

Now the economic significance of marriage has an additional effect as regards sexual morality. I have said above that some form of sexual control has to be devised for a society that has so many unmarried men and women hanging around. But, when marriage acquires a prominent economic significance, when it is on the occasion of marriage that major economic transactions take place, it is the women's sexual activity, rather than the men's, that seems to deserve special attention. Some authors have contended that the reason lies in the nature of those economic transactions and in women's role in them. In his well-known analysis of marriage payments, Jack Goody pointed out that the prohibition of premarital sex and concern over one's daughters' virginity should be linked with the emergence of diverging devolution (Goody 1973: 25). It is the fact that women can inherit property that turns the control of their bodies' reproductive capacities into a social necessity. A similar point has been made concerning the association of partible inheritance and severe sexual morality in the bourgeois culture of Victorian

England: an adulterous wife (and an unchaste unmarried daughter) may endanger family property by multiplying its potential claimants (Weeks 1989: 30).

Can we apply this argument to the Irish case? Dowry payments were widespread in traditional rural Ireland but they never involved women's access to property since they were appropriated by the wife's father-in-law in order to endow his daughters (Breen 1984). What we actually see in the Irish countryside of the late nineteenth century is not the proliferation of diverging devolution but of patrilineal, indivisible inheritance, dotal marriage and matchmaking practices. Under these conditions, the ideological value of women's premarital virginity cannot be readily explained by the prevailing inheritance system. The fact that a man's daughter had plenty of sexual liaisons before marrying and bore a few illegitimate children does not seem to affect in any significant way that man's property. Only when the daughter is legitimately married will she receive her dowry, which will be handed down neither to her legitimate nor to her illegitimate children but to her father-in-law and, eventually, to her sisters-in-law.

So why this great concern for women's premarital virginity, then? The specific surveillance of women's sexual conduct, particularly the unmarried woman's sexual conduct, has been so widely analysed in the ethnographic literature that it is worth having a quick look at it. To begin with Ireland itself, double standards in what concerns sexual morality (i.e. that men's and women's behaviour seems to be evaluated following different criteria) did not go unnoticed by Arensberg and Kimball. 'Premarital virginity is the ideal,' they remarked, but 'the young lads are not, or were not until recently, expected to be so pure as the girls' (2001: 206). So it is the unmarried women's chastity that is important. This is what is referred to as the woman's 'character':

> The young woman's 'character' is her full status as a social being because the familistic system is such that sexual activity, no less than economic, is completely integrated with one's role in social life. Consequently her sexual conduct is no concern of hers alone ... To 'destroy a girl's character' in the countryside is to upset the pattern of family and community life by overthrowing the possibility of an orderly change in farm succession. Much more than a shooting or a fight, a sexual irregularity, which cannot be righted in a match, is capable of destroying the intricate mutual obligations and expectancies of rural familism. (Arensberg and Kimball 2001: 208)

According to these authors, a woman who loses her virginity has lost two fundamental potentialities: potential motherhood of a familistic line and potential transmission of an advantageous marriage alliance. But in the 'familistic order' of rural Ireland these two potentialities are identical, and they are both based upon sex, since:

> They make of the unmarried girl a sort of symbol of familistic aspiration. To use the symbol for any but its proper purpose of procreation and alliance is to destroy not only its efficacy but the aspirations that are attached to it. Rural Ireland, indeed, provides a sort of archetype or 'pure' form of this sexual outlook, the congenial western European ideal of premarital virginity. It is important here as a living function of a closely integrated social system. (Arensberg and Kimball 2001: 210–11)

They were right. I do not know to what extent we can see an 'archetype' in rural Ireland (see McLoughlin 1994), but concern over women's premarital virginity is definitely a widespread phenomenon in European societies, especially southern European societies. Jane Schneider was one of the first authors to relate the honour-and-shame syndrome that is said to be so emblematic of the Mediterranean region (see Peristiany 1965) with the functional needs of the inheritance system. Specifically, her argument was that with partible inheritance families have a strong centrifugal tendency, which can only be counterbalanced by the common interest of male family members in their daughters'/sisters' virginity. 'A woman's status defines the status of all men who are related to her in determinate ways. These men share the consequences of what happens to her, and share therefore the commitment to protect her virtue. She is part of their patrimony' (Schneider 1971: 18). Similar observations have been made more recently by Goddard in relation to Naples. According to this author, when a woman is formally engaged to a man, her father becomes her 'guardian' – as a substitute for her future husband – and her misconduct can dishonour him, as the misconduct of a married woman dishonours her husband (Goddard 1996: 150).[2]

Perhaps Jane F. Collier (1997), in her ethnography of an Andalusian community, is the anthropologist who has most cogently related concerns regarding women's sexuality with the constraints of a social structure, in particular, as she herself puts it, with an organisation of social inequality based upon inherited property. A social order, Collier sustains, wherein inequality is based on inheritance has direct repercussions on the conception of women's sexuality. Men have to protect their female relatives' bodies because otherwise inheritance patterns (patrilineal inheritance) could be disrupted. In a patrilineal system, inheritance is based on paternity and 'the best way to establish paternity, and thus to determine the child's paternal inheritance, is to ensure that a child's mother has sexual relations with only one man' (Collier 1997: 71). That is why

> a man's honor depends on the chastity of his close female relatives. A man whose mother's chastity is open to question is at a disadvantage if someone challenges his right to the property or political privileges he claims to have inherited from his father. Similarly, a man whose wife is unfaithful may find himself ridiculed for working to enhance or preserve property that another man's children will inherit. (Collier 1997: 71–72)

Collier believes that an unmarried women's virginity is crucial in this particular context. Whereas men can go with prostitutes if they cannot repress their sexual desires, women have to avoid all physical contact with men until they marry for fear of losing their 'honour' (1997: 87–89).[3] A man who makes his fiancée pregnant must marry her as soon as possible, for if he refuses to marry her she will be disgraced for the rest of her life. And he himself will have to emigrate since his conduct will be seen as a betrayal by a local family. So some women might try to get pregnant on purpose as a way of forcing their boyfriends to marry, but it is obviously a big risk for them too (Collier 1997: 94–95; see also Goddard 1996: 148).[4]

The parallelism between these examples and the Irish case is beyond question. But from what we have seen it appears that, at least as far as Collier's ethnography is concerned, whether women inherit property or not does not seem to be very relevant, for the key point is the identification of paternity as a requisite for the constitution of a patrilineal descent line through women. Accordingly, it is clear why a married woman should have sex only with her husband, but I fail to see in what way women's premarital virginity has anything to do with the constitution of patrilineal descent. I shall come back to this in a minute. Furthermore, paternity is established by controlling women's sexuality in such a way that the need for that control, which explains the existence of this particular sexual morality as regards women, turns out to be precisely the social functions attributed to the institution of paternity: the establishment of a patrilineal descent line. To my mind, the problem with this argument is that it is based on an assimilation between the control of sexuality and the control of women's reproductive capacities. Sexuality must be kept under control because we need to control reproduction. But procreation and sexuality are two different phenomena, though closely interconnected (see Frigolé 1998). As Frayser (1999: 11) argues, if 'sexuality is equated with reproduction, this is more a matter of cultural definition than of biological fact'. My point is that the control of sexuality, men's or women's, and the control of procreation or reproduction are two separate things, in such a way that the need to control sexuality cannot be explained only by the need to control reproduction. Undoubtedly, this is part of the explanation but not the full explanation. I shall try to clarify why I think this should be the case.

We must move on to the other reason that presumably accounts for the existence of a repressive sexual morality in Ireland: the need to keep at bay bachelors' and spinsters' sexual activity. Consider again the correlation that can be established between widespread celibacy and sexual repression (in a pre-contraceptive environment). In post-Famine Ireland, a sexually inhibitive or repressive moral code was needed, so the argument runs, because, both late marriage and a high celibacy rate being requisites of the social structure of that time, how could a human society prevent social unrest with a high proportion of its adult population being debarred from any sexual contact, sometimes for a very long time, sometimes for life? A powerful cultural code must be in force that turns sexuality into something unnecessary or even undesirable, at least for the unmarried. This is precisely the reason why the Catholic sexual doctrine, for all its rigidity and harshness, was so easily accepted. In R. Kennedy's words:

> by the mid nineteenth century increasing proportions of Irish men and women decided to postpone marriage primarily for economic and social status reasons; they wished to avoid the emotional entanglements with the opposite sex and such temptations were more easily resisted with the help of a strong moral code; and in spite of official Roman Catholic doctrine which encourages marriage among lay persons and considers sexual union within marriage as sacred, the Irish desired and received from the clergy very strong emphasis on the dangers and sinfulness of sex among single persons. (Kennedy 1973a: 14–15)

First there are economic and social status reasons for celibacy and delayed marriage, afterwards there is the ideological justification in terms of an austere sexual doctrine. I wish to make two comments on this argument: one historical and another theoretical. Historically, a harsh code of sexual conduct has been documented in Ireland prior to the Famine (Connolly 1979, 2001: 176–82; Connell 1968: 51–86); so it is unclear how the post-Famine adjustments can be seen as the sufficient cause of a moral ideology that already existed when they were put into practice. But there is a seemingly more trivial, and rather theoretical, question that I wish to discuss now. It is not at all self-evident that the mere abundance of unmarried adults calls, by itself, for a sexually repressive moral ideology. A priori, one could think that just the opposite might very well be the case, to wit: a sexually 'disinhibitory' moral code that would allow for non-marital liaisons to take place between those people who had few possibilities of having sex within marriage. In other words, my contention is that the mere existence of high permanent celibacy rates and delayed marriage are in themselves neither necessary nor sufficient reasons for the emergence of a repressive sexual morality. Why is it, then, that my a priori assumption – the possibility of a sexually disinhibitory moral ideology – is never seriously taken into consideration? Simply because it would give rise to a regime close to sexual promiscuity and subsequent soaring rates of illegitimacy, with the socially disruptive effects that, presumably, all this may produce. We should not forget that, in a pre-contraceptive culture, sexual promiscuity is causally related to illegitimacy, and late nineteenth-century Ireland was still to a great extent a pre-contraceptive culture, though this is precisely what was going to change in the following decades, as we will see.

But let us have a closer look at the connection between sexual promiscuity and illegitimacy in a pre-contraceptive environment. This connection is based upon a particular, and distinctively Western, conception of marriage and the attribution of patrilineal descent and inheritance rights. By virtue of this conception, marriage establishes patrilineal descent on the assumption that it presumes the occurrence of fertile sexual intercourse between the marriage partners. It is because the wife has been fertilised by her legitimate husband, and thus will bear a child consanguineously related to him, that a relation of patrilineal descent can be

established between the husband and his wife's child. Now this act
of fertilisation through sexual intercourse is, from the social point of
view, not only invisible, as Friedl (1994) has pointed out, but also,
and more crucially, it is an imagined behaviour. It is a behaviour
legally presumed by the existence of the legitimate marital bond.
And, being a presumption, it can be invalidated if it can be proved,
for instance, that the wife has had an adulterous relationship with
another man.

From this, it is clear why, when contraception is not available, a
married woman's relationship with a man who is not her husband
can be so pernicious. Patrilineal descent cannot be established
because the presumption on which it is based – imagined sexual
intercourse between husband and wife – clashes with the actual
sexual relationship that that woman had with her lover (imagined as
well, but by other means). It is less clear, however, and this is the
point I wish to stress, why sex between the unmarried should be
equally punishable.

Now the situation sexual repression was supposed to 'solve' in
post-Famine Ireland, according to the argument that we are
following, was that of an abundance of bachelors and spinsters
caused by the prevailing family system. Thus, it is the unmarried
having children that we want to prevent with that particular sexual
ideology, rather than the married having them with the 'wrong'
person. But notice that no reason for the social stigmatisation of
non-marital children can be derived from the need to establish
patrilineal descent in the above conditions. An unmarried woman's
child does not threaten in any way either patriliny or inheritance
rights. In the absence of marriage, there is no (legitimate) paternity
to be established; her real sexual act did not clash with any imagined
act (legal presumption). By being illegitimate, the child is legally
debarred from all inheritance claims or paternal rights, but this does
not jeopardise in any way the legally recognised rights of those who
are legitimate children. This is what the difference between
legitimate and illegitimate children is all about. In actual fact,
illegitimacy can be perfectly functional in social systems based on
patrilineal inheritance, as has been observed in several European
rural societies: by systematically disinheriting a substantial part of
the population, it provides a source of cheap labour for landowners
(see O'Neill 1987). Admittedly, the social rejection of illegitimacy is
not distinctively Irish. There are many other societies, in Europe and

elsewhere, in which we can hit upon a similar set of attitudes concerning non-marital children. But we still have to find a reason why this should be the case, especially taking into account the absence of any visibly damaging consequences for the social system as a whole and, furthermore, the possible functional advantages that a population of disinherited men and women can bring for the 'legitimate' children in a community of landowners.

My point is that illegitimacy is socially unacceptable not for economic reasons. It is not because it threatens any inheritance or property system, but because it discloses an irregular sexual act, non-marital children are the signifiers of an activity that contravenes sexual norms. Illegitimate children are not 'evil' in themselves but they stand for, they evoke, an evil act. In short, illegitimacy is an abduction of immorality. This means that it is the prevalence of a particular sexual morality in a particular society that makes illegitimacy undesirable, and not the functional needs of this or that inheritance and land tenure system. This might sound rather obvious to some readers, but there are important consequences to be derived from it. It has been argued that the existence of a repressive sexual morality in post-Famine Ireland found its rationale in the need to prevent an excessive rate of illegitimacy, given the high proportion of unmarried adult population. But now this argument turns out to be curiously circular. We need a stern sexual morality because we do not wish to have illegitimate children, and we do not wish to have illegitimate children because our stern sexual morality does not allow us to have sex outside marriage and, thereby, to have illegitimate children. The functional argument, the argument according to which we need sexual repression to avoid the birth of illegitimate children, includes in its explanation the element that it is supposed to explain: sexual morality.

Notice, on the other hand, that this particular type of sexual morality is likely to produce a conspicuous gender imbalance in what concerns its disciplinary effects. It is a woman's improper pregnancy that discloses irregular sexual conduct by making it 'imaginable'. This is what explains why women's premarital virginity is particularly valued in Ireland and probably in at least some of the other societies we have seen. As I have endeavoured to demonstrate, it has nothing to do with property rights, the establishment of patrifiliation or inheritance; it simply has to do with the greater visibility of women's irregular sexuality. Without a doubt, it may be partially related to the asymmetry created by a system of gender relationships. But this is only a partial explanation, since it does not tell us why women's sexuality has to be the object of specific surveillance, and not any other part of their conduct. Stated otherwise, gender inequality explains why women are treated differently, but it does not explain why this different treatment has to focus on their sexual behaviour, and this is what we are interested in here.

We have seen so far that none of the functional arguments that presumably account for the existence of a repressive sexual morality in rural Ireland after the Famine are at all satisfactory. But there is one further element that might show even more clearly that sexuality and reproduction should be kept separate. I have contended that what has traditionally been considered as an explanation for the existence of a particularly stern sexual morality – the economic significance of marriage, the need to establish patrilineal lines of inheritance and the need to prevent soaring rates of illegitimate births – consists, in fact, of factors related to the reproduction of a particular social system, and all this explains very little because the curtailment of sexual activity does not seem to have a substantive effect on the working of that reproduction. Yet the separation between sexuality and reproduction is never complete in a pre-contraceptive environment. We can say that non-marital pregnancies do not threaten in any serious way the reproduction of the social system, but it is true that they are likely to produce some socially significant effect that goes beyond the mere abduction of an irregular sexual act. They will produce human beings for whom some sort of social arrangements should be provided, even if those social arrangements happen to be perfectly innocuous, or even functional, to the society where these children are born and are going to grow up. What we need to consider now is the fact that contraception was about to become a widespread phenomenon in European societies from the late nineteenth century (McLaren 1990: 178–214; Santow 1995). Now, if the sole concern with the control of sexual activity were the control of reproduction, the practice of non-reproductive sexuality would have gone unnoticed, if not openly encouraged as a way of controlling one's reproductive capacities. And yet the truth of the matter is that parallel to the increased availability of birth control methods there has been a formidable and conspicuous opposition to their use from traditional moral authorities, especially from the Catholic Church. Contraception confers full autonomy and visibility on the cultural logic of sexual morality,[5] and its prohibition clearly suggests that the ultimate rationale for the control of men's and women's sexuality cannot lie (only) in the constraints of reproduction.

So, if the political and economic constraints of marriage and the procreation intrinsic to the SFS (i.e. the functional needs of a particular social structure) cannot in themselves explain the lack of sexual liberty, how are we going to account for it? The crucial factor that is missing in this picture of traditional Irish society, and a rather obvious one at that, is the Catholic Church. The power of the Catholic Church in Ireland at practically all levels of the social structure is well known. This fact has been widely documented in general terms and also with particular reference to the area of sexuality.[6]

Ireland is not the only country where Christian sexual doctrine has prevailed. Concern with human sexuality has pervaded Christian ideology everywhere for a very long time, though it was accentuated in Catholic countries after the Counter-Reformation. Several principles of Christian sexual morality can be traced to pre-Christian Stoic philosophy, but it seems that the main body of Christian sexual doctrine, specifically in what concerns the institution of virginity and chastity as supreme moral values, was produced by the Church Fathers from the fourth century onwards (see Flandrin 1983). Now, if it is undeniable that concern with human sexuality is a general characteristic of Christian thought, it should be pointed that in Ireland the stress on the value of sexual chastity has apparently received specific attention. It is commonly understood that the particularly rigid sexual ideology of the Irish Church comes from the monastic tradition of Irish Christianity and the influence of French Jansenism in the seventeenth century, all working together to give rise to 'a penitential version of Christianity – a tradition emphasizing sin, guilt, the innate weakness of human nature, the need for purification and rituals of self-mortification, a distrust of reason, a fear of sex, and a high regard for fasting and sexual abstinence' (Scheper-Hughes 2001: 249).

It is far beyond the objectives of this study to carry out an analysis of the history of the Church's sexual doctrine, not even of the Irish Church's sexual doctrine (see Brown 1988), but there are certain aspects of this history that I believe are particularly informative. Before examining Catholic sexual ideology in Ireland, two observations are in order concerning the history of Christian sexual morality. According to the French historian Jean-Louis Flandrin (1983), sexual prohibitions and restrictions during the Middle Ages in Europe were so overwhelming that they must have had noticeable repercussions in the evolution of the birth rate and thus demographic growth. The interesting thing, however, is that the enforcement of these stern regulations had no connection whatsoever with what we might call the objective demographic needs of the population at that time.[7] In other words, the Church's sexual doctrine was clearly non-functional in demographic terms. There is no need to remark on the meaningfulness of this 'weird' phenomenon in relation to what we have been looking at in the previous paragraphs.

I shall now briefly refer to Jack Goody's analysis of the Church's role in the regulation of marriage in historical Europe (Goody 1983). Goody's main thesis is that the Church had to take the regulation of marriage under its control in order to break the solidarity of corporate kinship groups and thus gain access to their property. Can a similar point be made as regards the regulation of sexuality? It could be argued – and this would seem to apply especially to the Irish case – that the impossibility of the Catholic Church's seizing marriage control from kin groups, and therefore the permanence of matchmaking practices, would lead to a greater concern with the control of sexuality. In other words, if marriage cannot be used by the Church as an instrument of power, sexuality will be used instead. This is apparently a plausible explanation. Notice that the definition of illegitimacy, for instance, involves a regulation of sexuality (i.e. its prohibition outside marriage) that may have direct economic effects for the Church: its potential appropriation of family wealth that otherwise would have been inherited by the illegitimate children.

But things are not so simple. Full control of sexual activity, both inside and outside marriage, cannot be said to have the same economic effects as the control of marriage, following Goody's analysis – access to property. Consider the Church's insistence that the couple's consensus was a necessary and sufficient condition for marriage: it could very well provoke inter-generational conflicts if children decided to marry against their parents' will. These conflicts might end up with children's disinheritance and the subsequent appropriation of family property by the Church. Nevertheless, and this is the point I wish to make, if the sole interest of the Church in the regulation of marriage and sexuality was to secure ways of access to family property, we run up against a bewildering contradiction: the prohibition of contraception. The use of contraceptive methods, in so far as it increased the possibility of childless or heirless marriages, militated clearly in favour of the Church's economic interests since it could inherit the family property that otherwise would have gone to legitimate children. The underlying rationale for this obsessive and very explicit prohibition, taking this politico-economic approach, remains obscure.

And now let us have a closer look at the situation in Ireland. As I have just pointed out, it is widely recognised that the stern sexual morality of Irish traditional culture has a lot to do with the teachings of the Irish Catholic Church. Tom Inglis has argued, following Foucault's conceptual framework, that, unlike what took place in most Western European countries, wherein sexuality became, from the end of the eighteenth century, the object of medical scrutiny and scientific regulation, 'in Ireland the *deployment of sexuality* remained, until the end of the twentieth century, within the "thematic of sin"' (Inglis 1997: 12). There were certainly other discourses on sexuality apart from that of the Church; yet 'the language of medicine – the way doctors spoke to their patients about sexuality – was not significantly different from the discourse of the Church and, in most cases, supported and reproduced it' (Inglis 1997: 19). Until very recently, the Church has had an absolute monopoly on anything concerning sexual matters in Ireland. Just to bring in a very persuasive illustration: in 1950 the Minister of Health of the Irish Government tried to implement a mother-child health service that had to face the Church's most impressive and unyielding opposition. In a letter sent by the Secretary to the Hierarchy to the Taoiseach (Irish Prime Minister) we can read the following:

> Education in regard to motherhood includes instruction in regard to sex relations, chastity and marriage. The State has no competence to give instructions in such matters. We regard with the greatest apprehension the proposal to give to local medical officers the right to tell Catholic girls and women how they should behave in regard to this sphere of conduct, at once so delicate and sacred. (quoted in Connell 1968: 156, n.3; see also Whyte 1980: 196 ff.; Hug 1999: 84–85)

Very few would doubt, then, that the Church has been responsible for the historical characteristics of Irish sexual culture. But, at the same time, most authors seem also to accept that the Church's role in this respect has been mainly instrumental. Of what? Of the functional requirements of Irish rural social structure. 'The Catholic Church's teachings, especially those on sexual morality, were the means by which the emergent stem family kept its sons and daughters from marrying, and thereby increased its standard of living' (Inglis 1998a: 168). 'The Catholic Church's teachings on sex outside marriage dovetailed neatly with the peasant's economic interests' (Guinnane 1997: 260). 'But for all the power of Church and State,' Connell (1968: 158) argues, 'so formalized a code would hardly have been adopted if it were at variance with social and economic needs: indeed, the peasant's respect for the Catholic code as transmitted to him has sprung, not least, from its compatibility with his patriarchal and material ambition.' Exactly the same argument has been put forward by Lee (1973: 5), for whom the Church's doctrine concerning sexuality merely reflected 'the dominant economic values of post-famine rural society ... Priests and parsons, products and prisoners of the same society, dutifully sanctified this mercenary ethos, but they were in any case powerless to challenge the primacy of economic man over the Irish countryside' (see also Inglis 1997: 13, 1998b: 169–70). This is not to deny, I assume, that the curtailment of sexual activity has been one of the fundamental tenets of Christian morality everywhere right from the days of the early Church. It is just that the specific efficacy of this doctrine in Irish society could only be explained on the basis of some sort of coalescence between Christian principles and certain 'social and economic needs'.

As Humphreys (1966: 26–27, n. 26) pointed out in his ethnography of Dublin rural immigrants, 'a purely structural-functional analysis is hard put to explain adequately the quite ascetic sexual morality of the Irish countryside ... Structural-functional explanations of attitudes do hold up to a point. But world-views and their ethical consequences also have their special effect.' It seems to me that the Church's sexual policy and ideology were very far from meeting all the requirements of the post-Famine social structure. There was certainly some complicity between the functional needs of the SFS and the sexual regime prevailing in rural Ireland at the time. There was, furthermore, as several authors have pointed out (see Connell 1968: 122 ff.) a sociological accommodation between those functional needs and the provision of new recruits for the Catholic Church, since the priesthood (and the convent for girls) was a respectable option for the non-marriageable children from peasant families. And yet the apparent elective affinity between Catholic sexual morality and the SFS was far from complete, and in fact it is precisely the dysfunctional aspects of that sexual regime that might give us a clue to its deep cultural logic. The 'magic' of the social structure can turn our search for intelligibility into blatant mystification. There is something in the cultural analysis of sexual morality in rural Ireland that is not easily reducible to a simple functional requirement of a set of social relations. The undeniable power of the Catholic Church, in my view, hints at something different, which I will try to elucidate little by little.

The common characteristic of these somewhat classical socio-structural accounts, as far as the anthropology of sexuality is concerned, is that they are based on a conception of human sexuality very close to the Freudian approach. As I stated at the beginning of this chapter, we can see in them a sort of 'mild' Freudianism in that sexuality is taken as a biological given and the only thing that culture, or social structure, can do with it is to repress it. Thus, making sense of a particular form of sexual culture, to the extent that it must always be a form of repression, inevitably entails making sense of a particular form of repression. This is actually what the above socio-structural analyses have been doing as regards the history of sexuality in Ireland. This is 'mild' Freudianism since the social structure of post-Famine Ireland was not specifically conceived, so to speak, to carry out sexual repression. It had to fulfil other, perhaps more important, structural requirements stemming from certain ecological, economic and political conditions. But, following this conventional analysis, sexual repression was definitely instrumental in the fulfilment of those requisites. But then the paradox is that the institution that has most clearly been in charge of this repression, the Catholic Church, does not seem to comply with the demands of the almighty social structure. Does this mean that sexual repression is carried out irrespective of the needs of the social form wherein it develops? What is the purpose of repression then? What does 'sexual repression' actually mean, if anything?

Let me finish with a quotation from one of our dearest ancestors. After an excellent sociological analysis of Nuer religious beliefs, Evans-Pritchard ended his renowned book with these quite unexpected theoretical reflections:

That Nuer religious thought and practices are influenced by their whole social life is evident from our study of them. God is conceived of not only as the father of all men but also under a variety of forms in relation to various groups and persons. Consequently we may say that the conception is co-ordinated to the social order. Also, he is conceived of not only as creator but also as guardian of the social order who punishes transgressions, which are breaches of interdictions which serve to maintain the social order. But the Nuer conception of God cannot be reduced to, or explained by, the social order ... When the purely social and cultural features of Nuer religion have been abstracted, what is left which may be said to be that which is expressed in the social and cultural forms we have been considering? It is difficult to give a more adequate answer to this question than to say that it is a relationship between man and God which transcends all forms. It is not surprising therefore that we cannot give any clear account of what for Nuer is the nature of this spiritual relationship. We feel like spectators at a shadow show watching insubstantial shadows on the screen. (1956: 320–21)

Notes

1. As the Irish playwright J.M. Synge observed in the Aran islands:

   The direct sexual instincts are not weak on the island, but they are so subordinated to the instincts of the family that they rarely lead to irregularity. The life here is still at an almost patriarchal stage, and the people are nearly as far from the romantic moods of love as they are from the impulsive life of the savage. (Synge 1979: 122–23)

2. See Frigolé (1998: 37–38) for further references from European rural ethnography.
3. From here Collier draws an interesting contrast between 'modern' and 'traditional' societies in relation to the values attached to marriage. In market societies both men and women are supposed to marry for love because inheritance is not, or should not be, decisive in what concerns social status. But to the extent that a woman's income is more than likely to depend on the money she receives from her husband, women are always suspected of marrying for money instead of for love (Collier 1997: 74–75). In the traditional setting, in contrast, it is precisely the opposite. In Arensberg and Kimball's words: 'in discussions of immorality, illegitimacy, premarital intercourse, the question would arise: Would you believe such a thing could happen in Ireland? In such countries as England and America well it might be, for these, the country people hear, the boys and girls just take a liking for one another and go off and marry and "never mind the money"'. (2001: 203)
4. According to Ross and Rapp, in English and Welsh farming communities of the early modern period: 'Bridal pregnancy may have been a trump card in

children's hands as they asserted autonomy from the family economy via their own sexuality' (Ross and Rapp 1981: 59). Generally speaking, social historians are normally keen on relating sexual mores, specifically female sexual mores, with systems of land-ownership. To mention just two classical examples, both Shorter (1977) and Stone (1977), despite their vociferous disagreements, accept that the increased sexual permissiveness in late eighteenth-century England and Western Europe can be seen as the result of a decrease in the number of small property owners.

5. According to Russell and Thompson (2000: 20), the availability of contraceptive techniques 'means that people can now "make mistakes" that are seen as inexcusable, even pathological ... "Choice" is thus a double-edged sword insofar as it puts responsibility for controlling fertility back in the hands of individual men and women, with moral approbation and social penalties accruing to those who do not appear to take these responsibilities sufficiently seriously.'

6. See the recent edition of Inglis's excellent work (1998a).

7. 'On pourrait sans peine allonger la liste de ces interventions contraires aux nécessités démographiques de l'heure. Elles suggèrent que l'Église, qui fondait pourtant le mariage sur les besoins de la reproduction de l'espèce, ne s'est en réalité jamais souciée des problèmes démographiques – dont elle n'avait sans doute pas conscience – ni des conséquences de sa doctrine pour l'avenir de la société' [The list of these interventions against demographic needs could be easily prolonged. They suggest that the Church, which nevertheless founded marriage upon the needs of the reproduction of the species, has in fact never been worried about either demographic problems – without a doubt, she was not aware of them – or the consequences of her doctrine for the future of society] (Flandrin 1983: 70).

CHAPTER 6

The Peculiarities of Irish Demography

Our exploration of the nature of sexual morality will lead us now along a different detour. We have seen how sexual morality as a cultural form gains some sort of epistemological autonomy from its social and economic conditions. Thus we are beginning to see the 'empty space' left by the structural-functional interpretation. Let me advise the reader that this is a key point in the present discussion. In order to fully appreciate the implications of this presumed autonomy of sexual morality as a cultural form some closely interrelated questions should be investigated. In this and the following chapters I wish to look at the ways in which this autonomous sexual morality can be related to sexual acts.

How can we relate meaning with social behaviour? This is perennial subject-matter for the social sciences and for social anthropology in particular. The concept of history has a very prominent role to play if we want to look at the relationship between culture and social action. Generally speaking, history is the product of social action, hence, any theory that lays down an interpretation of historical events implies a theory of social action, it is in itself a theory of social action. Now my purpose is to make this somewhat abstract principle a bit more concrete. I have already stated that my view of social structure is inherently diachronic. This is not the only way in which history is relevant for anthropological analysis or, at least, for an anthropological analysis of a Western literate society. This issue will be dealt with at some length in the next chapter. But first I would like to start from the opposite end, so to speak. I would like to tackle first the ways in which anthropology is said to be relevant for historical research. Specifically, I am interested in looking at the way 'culture' (sexual culture) is supposed to explain, or explain away, the peculiarities of Irish demographic history.

'Of all the concepts employed by demographers, it is the treatment of culture that has left anthropologists most dissatisfied' (Greenhalgh 1995: 19). Historians and demographers normally make use of what we might define as a residual culture concept. Those who deal with the evolution of Irish demography in the nineteenth and twentieth centuries normally attribute a noticeable explanatory power to the social structure depicted in the previous chapter (Kennedy 1973a; Clancy 1992; Ó Gráda 1994: chap. 9; Guinnane 1997). Late marriage, high celibacy rates and high marital/low non-marital fertility are said to be the peculiarities of Irish demographic history from the second half of the nineteenth century until practically the present day. To account for them the SFS seems to be impeccably suited, amongst other reasons, due to the specific kind of sexual morality and sexual behaviour that go with it. But, while discussing the ways in which this powerful social structure helps us understand the evolution of Irish demography, an additional and seemingly autonomous notion of culture is normally brought into the picture, either as an all-too-facile and apparent explanation that should be dismissed in favour of more substantial, quantitative or empirically testable factors or, alternatively, as an explanatory last resort when all else has failed. 'Culture is treated as a grab-bag of non-demographic, non-economic characteristics that influence behavior without themselves being susceptible to economic or demographic explanation' (Kertzer 1995: 29). Interestingly, when historians and demographers talk about culture they normally refer to some sort of mixture of religious beliefs and sexual mores or, more precisely, the sexual mores that have been shaped by a specific set of religious beliefs.

We saw a clear example in the previous chapter. Because the SFS obliged so many people to remain celibate and chaste, a 'culture' of sexual control or inhibition was necessary to prevent social unrest. I have already criticised the underlying assumptions of this argument. But now I wish to make a different point, or rather I wish to look at this same problem from a different angle. First of all, even if we accepted that the culture of sexual inhibition was a functional requirement of the SFS, it is obvious that this culture did not originate in the SFS itself (since being a functional requisite does not mean being a necessary consequence) but must have come from somewhere else – from the Church, for instance. Now my question is: can this culture of sexual inhibition, irrespective of whether it is functional to the SFS or not, be held responsible for the production of any identifiable historical effect? In other words, is there something in the history of Irish demography that can only be put down to the existence of this particular cultural complex? I am trying to find out whether religious sexual morality could be seen, or should be explained, as a mere legitimation *ex post facto* of a situation resulting from other causes, or if it had some additional behavioural consequences.

A very heated debate between demographers, historians and anthropologists has taken place concerning the ways in which culture might account for demographic patterns (see Handwerker 1986; Greenhalgh 1995). Ever since the Princeton European Fertility Project failed to correlate their socio-economic variables with the decline in fertility in Europe (Coale and Watkins 1986), several demographers have been calling for an analysis of the 'cultural factors' that in their view inform demographic behaviour. This is only marginal to my interests here, but the reasons why are theoretically worthy of note. My purpose is not to find the causal factors that account for Irish demographic patterns, whether they be 'cultural', 'political', 'economic' or whatever it may be; I am only interested in looking at the ways in which, while trying to explain those demographic patterns, culture is thought to be relevant. But it should be clear that the explanation of a particular demographic fact (fertility decline, for instance) is a specific analytical endeavour and it has an entirely different analytical aim from the study and interpretation of a particular cultural form (sexual morality, for instance). The fact that both types of analysis can in many ways illuminate each other, because of the obvious empirical connection between demographic behaviour and sexual norms, should not lead to theoretical confusion between the two. A great deal of the discussions that have taken place between 'culturalist' and 'materialist' accounts of demographic patterns are precisely the consequence of this recurrent danger of cross-disciplinary studies: the confusion between diverse theoretical objectives that are empirically related or coincident.

After these preliminary warnings, let us see in what way the culture concept can be useful in explaining Irish demography. We know that late marriage and, above all, high celibacy rates can easily be accounted for as a result of a particular social structure. These are not specifically Irish demographic patterns since, according to Hajnal's seminal analysis (1965), a high age at marriage and a high proportion of people who never marry are common Western European characteristics. Interestingly, Hajnal also maintained that the probable reasons that might account for this Western European marriage pattern lay in the development of the stem family and an agrarian structure of small landowners, from the sixteenth century onwards (1965: 130–35). Much the same argument can be, and has been, applied to Ireland, with the qualification that here the SFS and peasant land-ownership only started to develop towards the end of the nineteenth century. Hence, in this connection Ireland seems to provide merely a late and extreme case of a characteristically Western European arrangement. 'Culture' as a separate phenomenon from social structure does not seem to play any role here.

In trying to offer an explanation for Irish celibacy, some authors discuss the possibility that Catholicism and its typically repressive sexual ideology might be responsible for it. But they immediately reject this explanation in view of the undeniable fact that the characteristics of the social structure, of the SFS, can account for Irish celibacy without further ado. Kennedy, for instance, after discarding the influence of Catholicism in the configuration of Irish marriage patterns (1973a: 145–48), holds that permanent celibacy and postponed marriage can be accounted for by a combination of what he calls the standard-of-living thesis and the stem-family thesis. On the one hand, the heir had to wait in order to obtain the land from the father and also in order to find a suitable partner with the appropriate dowry. On the other, celibacy increased because in order to keep their living standards those who did not get the land from the SFS preferred to remain celibate at home rather than marrying and becoming landless labourers (Kennedy 1973a: 153–63). The American historian Timothy W. Guinnane has recently criticised both Kennedy and Connell for what he sees as a Malthusian interpretation of Irish historical demography (1997: 195 ff.). He agrees with Kennedy, however, in rejecting Catholic social teaching, 'cultural and religious explanations', as a possible cause of Irish demographic patterns (Guinnane 1997: 216–17). For Guinnane, in what he defines, following Hammel, as a 'culturally smart' microeconomic perspective (1997: 17) so many people opted for permanent celibacy in Ireland because the balance of costs and benefits of getting married became somehow negative in the course of the second half of the nineteenth century. In pre-Famine times, people married and bore large numbers of children in order to have someone who would look after them in their old age. But by the end of the nineteenth century these benefits of marriage were increasingly provided for by what Guinnane calls 'marriage substitutes' (1997: 225). The Land Acts gave better security to tenants, turning them eventually into landowners, and the poor-relief system and the old-age pension had the same effect: they all made marriage and children less attractive as a way of providing security (Guinnane 1997: 239–40).[1]

But a culturally sensitive point of view should take into consideration the 'noneconomic implications of marriage' as well, namely, sexual activity (Guinnane 1997: 234–35). It is true that late marriage and a high celibacy rate have been common features of Western European demography. But what does seem to be somewhat more peculiar of the Irish is that, together with late marriage and a high celibacy rate, there is also a (by European standards) very low rate of non-marital fertility.[2] The Irish did not marry, or married very late, and while unmarried they, apparently, remained chaste. It could be argued, as I said in the previous chapter, that before contraceptives became available chastity for the unmarried was needed in order to prevent soaring rates of illegitimacy, but then how is it that the same thing did not happen in the other European countries with similar marriage patterns? Could it not be the case that a specific form of sexually repressive, or at least sexually inhibitive, morality was in force to discourage the Irish from indulging in so disruptive a practice? Guinnane, who sees only 'economic interests' in Ireland's unusually low rate of non-marital births, specifically those related to 'lineages and intergenerational transfer of property' (1997: 260), also addresses the question of sexual repression as a possible cause of Irish celibacy. He rejects Messenger's and Scheper-Hughes's theses and claims that there is no historical evidence that the Irish have been sexually repressed, or more sexually repressed than any other European people. In fact, he even uses a quotation from Arensberg and Kimball's work to suggest that the rural Irish were much less inhibited in sexual matters than is normally assumed (Guinnane 1997: 222). But given the lack of sexual outlets outside marriage, was it possible to remain celibate in Ireland without falling into some sort of deep neurosis? Guinnane thinks that it was. We are a sex-ridden culture that can only see 'repression' wherever sexual activity is not as widespread as it is among ourselves, but this is very far from being the case in nineteenth-century Ireland (see Fitzpatrick 1985: 128–29).

No matter how they look at it, demographic historians find it impossible to account for the peculiarities of Irish demographic patterns, at least in what concerns high permanent celibacy rates with a low non-marital fertility, without some notion of culture being smuggled into their argument. Widespread permanent celibacy seems to be a structural requirement of the SFS, but what about its attendant low rates of non-marital fertility? Religious morality – the 'cultural' factor – is thrown of out the door as an explanation for permanent celibacy but it returns through the window as the cause of low illegitimacy.[3] We are faced with a slightly more complex situation when we turn to another of the alleged peculiarities of Irish demographic patterns, namely, high marital fertility.

Ireland's fertility seems to have been high ever since demographic records have been available. According to Connell (1965), before the Famine, Ireland's fertility was high due to high nuptiality and early marriage. Later researchers have qualified Connell's thesis: there does not seem to be much empirical foundation for the existence of early marriage in pre-Famine Ireland, but high nuptiality and high marital fertility are still considered its prominent demographic characteristics (Coleman 1992: 59; Guinnane 1997: 81–85). The result was the unprecedented population growth that we have already seen. After the Famine, the population decreased steadily up to 1961, though this was due to emigration, since births exceeded deaths throughout the period. Yet, despite this natural increase, the Irish birth rate for the second half of the nineteenth century was comparatively low. Ireland seems to have followed other European countries in controlling population growth, but with notably different means. Whereas in other European countries it was the practice of contraception that presumably accounted for their fertility decline, so that high nuptiality could combine with low marital fertility, the low birth rate in Ireland was the result of widespread celibacy combined with persistent high marital fertility (Clancy 1992: 165). Once again, a 'cultural explanation' insinuates itself: Catholic morality forbids contraception, so the Irish had large families simply because they followed the dictates of the Catholic Church. But, once again, this explanation is rapidly called into question for being too simplistic. Other Catholic countries such as France experienced a fertility decline, and at a very early date. Furthermore, and this is an interesting point, Catholicism does not encourage large families *per se*; it only prohibits certain sexual practices as contrary to natural law, but sexual abstinence is perfectly acceptable to the Church as a way of controlling marital fertility (Guinnane 1997: 261). Furthermore, there is evidence that by the end of the nineteenth century the Irish did practise contraception, especially in urban areas. Therefore, Irish marital fertility was high not because contraceptive techniques were unknown or deliberately ignored, but simply because the Irish wished to have large families (Guinnane 1997: 254–59; see also Kennedy 1973a: 189–90).

So why did the Irish wish to bear so many children? Kennedy held that Irish families were so large mainly because, thanks to systematic and massive emigration, there was no reason why they should be smaller to begin with. 'The Irish were able to persist in their high rates of marital fertility because they did not have to face the problems of rapid population growth usually associated with such reproductive behavior' (Kennedy 1973a: 173). Guinnane has proposed an interesting 'marginalistic' approach to the problem of Irish fertility. Because marriage in Ireland implied a very high fixed cost – dowries, farm, etc. – the cost of each additional child became progressively lower. In contrast, under different structural conditions (an urban setting, for instance), marriage has lower fixed costs and, consequently, the marginal cost of each additional child increases. That would explain why in Ireland we find either large numbers of people who do not marry or people who marry and have large families, whereas in an urban environment, let us say England, the opposite situation is true: large numbers of people marrying but with small families (Guinnane 1997: 265–66).

Still, neither Kennedy nor Guinnane have entirely dismissed the influence of Catholic teachings. Let us assume that Catholic sexual morality, even though it does not forbid the control of marital fertility, indirectly causes the appearance of large families by outlawing non-reproductive sexuality. Now, unlike other Catholic Europeans, the Irish had two ways of circumventing the deleterious effects of this doctrine. First, the most rebellious could simply emigrate: it has been proved that Irish emigrant women to the USA were likely to practise contraception more than any other immigrant group, even more than native-born whites. Secondly, the less defiant could stay in Ireland celibate, and chaste, due to the social acceptance of the unmarried status. In other words, those who remained in Ireland had such large families precisely because those who were more prone to marry and control their fertility simply emigrated (Kennedy 1973a: 192–95; Guinnane 1997: 263–64).

Thus religion, the cultural factor, was important after all: it did not prevent many Irishmen and women from marrying and practising contraception but it prevented them from staying in Ireland if they decided to do so. Perhaps the best way to prove the actual incidence of the cultural factor in the determination of Irish fertility patterns is to examine the demographic characteristics of populations that differ only in terms of their cultural backgrounds. Northern Ireland offers the perfect arena for such an analysis. Needless to say, by different cultural backgrounds what is meant here are different religious denominations. According to Paul A. Compton (1982), who uses evidence provided by the 1961–1971 censuses, the Northern Irish population presents two distinct demographic patterns: a low-fertility/high-nuptiality regime in the Protestant population and the high-fertility/low nuptiality regime of Roman Catholics. Now despite their lower nuptiality the birth rate of Catholics in Northern Ireland is higher than that of Protestants. This is not because Catholics are poorer, as is sometimes argued, since 'high-income, high-status Roman Catholic families are nonetheless larger than the families of low-income, low-status Protestants' (Compton 1982: 211). It is not because Catholics are a minority in the North, since their fertility rates are similar to those in the Republic (Compton 1982: 210; see also Kennedy 1973b; Coward 1980). Hence we are left with a 'cultural' explanation: 'we should therefore conclude that it is the shared cultural norms of the Roman Catholic population throughout Ireland that hold the key to an understanding of high Roman Catholic fertility within Northern Ireland' (Compton 1982: 211). Ó Gráda (1985) reached a similar conclusion using this time the censuses of 1901 and 1911: 'Catholics have inherited or developed a different set of values as regards fertility and family size' (1985: 80). For this author it is clear that 'economic explanations' are 'only of subordinate importance' (Ó Gráda 1985: 83; see also Ó Gráda 1991; Ó Gráda and Duffy 1995). More recent evidence has been provided by the

1991 census, studied by Ó Gráda and Walsh (1995), who observe that the fertility rate of Northern Irish Catholics continues to be higher than that of other confessions, even though the differences between Protestant and Catholic fertility are declining (1995: 279). Their conclusion is again that 'Catholic religiosity or "culture" remains the best explanation for the gap' (Ó Gráda and Walsh 1995: 278).

I am intrigued by the way in which demographers posit 'culture' as an explanation. It does not really make much sense to argue that some human behaviours are culturally determined whereas some others are not. If by human behaviour we understand meaningful social action (i.e. something ontologically distinct from, say, a human individual or a set of human individuals moving their bodies in a certain way), culture is inherent to the concept of human behaviour. But understanding human behaviour does not necessarily mean understanding its cultural wrapping, and understanding the cultural wrapping of human behaviour is different from looking at it as a necessary effect. These issues will be taken up later.

Culture is eschewed in demographic and historiographic explanations because culture comprises the 'irrational'. Consider an Irish peasant who has many children because he has no access to contraception, or a bachelor who remains chaste for the same reason and also because he is afraid of the social and economic consequences that might ensue if he fathers an illegitimate child: neither of these men seem to follow a 'cultural' principle in their behaviour. In contrast, the man who rears a large family, perhaps to the detriment of his standard of living, when contraception is freely available and the bachelor who has no sexual liaison because, as a devout Catholic, he does not agree with having sex before marriage are both presenting a 'cultural' behaviour. Clearly, what is involved in this type of argument is that what is 'cultural' is simply not rational. Why is the individual who behaves in accordance with a particular moral principle considered 'irrational' whereas the one who pursues some sort of apparently selfish or short-term material interest becomes 'rational'?

To explain irrational human behaviour, behaviour that cannot be accounted for in any other way or by any other discipline, is a time-honoured way of looking at the object of anthropological knowledge. But how is it that human beings behave 'rationally' at one particular time and 'culturally' at another? We all have rational and irrational behaviours in our everyday lives but this is certainly not the point that is being discussed here. It is not the point because the irrationality in everyday behaviour is a structural fact whereas our demographers and historians are concerned with the explanation of historical events, of a particular historical process. When historians and demographers argue that a particular demographic behaviour or demographic pattern can only be accounted for by invoking the 'cultural factor' they are actually admitting that there is no available explanation for it, since to consider that certain human behaviour is 'irrational' means simply that it cannot be explained. That is the reason why demographers are so reluctant to accept 'culture' as an explanation for demographic facts and behaviours, and they will only invoke it in the last instance, that is to say, as an implicit acknowledgement that there is no explanation.

Let us hold on to the principle that demographic explanations are concerned with the explanation of demographic events. The events that comprise demographic growth – low nuptiality, high marital fertility, etc. – are specific manifestations, instantiations in Sahlins's words (2000a: 321), of human conduct, they are not the values, beliefs, moral ideas, etc. within which this or that human conduct takes place. Stated otherwise, the fact or event of having sex is different from the cultural significance that sex might have in a particular society, in the same way as the fact of having a child is different from the cultural significance that this child has in any one particular society. But, if cultural meaning is clearly different from actual behaviour (i.e. behaviour as an event is different from behaviour as a structure), does this mean that we can explain actual behaviour while ignoring its cultural meaning and, conversely, that we can analyse cultural meanings while paying no heed to the actual behaviours they gave rise to or that went with them in a particular place at a particular time?

Suppose that a demographer succeeds in explaining Irish demographic history with no reference to any independent 'cultural factor', that is, making exclusive use of what we might call 'social and economic' determinants. Would that mean that Irish demographic behaviour takes place in a cultural void? Certainly not; it would simply mean that the cultural values that enfold such behaviour can be taken for granted. Imagine a man who has a small family because he uses contraception. No 'culture' seems to be involved in this type of behaviour because we take it for granted that once contraception is available nobody will want to rear a large family. The same applies to the bachelor who has sex with his next-door neighbour and fathers an illegitimate child. Why is this behaviour less 'cultural' than that of the men or the women who simply abstain from sex because they cannot marry?

Perhaps it is time for me to state a very fundamental principle concerning the concept of culture that I wish to clarify in this essay, a concept that is beginning to insinuate itself in the interstices of the social and economic processes we have been looking at. Culture is not an object that stares any observer in the face; it is a perspective, a matter of changing perspectives. What looks like culture from one point of view is no longer culture from another point of view; it becomes 'social and economic' conditions. Much of what took place in Irish demographic history merely replicates European demographic history of an earlier age. In other words, it can be reduced to 'social and economic conditions'. Yet, as we have seen, there are certain facts clearly at variance with this Western European model, or any other subsidiary model that could be worked out from it. Hence the need for the 'cultural factor'. This is the first intimation of the perspectivist approach to the culture concept that will be fully developed in part III of this essay. It is worth emphasising that, following this approach, the distinction between the cultural and the non-cultural, equivalent to the distinction between the rational and the irrational, depends as much on the object to be accounted for, the form of behaviour to be analysed, as on the subject that carries out the analysis.

Notes

1. See the new edition of Bourdieu's (2002) classical studies on rural celibacy in Béarn.
2. Kennedy's figures are unequivocal: marital fertility has accounted for 96 per cent of all births in each inter-censal period since 1871 until the 1960s (Kennedy 1973a: 174); even though, as I have argued elsewhere (Salazar 1999), documented evidence on illegitimacy does not constitute reliable proof of the non-existence of births out of wedlock, and a fortiori of the lack of premarital sexual activity. As we will see later, things have radically changed in recent years.
3. Guinnane concludes his work by underlining his agreement with most Irish historians 'in thinking that cultural differences and cultural change did not play a large role in Irish demographic patterns', but then adds an interesting remark: 'From a slightly more distant perspective, however, Ireland's demographic history suggests that to the historian the distinction between culture or institutions or economics is a bit artificial' (1997: 283).

CHAPTER 7

Imagining Sexuality: History as a Cognitive System

In this chapter, we will examine the nature of the cultural factor that seems to be so significant in Irish demographic history. But first let us pause for a moment and have a cursory look at the ways in which history is said to be relevant for anthropology. I argued elsewhere (Salazar 1998: 374) that there are two ways in which history, or a historical perspective, should be taken into consideration. On the one hand, history constitutes an objective process that leads to a particular point in time, to the so-called 'ethnographic present', for instance. It is the causal concatenation of events that enables us to explain or to understand what has happened. On the other hand, there is history as a people's discourse about themselves, history as a set of meanings that transmit intelligibility to the world. In this sense, history is learned in the process of enculturation in the same way as language or moral and religious beliefs are. It could be argued that what I did in chapter 4 was history in the first sense, the analysis of the 'causal' antecedent of the present situation. I did this to an extent, but that was not my main purpose. In fact, I believe now that there are not two but three ways in which history can be engaged with anthropology. Let me try to spell them out in some detail.

Gellner (1973: 101–6) has drawn an important distinction between genetic accounts of a particular social situation and the historical depth that a synchronic account of a social structure should have. A genetic account is an explanation by antecedent, the normal *modus operandi* of historians after careful documentation of the succession of events that define a particular time sequence. But

Gellner understood that historical evidence was also needed for the sort of structural analysis that anthropologists normally carry out. Only a historical perspective enables the anthropologist to identify the structural elements he or she is looking for: 'the structure of the present is not fully revealed without reference to its development over time' (Lewis 1968: xviii). 'I would say that a term like "structure"', Evans-Pritchard wrote, 'can only be meaningful when used as an historical expression to denote a set of relations known to have endured over a considerable period of time' (1962: 55). Quite obviously, if structure is a *longue durée* phenomenon only some measure of temporal depth can tell. This is different from a mere genetic account even though in both cases we might be using the same sort of data. And this is the sense in which 'objective' history becomes relevant to an anthropologist.

In chapter 4, I was not interested in the Famine as an 'event' but rather in its structural contextualisation: the way in which the Famine helps us to understand the meaning of certain aspects of the social structure of the Irish countryside, not the way in which the Famine event may causally explain subsequent events in Irish history, in the same way as the Famine is itself explained by antecedent events. The difference between the Famine as an event and as a 'structural index' might seem trivial, or perhaps too subtle to be of any importance. It is certainly a purely theoretical distinction with an exclusively theoretical significance, that is, it is important, or I take it to be important, only to the extent that I am interested in pursuing a theoretical argument concerning the nature of anthropological knowledge. (But, for anyone who is interested, say, in the history of Irish rural society, even in the 'structural' aspects of this history, this distinction is of little use.)

Apart from this objective-structural history and the genetic history recounted by professional historians, there is the 'subjective' history, history as a people's discourse about themselves.[1] Subjective history is a form of historical knowledge that is used to understand and to explain a state of affairs. This is the account of past events that anthropologists learn from their informants when these try to make sense of their present situation. It so happens that the difference between this subjective history and both the genetic and structural histories is not as clear-cut as it might seem, if only because in a literate society the objective history, as written by historians, for instance, is fed into people's understanding of their past by schooling, by the mass media, by popular history books and by all sorts of other means. As with the majority of cultural beliefs, this is largely an almost unconscious, non-discursive, understanding in so far as it is not normally immediately apparent to the foreign observer. But any anthropologist doing ethnography in a literate society without being familiar with its history will soon realise that he or she is missing something crucial, something like a historical *conscience collective*, a particular system of meanings that colours, sometimes in subtle ways and sometimes in more explicit terms, his or her informants' world-view. In this connection, the apparent historical reconstruction of chapter 4 can also be seen as an indispensable part of a (synchronic) cultural analysis, an exploration of a bit of the Irish historical collective unconscious.

Keeping in mind, therefore, that the difference between 'objective' and 'subjective' histories is never clearly established, that the two histories overlap and merge into each other in all sorts of complex ways, in this chapter we will look at a particular form of subjective history, or a particular form of historical narrative that clearly runs closer to the subjective pole. This is precisely the 'cultural factor' alluded to in the previous chapter, the cultural factor, or parts of it, that for some demographers might explain the peculiarities of Irish marriage and fertility patterns.

This cultural factor is, interestingly, a form of historical knowledge but seen from the opposite end. While discussing the peculiarities of Irish demography, we examined the ways in which a particular set of cultural values – sexual mores playing an important role among them – became salient when we tried to explain certain historical facts. We could now try to examine the opposite situation: how a historical process might account for a cultural form. We saw how structure shaped the production of events; we will see now to what extent events impinge on our understanding of structural phenomena. For the complex issue involved in the alleged cultural determination of human behaviour can only be properly addressed, I believe, if we look at it both ways, so to say. As I will attempt to show, both questions are simply two sides of the same coin, even though their analysis will take us into apparently very divergent lines of reasoning. Remember that our purpose now is to see how a set of beliefs, in this case concerning sexual behaviour and sexual morality, manifest themselves as historical knowledge.

When Nancy Scheper-Hughes returned to her fieldwork site in western Ireland in 1999, twenty-five years after her first visit, she was struck by the extent to which, among other things, sexual mores had changed, even in the remotest rural communities on the western shore. She sadly admitted that there was no way she could have predicted this radical transformation in her initial enquiry, since 'as dedicated historians of the ethnographic present (and therefore wedded to a particular representation of local and national life and culture), anthropologists are poor at predicting new trends, let alone cataclysmic ruptures and transformations in social and cultural life, such as these represent' (Scheper-Hughes 2001: 56). In effect, no ethnographer of contemporary attitudes towards sexuality in rural Ireland can miss what in my view constitutes its most prominent cultural theme: the ever-present feeling that things have been changing radically over the last few years. For all the severity and harshness of the Church's sexual discipline, for all the sexual repression that for so long was such a salient feature of the Irish cultural landscape, it all appears now as belonging to a recent past against which current narratives can be contrasted. The past, with its characteristic repression and backwardness, has now become a backdrop, which highlights, by means of the contrast it produces, the shapes and contours of the modern discourse. Sexual mores are believed to have radically changed in the last decades in line with broader changes that have taken place in Irish rural society and in Irish society at large. Modern views, therefore, always appear modelled as a sharp contrast against what are held to be the characteristic values and mores of bygone times.

In what concerns the subjective history of Irish sexuality, however, the past/present dichotomy, despite its pre-eminent role, runs unevenly interlocked with a series of other conceptual dichotomies – binary oppositions, if you wish – which provide it with form and content in a rather complex way. Freedom/repression, knowledge/ignorance, visible/invisible, pleasure/responsibility, control/lack of control could be seen as examples of those dichotomies, sometimes cutting across, sometimes coextensive with, the dichotomy between the past and the present. None of them has sexual activity as its exclusive referent but they all operate as cultural mediators in the local definition of sexual norms.

History is taken here as a meaning-producing machine in the same way as any mythological narrative would be (see Lewis 1968:

xv, xvii–xviii). In history the main binary opposition is between past and present, which plays a similar role to the opposition between consonants and vowels in structural phonology, or between elementary and complex kinship structures in Lévi-Strauss's well-known analysis. In what follows we will take a closer look at the way this contrast between past and present is portrayed. I will indiscriminately use direct quotations from my informants, indirect speech and different forms of ventriloquising. What has already been stated in the Introduction should be repeated now: none of the views that I will present should be seen in any way representative of Irish society, not even of the farming community where I did my fieldwork. Ethnographic subjects are only representatives of themselves – even though it is my surmise that much of what I observed could be extrapolated to other similar contexts, in Ireland and elsewhere in Europe. My purpose is to evoke a particular cultural environment meaningfully related to the images of Irish society we have already seen.

The Catholic Church and its priests are without a doubt the main character of our story. According to local narratives, sexual repression and ignorance of sexual matters originated in the all-pervasive power of the Church in the past. The power of the Church, in sexuality as well as in all other aspects of social life, was supported by people's generalised ignorance and fear. The Church is seen as responsible for keeping people ignorant of sexual matters in such a way that this ignorance appears as the justification for the very power that kept them in this ignominious mental darkness. I shall attempt to provide some ethnographic taste of this gloomy atmosphere.

My informants underlined in different ways how ignorance and fear fed on and reinforced each other. They told me that in the past people were highly religious because they lacked education; they did not enquire about things and just believed what the priests told them. They did not make enquires because they were afraid to make choices and they were terrified of the priests and the hierarchy. Even those who did not believe would pretend that they did, such was their awe of the clergy. Tales of the priests' supernatural powers are not uncommon, even though they might be recounted with some disbelief (see Taylor 1995: 145 ff.). Fear of the priests was not so much a consequence of their alleged powers, supernatural or otherwise, but is explained as a way of showing respect. To respect a priest was to be afraid of him. In this context, it is understandable that the priests' (hypothetical) sexual activity is seen with a mixture of scepticism and cynicism. A priest was murdered in a nearby parish, people told me once, and they said that he was killed by a man who found him in bed with his wife. The man managed to prove his innocence. It was a very sad story; everybody in the village talked about it for a long time.

My belief is that the priest's chastity was seen by many as an indication of his superior status, as if by renouncing sexuality some kind of supernatural nature could be proved. While discussing the Catholic priests' enforced celibacy with a married couple, the wife argued that they should not marry because, if they were allowed to, then 'they would be like everybody else'. But in her parish, she went on, there was a priest who took an unmarried mother and her child under his protection, and people thought that she was actually the priest's mistress. And yet they were all very happy with that priest, she concluded enigmatically. 'That's all gossip,' her husband interrupted. Priests used to have a 'lady' in their houses who would prepare meals for them and do the housework, that's all, he explained. But neither of them denied the possibility of some sort of sexual liaison between the priests and those women.[2]

In any case, the priest's image as an all-powerful, fearsome and mysterious character is seen as belonging to the past. Recent discoveries of priests' sexual abuses and affairs, such as the case of the Bishop of Galway, have certainly contributed to their discredit. Everybody agrees that today people are too educated, too clever to believe everything they are told. They have knowledge, they are more 'civilised', they are more affluent. The more money they have, the less religious they are – linking thus their parents' poverty with their extreme religious zeal – and so they are more selfish and pleasure-seeking. The fears of earlier times have disappeared and along with them the kind of moral certainty and security they seemed to imply. No one actually wishes to turn the clock back, but people's depictions of the situation today are by no means devoid of nostalgia. Too much knowledge can have unfortunate side-effects. Consider the case of a man who committed suicide by taking weed poison, a young mother commented to me. He was well educated, the son of a politician, and he had probably learned about that poison at university. Otherwise he would not have known about it and he might not have killed himself. For her, this event clearly illustrated the damaging consequences of an excessive concern with learning and education. But the argument about general knowledge gradually slipped into the particular case of sexual knowledge. 'We didn't know nothing at all,' she said referring to her childhood (she was about thirty-three when interviewed), 'and it was much better, you know, because now they [children] know everything and then want to try everything ... Now children are very bold, even my own, I admit that, they know too much. There is no respect and no manners. Now they even answer back to a priest! No way we would have done that ourselves; because we were afraid, and we were as better off. Now children know too much, I always say that. I've heard that a girl of fourteen bore a child in the school, and her parents didn't even know that she was pregnant.'

The excess of sexual knowledge brings about unwanted children: the problem of illegitimacy. We already know that according to documentary evidence the number of non-marital births in Ireland has historically been low. But things have changed: fertility outside marriage has risen from a moderate 5 per cent in 1980 to 32 per cent in the year 2000, one of the highest in Western Europe (Fahey and Russell 2001: x). This relatively rapid and quite remarkable increase in non-marital births figures prominently in people's descriptions of the current situation.

People often emphasised priests' severe attitude to illegitimate births in bygone times. A man told me the following story. Years ago, a farmer was accused of getting a young unmarried girl pregnant. He was the son of one of the wealthiest farming families of the neighbourhood, whereas the girl came from a modest family of small landowners. There was a trial but nothing could be proved. Nevertheless, the parish priest – who, incidentally, was said to possess some sort of supernatural curative powers – publicised the affair. The man married another woman some years afterwards but he could never bring her to his house while his parents were alive because of their strong opposition to the marriage. Once they were dead the wife finally went to live with her husband, but he died soon afterwards, leaving a widow and two children. Nobody could affirm that the priest's mysterious powers lay behind this ill-fated story, but some definitely envisage some sort of connection.

So it was in the old times. But today it is different. One of my informants admitted somewhat apologetically that today priests take no notice of unmarried mothers: they wouldn't be able to count them! But in the local world-view this does not make unmarried mothers any more legitimate. The schoolgirl got pregnant because she had 'too much knowledge' and too little sense of responsibility, and the same applies to the man who committed suicide. In moral terms, knowledge and responsibility seem to be directly correlated: responsibility appears as the desired ideal consequence of increased knowledge, in such a way that the lack of this desired ideal consequence turns the increased knowledge into 'surplus' knowledge, and thus morally abhorrent. In the past a certain level of sexual laxity could be somehow condoned due to the generalised ignorance about sexual matters so characteristic of former generations.[3] Only the priests, with their idiosyncratic severity, were an exception – a necessary exception, some might add – to this moderately compassionate attitude. But things have changed: everybody agrees that the Church has now lost much of its power, as people have lost much of their ignorance. Modern views on illegitimacy contain an implicit discourse on sexuality that links it with very basic definitions of the self as a knowledgeable agent and a responsible subject.

In another chapter I will deal with the relevance of modern conceptions of the self in the field of sexual morality. But now let me bring in one last story. An unmarried 22–year–old girl who had been studying in England returned to Ireland with a baby. It was a great shock to her mother, who had a son about to be ordained and who was said to be a very holy woman. But now she has accepted it, and she will take care of the baby while her daughter goes to Limerick to finish her degree. Neighbours pitied the girl for her distressing situation and her uncertain future. 'She is only twenty-two and she will be stuck with the baby being so young,' a woman observed. Nobody could understand how it had happened to her, a girl 'as educated' as she was, said another, while she was going to pay a visit to the unwed mother. 'You have to think of the day after and not only the night,' she asserted rather seriously. 'That would have never happened in my family, if any of us had come with a baby she would have been thrown out!' Interestingly, the same woman told me some time afterwards that one of her sisters bore a child only three months after her marriage. She was recalling the fact in a joking mood that contrasted with the sadness and gravity with which she had judged the previous event. But this time it was different, the pregnant woman married before giving birth. The funny thing was the advanced state of her pregnancy at the time of the marriage ceremony.

Quite paradoxically, lack of knowledge accounts for unwanted pregnancies of the past in the same way as too much knowledge (too much education) is the cause of the exorbitant number of unmarried mothers in the present. What has turned the knowledge differential of the present into surplus knowledge is the fact that it has not been matched by a corresponding degree of individual responsibility. In sexual matters, individual responsibility, which, it should be stressed, appears as a prominent characteristic of modern times, is culturally constructed by relating sexual conduct to the discourses of marriage and fertility. As I will try to show, in so far as discourses on marriage and fertility constitute the cultural symbols in terms of which an individual subject can be identified as a sexually responsible person, they can both be seen as idiosyncratic languages that make sexuality visible, or imaginable, by defining a particular sexual norm. Stated otherwise, it is by talking about marriage, its meaning, its purpose, its moral value, etc. and about marital fertility, specifically, whether it should or it should not be kept under control, that sexual conducts are imaginable and, consequently, a particular view on sexual morality becomes apparent.

According to local ideology, marriage erases the immoral qualification of a previous sexual encounter. 'Getting a girl in trouble is no longer a sin if you marry her,' a bachelor instructed me once while trying to illustrate the contrasting moralities between the old and new times. This does not seem to have been the Church's point of view. For, it is argued, the priests would consider as sinful any sexual activity involving two unmarried people, no matter what happened afterwards. And, as a result of the Church's power, my informants have no doubt that this is also how it would have been seen by the priest-ridden and brainwashed members of previous generations. But now people are more civilised, they add in a conciliatory mood, and they would condone the visible sexual incontinence of pregnant single women so long as they marry. Thanks to this moralising capacity of marriage, a pregnant woman who marries removes the indecency of her sexual conduct by counteracting her 'excess' of sexual knowledge with a paramount act of moral responsibility: marriage – which prevents that differential knowledge from becoming 'surplus' knowledge.[4]

My informants see marriage as a fundamental watershed in a person's life, marking the entrance into adulthood. Moral credentials accrue to married men and women, who are held to be responsible subjects. Bachelors, in contrast, despite their relative abundance, are pitied for their lonesome condition but censured as well for their allegedly irresponsible behaviour: they have a good time while they are young and then when they want to marry it is too late. When asked about the pros and cons of non-marital unions a middle-aged married woman expressed her support by arguing that 'you can see how it works and then if you don't like it you just leave it'. She recognised that the Church would not approve it – 'they say it is a sin' – but her attitude, always respectful and uncritical concerning religious matters, did not seem to involve a blind acceptance of the Church's prescriptions. Her support of a consensual union as a kind of trial marriage, however, is very far from a libertine posture as regards premarital sex, but it should be interpreted in connection with her firm rejection of the possibility of divorce – which at the time of my fieldwork was still unauthorised in the Irish Republic. It is important to note that rejection of divorce is very widespread among the rural population of the west of Ireland, especially among women, both young and old (see Coulter 1997). Thus my informant's positive views on consensual unions clearly resulted from her understanding of such a practice as a sort of antidote against marriage breaking. A broken marriage was seen as a consequence of the spouses' lack of responsibility, all the more so if they had children; but in any case separation always appeared as morally abhorrent and the spouses were the only ones to blame.

The contrast between past and present provides again an appropriate framework to interpret local views on marriage as a supreme moral and moralising act. Matchmaking practices were the prominent characteristic of marriage in bygone times. Now they are firmly condemned as backward, oppressive and narrow-minded. Everybody agrees that parents should not have a say in their children's marriages, it is a matter solely for the young. Interestingly, however, this does not mean that marriage is seen as a bond exclusively linking two isolated individuals. 'You marry a family, not just a woman,' a married man informed me. He was talking about a previous relationship he had with a girl he was very much in love with. But eventually he broke it off because he felt he was not accepted by her family. People like to think of their marriage decisions as depending exclusively on their own free will. But the moral appraisal that those decisions will deserve seems to be contingent to a great extent upon family acquiescence. Thus, a young married woman did not have any doubt when in an informal conversation I asked her why she married her husband: 'because they liked him at home'. Be that as it may, as we saw when we were discussing the question of illegitimacy, what needs to be stressed here is that the moral aspect of marriage is closely associated with modern notions about the self as a knowledgeable and responsible subject.

We see therefore that sexuality outside marriage is not necessarily disapproved of and it may even be advisable in so far as it may help in the building of a stable marital relationship afterwards. We will see later, however, that the moral evaluation of premarital sexual activity is slightly more complex than that. In any case, when these sexual contacts lead to an undesired pregnancy they definitely spur severe moral criticism, especially of the woman, because it shows that her conspicuous sexual knowledge surpasses her sense of responsibility. A subsequent marriage, if it takes place before the birth, can expunge the immorality of the premarital pregnancy, thanks to the moralising capacity of the marriage act.[5]

Does this mean that sexual activity within marriage lacks any moral constraints? Not at all. Here we come across the second cultural discourse that intervenes in the definition of a sexually responsible person: fertility or, rather, fertility control. We have seen that high marital fertility is a well-known feature of traditional Irish demographic patterns. The decline of the birth rate in the last twenty years is taken as a clear indication of the modernisation of Irish society as a whole. In 1955, 31 per cent of all births were fifth births compared with only 5 per cent in 1998; in 1962, there were 2000 births to mothers with ten children and over, compared with 55 such births in 1998 (Kennedy 2001: 30; see also Fahey and Russell 2001: 30–32). Once again, people seem to be very much aware of this reduction in family size, and considerable moral and social significance is accorded to it. As I did for non-marital births, I shall explore now a little of the cultural context that surrounds the decline in fertility.

Until recently, in rural Ireland a very positive value was placed on having many children, viewed not only as an economic asset but also as a source of pleasure and status for both parents. And yet most of my younger informants invariably identified large families as a typical characteristic of bygone times. Thus, as with sexual repression, high marital fertility is also associated with the ignorance and backwardness of the previous generations. On the one hand, I was told that families were very large in the past because people were ignorant of contraceptive methods. But, perhaps more significantly, they say that it was not only ignorance that prevented people from planning their families but also their blind obedience to the dictates of the clergy. We already know that one of the most prominent aspects of the Church's sexual doctrine is its opposition to contraception. The unavailability of contraceptive methods is thus seen as a result of both the Church's stern prohibition and the people's lack of knowledge. Several people reported that a priest could very well ask in confession how many children a couple had and for how long they had been married, so that a discrepancy between the number of children born and the years of married life would be harshly interpreted as a sign that some sort of contraception had been practised. 'They say you cannot have the Holy Communion if you practise contraception, perhaps you cannot even go to church,' a woman told me while referring to the Church's bygone morality. 'But all this is dying out,' she rushed to add (see also Sweetman 1979: 119–20). It was not only the priests who had this negative view of contraception. Contraceptive methods could be obtained with a doctor's prescription, but prescriptions were only issued when pregnancy could seriously jeopardise the mother's health.[6] A mother of twelve children was unable to obtain the contraceptives prescribed by her doctor, one of her daughters told me, because the doctor was an old man, the old-fashioned type, she explained. He continued to say that she was a healthy woman and could bear children with no problem.

There is one further explanation for large families, which points even more directly to people's understanding of sexuality. As Sicilians told the Schneiders: 'sexual embrace is the festival of the poor' (Schneider and Schneider 1984: 263). My informants understand that lack of education and backwardness, as the main reasons for large families, lie at the roots of the sexual incontinency characteristic of former generations. In the past, they say that people had so many children because they knew nothing of contraception, they were utterly dominated by priests and the Church and, on top of that, as a man said to me while talking about the obsolete attitudes of the old people, 'they had no amusement other than sex at that time'. The conceptual opposition pleasure/responsibility now seems to be coterminous with that between past and present. Sexuality in the past, apart from being severely repressed, is seen very much as uncontrolled or boundless. In this context, people are now convinced that repression is what prevented their acquisition of the sexual knowledge necessary to become sexually responsible subjects and, as a result, the blind search for pleasure was the only force that informed their sexual behaviour. The way to reduce the dreadful effects of an entirely unbridled sexual activity was, paradoxically, to increase repression. They think that modernity has enabled them to escape from this deplorable vicious circle. Now everybody agrees that sexual repression, especially that exerted by the Church authorities, has been substantially reduced and has made way for sexual knowledge. And the clearest consequence of all this appears to be the reduction of marital fertility.[7] But notice that, as we saw earlier for premarital sex, the modern sexual morality that can be envisaged behind people's views on fertility is somewhat more nuanced than a mere opposition between sexual repression and sexual freedom.[8]

Let us stop here with this impressionistic account of some bits of Irish historical consciousness. I pointed out in chapter 5 that sexuality is, socially speaking, an 'imagined' behaviour. It is an imagined behaviour that can only be made visible through certain, let us call it, symbolic evidence that stands for it. The cultural discourses that make sexuality visible by defining a particular sexual norm are the discourses of marriage and fertility. Marriage defines the socially sanctioned way of having sex, marital fertility signifies the proper way of having sex within marriage. The discourses and ideologies of marriage and fertility are in this sense abductions of sexual acts. The interesting thing is that these signifiers can be used in different historical contexts to produce different meanings, specifically, different moral assessments. Sex outside marriage is differently evaluated 'in the past' and 'in the present', and the same applies to marital fertility. But we will explore all this in more detail in a later chapter.

At any rate, this is the 'cultural factor' that has given demographers so many headaches. But look at the way in which this cultural factor has been elucidated. I have attempted a very elementary structural reading of certain historical narratives in which my main concern was to pinpoint some form of underlying 'formal properties'.[9] As Taylor (1995: 162) has suggested, paraphrasing Geertz, in these narratives we see a model of history and a model for history. Several themes prominent in the 'objective' version of Irish history furnished in chapter 4 are echoed in these ideological constructs, so much so that to some extent it would be impossible to draw a clear dividing line between the two. In fact, I firmly maintain the one cannot be properly understood without the other. But my point is to show how these historical narratives constitute a template for the interpretation of the current situation, a meaning-giving mechanism to make sense out of day-to-day experience, a template from which moral judgements can be produced and out of which a certain sexual norm, sometimes explicit, sometimes implicit, takes shape. Without a doubt, these narratives embody an 'invented tradition'. Traditions are always invented, never improvised. They are definitely arbitrary, and yet we cannot swap them around any more than we can change the arbitrary meanings of linguistic signs. Traditions must follow certain rules if they are to be effective.

In the same way as our models of history are only arbitrarily related to the chain of actual events from which they originated, our models for history will never be the necessary and sufficient condition for the production of real history. 'Man's symbolic hubris becomes a great gamble played with the empirical realities' (Sahlins 1985: 149).[10] If, as Sahlins has contended (2000a: 27), 'history can be culturally ordered without being culturally prescribed', this means that the relation between symbolic models and social action is not causal but merely semiotic (i.e. the one is made intelligible in terms of the other but cannot be deduced from the other). Hence, events are irreducible to structure and vice versa (see Sahlins 2000a: 287). As an anthropologist, I do not know what the 'causes' of high marital fertility, low non-marital fertility or fertility decline in Ireland could possibly be (any more than I know the causes of the Irish Famine). I can only investigate the ideological and moral context that turns this demographic behaviour into a culturally sensible option.

The analogy with the biographical approach of Freudian psychoanalysis suggests itself. Could it be argued that the social anthropologist is not interested in the actual historical events that lead to the ethnographic present any more than the psychoanalyst is in his or her patient's real personal history? This is what in actual fact Freud himself tried to do in *Totem and Taboo*, or what in modern psychoanalysis corresponds to the distinction between 'historical truth' and 'narrative truth' (cited in Plummer 1995: 171). Freud was not so much interested in the real historical origins of certain cultural phenomena such as the incest taboo; he wanted to explore humanity's unconscious formation. But the analogies between the individual and the social have a limited scope, as some of Freud's critics were eager to underline. Although both analyst and anthropologist are concerned with some sort of mental constructs or representations, the mental construct that the anthropologist is interested in has an entirely different origin. That is why I believe that both subjective and objective histories can never be fully dissociated. Even at the risk of repeating myself, allow me to underscore the tenuous and foggy limits that separate one from the other.

Notes

1. This perspective on history is close to Nugent's concept of 'social memory', although I am not sure that it allows us 'to leave to one side the illusory distinction between anthropology and history' (Nugent 1985: 73; see also Collard 1989).
2. The priest's mistress (*ceile shagairt*) is a prominent figure in Irish folklore, always associated with paramount evil.
3. In a renowned Irish novel we read: 'No, I had to go and fall for a boozer with the charm, Peter Molloy, a champion pint drinker that had me up the pole and up the aisle when I was barely seventeen. I was ignorant, missus. We grew up ignorant in Limerick, so we did, knowing feck all about anything and, we're mothers before we're women' (McCourt 1996: 69–70). The Irish journalist Rosita Sweetman made the following observation some decades ago:

   Any gynaecologist in Ireland can regale you with stories of 'barren' couples, who when examined were found not to be having full intercourse at all. The stories have an apocryphal tone: the woman who arrived with a raw navel after five years of her husband's misgided attempts at entry via there; the man who attempted anal intercourse for eight years; the woman married for seven years with her hymen still intact, who explained that her husband ejaculated on her. (Sweetman 1979: 14)

4. In their analysis of crisis pregnancy Mahon, Conlon and Dillon found out that in 1995 95 per cent of all births to women under twenty were non-marital births, whereas in 1957 the figure was only 26 per cent. But 27 per cent of the 'legitimate' births were born to women within zero to eight months of marriage. So the proportion of non-marital conceptions was 53 per cent: these were the so-called 'shotgun' weddings. 'Thus the present increase in the proportion of single births', the authors conclude, 'is as much an indicator of a reluctance to marry at that age now as of premarital sex' (Mahon et al. 1998: 23–24).
5. The local view is that single pregnant women should marry because the child must have a father and a mother. If marriage is not possible then the child should be given in adoption, but a single mother should not be allowed to bring up her child in any circumstances.
6. A doctor in a working-class area of Dublin said to Sweetman: 'I get hundreds of letters every year from women in rural Ireland asking for the

Pill, saying their own doctors won't give it to them, and abuse them for it' (Sweetman 1979: 137). Contraceptive devices remained virtually unobtainable in the Republic of Ireland until recently, with some women going as far as to visit the North in order to obtain contraception. Only in 1973 did the Supreme Court decide that married couples had a constitutional right of access to contraception. But under the relevant 1974 Act the purchase of contraceptives by an unmarried person was made an offence, even though the law was made unenforceable. Under the 1979 Act non-medical contraceptives, like condoms, could only be secured on prescription from a doctor. Not until 1984 did these become more freely available.

7. The Schneiders' (1991) analysis of a Sicilian town provides an interesting comparative reference. They show how coitus interruptus was the commonest way of birth control until the 1960s. It was always seen as a 'sacrifice of sexual pleasure and the way to achieve a respectable way of life' (Schneider and Schneider 1991: 889) – interestingly, they point out that the local clergy had little interest in monitoring those practices (1991: 888). Those keenest on birth control were the artisans, who were also the most 'progressive' in political terms (1991: 890–91). In the 1950s and 1960s the poor peasants and landless labourers began also to limit their family size, at a time when the other classes already had small families. Why did it take them longer to limit their family size? The wife of a landless labourer said: 'the rich were governed by "brains, culture and civilization" whereas the poor were governed by "instincts"' (Schneider and Schneider 1991: 891). Invariably, all classes understood that large families among the poor peasants were a consequence of their 'ignorance'.

8. The Schneiders again have studied a remarkable instance concerning the definition of coitus interruptus in the history of European sexual morality. Traditionally it had been harshly condemned as a form of 'conjugal onanism' by all the main Churches. But, when Malthus spread the alarm in the early nineteenth century, birth control began to be seen as highly beneficent and coitus interruptus as one of the best ways to achieve it. But the interesting thing to note here is that this re-evaluation of coitus interruptus was not considered to be in opposition to the previous moral condemnation of free sexuality. In other words, coitus interruptus was 're-signified': from an aberrant practice that encouraged free sexuality to a civilised and rational way of limiting births by 'restraining' the free development of sexual activity (Schneider and Schneider 1991: 886–88).

9. The possibility of this structural reading of Irish history has been suggested by Buckley as regards the Ulster Protestant perspective (1989: 186–87). See also Shanklin (1985: 154–55).

10. See Sewell (1999: 46–47) for an interesting critique of the somewhat mechanistic relationship envisaged by Geertz between the 'models of' and the 'models for' reality.

CHAPTER 8

Coercion and Meaning

The problem of the relationship between culture and social action, between models of/for history and actual history, can be rephrased as the problem of the relationship between coercion and meaning. To what extent are cultural forms coercive forms? The purpose of this chapter is to explore the long-established opposition between power and culture, or power and meaning. This is a question closely related to what we have just discussed, the relevance of history to anthropology, but in more directly political terms. It is currently assumed that traditional obliviousness of history by structural-functionalist paradigms in anthropology were to the detriment of a proper understanding of the significance of power relations in human societies. The contention is that traditional anti-historicist approaches in anthropology simply removed all signs of power from their accounts. The 'hidden history' that those static models were so carefully screening was a history of power relations, of domination of the colonised by the colonisers.

Not only are traditional structural-functionalist theories to be blamed for this unpardonable inattention. The more fashionable symbolist approaches are equally guilty, since, according to a widely held view, an excessive concern with meaning and culture has also led many anthropologists to ingenuously neglect, or perhaps to maliciously obscure, the weight of power relationships (see Roseberry 1982). As Gellner (1979: 128) once wrote, 'a man with the more powerful weapon can impose his will, whether or not the social syntax condones it'. Gellner felt very little sympathy for those who would like to turn anthropology into a political weapon of sorts, so by no means can he be considered as a representative of, at least, the most ideologically charged versions of the historicist perspective. In the text from which that quotation comes he was actually turning his powerful intellectual guns not against traditional social anthropology but against one of its, in his view, perversions: French structuralism. Specifically, it was the structuralists' all-pervasive concern with language and its rules that Gellner attacked. Social life cannot be reduced to a form of syntax since there are many aspects in human conduct that are not a product of any one language. 'Actual conduct, unlike speech, is a by-product of two different sets of factors – the cultural conventions within which the conduct takes place, and the real-world causal connections which are quite independent of those conventions' (Gellner 1979: 128–29). The man with the more powerful weapon can be taken as an instance of the real-world causal connections independent of cultural conventions, and can also be taken as a synecdoche – if I am allowed to use a linguistic concept – for power relations in general terms. There is no culture to be interpreted, no meaning to be grasped when power – when 'causal connections' – comes to the fore.

Thus anthropologists who claim that the object of their discipline should be the analysis of meaning, or culture, are guilty on at least two accounts. First, they have forgotten history, the chain of events that underlies the production of meanings. Secondly, by forgetting history they have concealed the political conditions of possibility of anthropological knowledge – i.e. Western domination over the world. These are their ideological or moral sins. But there is more to it than that, because by committing those moral sins they are also responsible for an epistemological offence, they have blocked themselves from access to a set of very real causal connections that lie behind human conduct: power – and presumably other material, extracultural, conditions that can also be included within the category of causal connections. 'Cleaving to a notion of "culture" as a self-generating and self-propelling mental apparatus of norms and rules for behavior,' Wolf (1999: 19) contends, 'the discipline has tended to disregard the role of power in how culture is built up, maintained, modified, dismantled, or destroyed.'

Power has been present all along in the previous accounts. Chapter 5 ended with a somewhat elusive remark about the 'undeniable power of the Catholic Church' that was hinting at something different. The main point in that chapter was to highlight the way in which the historical constitution of sexual morality in rural Ireland could not be explained by reference to conventional socio-economic determinants. The reader could very well reach the conclusion, then, that it was all a matter of power, of the bare power of the Catholic Church that did not seem to obey any other logic but its own internal rationality. In the following chapter an analysis of the Catholic Church, of this mysterious source of autonomous power, should have been provided. Surprisingly, however, in subsequent chapters the analysis of sexual morality was undertaken from a different angle. The power of the Catholic Church was undeniably present but in a rather oblique way, only through the narratives of its own subjects. Where is that dreadful power, then? Should we conclude that the power of the Church was mainly, or even exclusively, in people's minds? I will leave that as an open question. There is something definitely subtle in the way the Catholic Church has wielded its power in Europe throughout the centuries, and this is precisely what, in my view, renders it particularly suitable for an anthropological reflection on the relationship between power and meaning.

Let us go back to Gellner's assertion, which I believe epitomises in very simple terms the key point of the power/meaning opposition. A man with the more powerful weapon imposes his will irrespective of any cultural code because, Gellner explains, actual conduct is a by-product of two different factors: cultural conventions and causal connections. Since the armed man falls within the category of causal connections he is, by definition, outside what Gellner calls 'cultural conventions'. In a word, power is outside culture and, in many circumstances, it can be in opposition to culture. Besides, since the powerful man can impose his will simply because he has a weapon, as far as the analysis of human conduct is concerned there does not seem to be much room left for the explanatory potential of cultural conventions when confronted with power. Human beings would behave following their cultural codes as long as there is no power to prevent them from doing so. There is still some residual explanatory capacity accorded to culture in this scheme: culture matters, definitely, but only in the absence of power.

It all hinges on what exactly we wish to explain when we refer to cultural conventions and real-world causal connections. In other words, what do we mean – or what did Gellner mean – when we talk about 'actual conduct'? Is actual conduct an event, i.e. so-and-so's conduct in a particular place at a particular time? In this case there is no doubt that any account of human behaviour that only included its cultural constraints would definitely be insufficient. Events are always the consequence of multifarious causal connections. I would dare to say that there are infinite causal connections that account for the production of any specific event – that may be one of the reasons why events are contingent. In any case, it is up to historians, or to anyone working on a historical explanation, to decide which of those connections is more relevant for any particular argument. Economic historians may wish to underline the significance of economic causal connections, political historians may be inclined to highlight the power of political struggles, general historians may stress the complex interaction among different causal factors, etc. We would be hard put to it to pinpoint a unique and irrefutable cause for any single event. It would all depend on the quantity and quality of the records we have been able to amass. Historical records help you to substantiate one particular historical explanation or interpretation, but they will never (or very rarely) tell you the real 'cause' of anything.

Now power is just another way of interpreting the course of history. There are two aspects of power that Foucault has cogently highlighted and that happen to be specifically relevant to the present discussion. First of all, power is coextensive with every social relationship (Foucault 1983a: 224) and, secondly, 'power exists only when it is put into action' (1983a: 219). Two consequences can in turn be derived from this characterisation of power. First, if all social relationships are power relationships, there is no point in defining any particular relationship as a relationship of power since, by definition, power is everywhere. This would be as redundant a definition as to say that a particular social relationship is 'social'. I shall return to this. Next, because power can only be seen 'in action', the analysis of events, of the specific enactment of a form of behaviour within time-space coordinates, happens to be a privileged instance of the perception and documentation of power (Barrett et al. 2001: 473).

It could be argued, as Gellner himself has done in several of his writings (e.g. Gellner 1995), that in what concerns the analysis of coercive institutions, namely, the political system, a structural approach will suffice, a structural approach that does not require us to go into the messy area of historiographical research. This approach would not need to take culture as such into account either, since it would concentrate only on the strictly coercive mechanism that preserves a particular social system. But, if, following Foucault's insights, we make use of a concept of power which is not limited to what goes on in formal coercive institutions – a concept of power which is not synonymous with political power – the need for a historical perspective, for an analysis of particular events and chains of events, becomes much more imperative. So we could conclude that power becomes historical in so far as we go beyond its formal-institutional manifestations. And, similarly, human social behaviour becomes over-determined by power relations to the extent that it is historically analysed. Stated otherwise, in any kind of social research, as soon as we leave the ethereal realm of formal systems of meaning and begin to deal with the hard core of real events, the analysis of power relationships must take its due prominence – alongside perhaps other material constraints. There is no wonder, then, that those that have been so eager to denounce the power-blindness of traditional social anthropology, and of more recent hermeneutic approaches, have also championed the historicist perspectives.

Now, if a definition of social anthropology as a kind of structural (i.e. with all due qualifications, 'ahistorical') approach to human social life specifically concerned with the analysis of culture and meaning is accepted, or merely kept in mind, it must be conceded that the object of anthropological research encompasses neither the study of formal coercive systems – we may leave this to political scientists – nor the study of events, of historical events – which should be left to historians. In other words, neither power as the genuine function of political institutions nor 'power in action' as manifested in all kinds of historical events should fall within the field of knowledge of anthropology. Does this mean that an approach that takes as its object the analysis of systems of meaning should, *ex hypothesi*, be power-blind? Does it mean that power has nothing to do with the type of hermeneutic approach to anthropology that I am espousing? I don't think so. We would only reach this unpersuasive conclusion were we to start with the principle that power is by definition outside, or even in opposition to, culture. But this is very far from being the case. My belief is, following Foucault and many others, that power is coextensive with every social relationship. But I do not think – and I do not know whether Foucault would agree with this – that such coextensiveness only manifests itself in historical analysis. If social relationships are mere structural or behavioural manifestations of shared meanings, any cultural analysis of those shared meanings should be an analysis of a power form, even if it is carried out on a merely structural or ahistorical level. But, and this is the point I wish to underline, it is an analysis of a power form of a very special kind, a power form different from both the institutional power of the political system and the material power manifested in historical events.

Once again, recall Gellner's observation. Even in that extreme situation he imagined, the man with the more powerful weapon can only impose his will if the other understands what a weapon is and, perhaps more importantly, what his will is – try to force a dog at gunpoint to get off your couch. Admittedly, there is no need for much cultural communication when it is a question of understanding, and of making others understand, the power of firearms or of any other lethal weapon. But, when power can only manifest itself by means of mere physical constraints, can we still talk about the existence of social relationships? In other words, it is clear that in the plain existence and development of any form of society physical and material constraints of all sorts play their role, but can anyone think of a social system that is exclusively based on physical constraints? Would that still be a social system? Certainly, we will need some other form of enforcing conformity that is not merely physical or material power if social life is to exist even in its most rudimentary versions.[1]

Suppose that in all societies we can distinguish three kinds of relations: relationships between human beings and inanimate things (and non-human beings); power relations between human beings; and relationships of communication which transmit information by means of any system of signs (Foucault 1983a: 218). This can be reworded as the long-established distinction between economy, politics and culture. So many authors in the history of the social sciences have endorsed this or similar tripartite classifications that there is little need for further elaboration. The important thing is not that they constitute three absolutely separate domains but, as Foucault has argued, 'it is a question of three types of relationships which in fact always overlap one another, support one another reciprocally, and use each other mutually as means to an end' (1983a: 218). Furthermore, in any particular human action in which we can abstract its economic, political and cultural dimensions, they are likely to intervene with unequal weight. In some situations, it will all be a matter of sheer economic forces, or techno-economic forces if you prefer, with a totally insignificant role left to the strictly political or cultural. In others, in contrast, human action may only be intelligible if we pay special attention to its cultural component. Probably in the explanation or interpretation of most human actions, political, economic and cultural factors have some bearing. Say that anthropological analysis has to do with this cultural or communicative dimension of human activity. Because the cultural is unequally represented, so to speak, in all human acts, an anthropological approach might not always be relevant, or equally relevant, for the analysis of any one social relationship. And obviously the same applies to what we might call a political or economic approach. That is the reason why, in the same way as a strictly political and economic study of a culturally distant form of social organisation lays itself open to the accusation of ethnocentrism, an anthropological analysis of a form of life that happens to be too close and culturally familiar to the knowing subject – whoever he or she is – runs the risk of having very little intellectual or scientific value. It seems to me that this is a rather obvious statement that should not come as a surprise to anyone.

But here we are specifically interested in the relations between power and meaning. My point so far has been that power is only alien to anthropological concerns if we take a restrictive power concept, i.e. if we understand by power either the distinctive function of formal coercive institutions or the material constraints of all sorts that impinge on the production of historical events. But if we consider, with Foucault, that power is coextensive with every social relationship, it does not imply, if I understood him correctly, that all social relationships have an equally significant political dimension, or even an equally significant historical dimension – and in this I might be parting company with the distinguished French philosopher – but that power goes beyond its restricted political meaning and pervades both the economic and cultural spheres. In other words, economy and culture each have a distinctive way of embodying power. It is on power through the cultural system, or power through meaning, that I wish to focus my attention. Let us call this form of power, for lack of a better expression, power of signification.[2]

How are we going to deal with this power of signification in the field of sexuality? The reader will remember that in chapter 1 we were actually confronted with an example of a perfect assimilation

between power and culture concerning sexuality: culture as
repression. At that point of the discussion, I was specifically
interested in showing how this repressive view of culture excludes
sexuality from its ontological scope and turns it into a biological, pre-
cultural, given. But, if we are no longer happy with this pre-cultural
conception of human sexuality, by the same token we can no longer
sustain a repressive view of culture (repressive of what?). This means
that the idea that culture 'represses' in any way should be inimical to
an anthropological perspective that takes sexuality as a cultural
construct. It has been said that 'Repression remains an area of
misunderstanding between psychology and anthropology to this day'
(Stewart 2002: 281). Rather than misunderstanding, my belief is
simply that repression can be a useful concept from a
psychoanalytic, political, moral, historical, perhaps even sociological,
etc. perspective, but not from an anthropological viewpoint. It all
depends on the angle from which we decide to look at human affairs.
This is the way I have chosen to define the intellectual aims of the
anthropological project, which pivots on the notion of interpretation
that I shall elaborate in the final chapter. But now let me show in a
bit more detail why a repressive culture concept, despite the fact
that it encapsulates a very clear notion of power, is inappropriate to
our exploration of the power of signification.

I will take as an example the famous ethnography of rural Ireland
done in the 1970s by the American anthropologist Nancy Scheper-
Hughes. It was not an ethnography specifically concerned with sexual
behaviour or sexual beliefs, but in the prologue to the 2001 edition,
Scheper-Hughes admits that her initial research interest was precisely
that, the 'problematic issue' of Irish sexuality (2001: 22–24). Certain
serendipitous events, she explains, altered her original focus –
notably, the information supplied by an Irish psychiatrist as to the
importance of schizophrenia in the Irish countryside. Nevertheless, a
very particular view of human sexuality, which happens to be rather
close to the Freudian conception discussed in chapters 1 and 2,
clearly, at times quite explicitly, permeates Scheper-Hughes's
account. Much of what I said in chapter 1 in relation to Herdt's work
applies equally to Scheper-Hughes's perspective as far as sexuality is
concerned. But here I am interested in something different, if not
altogether unrelated; I wish to look at her view of culture as being
responsible for the distinctive manifestations of mental illness in rural
Ireland. As a matter of fact, this is precisely the main thrust of her

argument: schizophrenia originates in this context, Scheper-Hughes
contends, not so much (or not only) in the individual's constitution,
as a psychiatric or psychoanalytic approach would have us believe,
but in the overall cultural model in which he or she has been brought
up, laying particular emphasis on the child-rearing practices derived
from this model.

Despite her open criticisms, Scheper-Hughes makes extensive use
of a noticeably psychologistic-psychoanalytic approach in her
research – again, very similar to Herdt's,[3] the only difference being
her substitution of a set of cultural patterns for individual experience
in her analysis of the aetiology of mental illness. This has the rather
unwelcome, if inevitable, effect of pathologising practically the
whole cultural system: almost an entire form of life becomes, in her
words, 'schizophrenogenic'. No wonder Scheper-Hughes's research
met with such a hostile reception when it was first published. It must
not be a pleasant feeling to learn that one's way of life is responsible
for the proliferation of disturbing psychotic episodes. Be that as it
may, I shall not question the capacity of any particular cultural
pattern for having such a negative effect on people's psychic health.
In fact, it could very well be the case that many psychological
disturbances have their foundation in, or are at least closely related
to, social maladjustments stemming from specific cultural settings,
in Ireland and elsewhere. What I should like to tackle in its stead is
the particular way in which Scheper-Hughes's repressive view of
culture holds back the development of what in my opinion amounts
to a genuine anthropological approach to power. The problem
originates, as I will try to show, in an unsuitable understanding of the
relationship between power and culture.

But how can a cultural form become pathogenic in the first place?
What sort of anthropological analysis can make us reach such an
upsetting conclusion? It has to be a type of analysis that sets out to
discover what is 'wrong' with a particular culture. It is obviously a
type of analysis with a strong resemblance to the clinical analysis
undertaken by an ordinary medical doctor. In medical practice the
physician aims at not merely understanding the patient's linguistic
utterances but at interpreting them as symptoms of an underlying
disease. 'While patients' symptoms may be coded in cultural
language, the primary interpretative task of the clinician is to decode
patients' symbolic expressions in terms of their underlying somatic
referents. Disordered experience, communicated in the language of

culture, is interpreted in the light of disordered physiology and yields medical diagnoses' (Good 1994: 8). Medical hermeneutics is clearly a 'hermeneutics of suspicion' in so far as the truth of disease always transcends the patients' symbolic expressions. Now the very idea of 'disease' rests on the assumption that there must be some malfunction or disorder in the human body that should be mended by the proper therapeutic course of action. A pathogenic agent, a virus, bacteria, etc., will be normally identified as the cause of the disease. A pathogenic agent is simply something that has the power to affect the normal functioning of the human body. Disease, therefore, always originates in an external power, external not necessarily to the body itself but to the way this body is supposed to work, to be in a 'healthy' condition (see Martínez-Hernáez 2000).

Similarly, a pathogenic culture embodies a form of power that, in the same way as any other pathogenic agent, must be capable of producing a particular disease; in our case, this will not be a somatic but a psychological disease. There is definitely 'power' in a pathogenic culture, a power that manifests itself in its capacity to modify a particular state of affairs that we understand as 'healthy'. In the final chapter I shall explore in a bit more detail the theoretical foundations of this way of conceptualising culture. But now I wish to show how it can be identified in Scheper-Hughes's ethnographic account. In accordance with some psychoanalytic approaches, Scheper-Hughes places considerable importance on the mother's role in the aetiology of schizophrenia. But 'as an anthropologist' she understands that her primary interest 'is not so much in the individual parent or child as in the *norms* of parenting shared by a culture. I wish, therefore, only to raise the issue of the apparent parallels between the stereotypic "schizophrenogenic" mother and the stereotypic rural Irish mother' (Scheper-Hughes 2001: 258). So it is not the behaviour of any one mother as an individual that the anthropologist is interested in but the way she adheres to a certain stereotype that would explain why she behaves the way she does. And this stereotype is precisely a particular cultural model:

> There is, in short, a public village consensus regarding 'proper' child rearing against which parents measure their own performance. And it is *this* set of cultural guidelines for parenting (rigidly adhered to by some, in modified form by most, and not at all by a 'progressive' minority) that I perceive as possibly laying the foundations for the psychotic episodes of the more psychologically vulnerable children. (Scheper-Hughes 2001: 258)

We see that the power of this cultural model is not an absolute power. People are not seemingly coerced into following the 'cultural guidelines' as they might be coerced by, say, political institutions or economic forces into doing something or behaving in a certain way. It could even be said that the power of culture appears as somewhat optional: you may follow it or you may not. But given the importance of schizophrenia in the way Scheper-Hughes has characterised her western Irish community, one would be inclined to surmise that, even in its 'modified form', the cultural model crucially affects people's conduct. If we took Scheper-Hughes's hints as to the optional, or nearly optional, nature of the cultural guidelines at face value, we would not be able to explain the aetiology of schizophrenia in the west of Ireland in the way she is actually trying to explain it. Far from it; we would come to the unimpressive conclusion that schizophrenia emerges because some people decide to behave in a schizophrenogenic way, i.e. they decide to adhere to a schizophrenogenic cultural model. Since schizophrenia is not just a theoretical possibility but an actual fact, something that is actually happening with uncommon frequency, this must be because the cultural model has a certain degree of power to impose itself despite people's alleged capability of disregarding it. The interesting thing to note here is that culture shows its power in a not altogether different way from the way in which power manifests itself in other, more explicitly coercive, instances. The power of culture manifests itself in making people do certain things that they would not have done were it not for the existence of this power.

Now, there is nothing wrong in this way of defining power, the only thing is that, as I say, I do not see any substantial difference between this form of power and the way power shows up in typically coercive institutions. In other words, since my concern is in identifying a specifically anthropological perspective on power, my contention is that Scheper-Hughes's approach does not add anything new to a customary way of understanding power that we can obtain from other, non-anthropological, perspectives. Arguably, there is something different, but hopelessly contradictory, in the way she envisions the working of the power of signification. Schizophrenia originates in child-rearing practices that go by a set of cultural guidelines, and yet nobody seems to be obliged to follow them. Yes, culture seems to be compulsory and yet not compulsory at the same time. Here we have a nice example of the ambivalence

between 'creativity' and 'normative regulation' with which Bauman
has recently characterised the culture concept (1999: xiv). The
misleading effect that this contradiction generates does not come so
much from a wrong understanding of culture but rather from an
attempt to see culture as the causal factor that accounts for the
production of a particular kind of behaviour, i.e. from seeing the
power effect of culture as if it were the power effect of a coercive
institution. Quite obviously, if we try to see in a cultural model the
cause of someone's conduct, it must be because the power inherent
in this cultural model is very close to the gunman's power in Gellner's
example: a coercive power. This is precisely what strikes me as a
wrong approach to the power of signification.

The danger with this 'coercive' approach is notably the reification
of the culture concept, something that has raised several authors'
concerns in recent times (Fox and King 2002). My point is that
reification is inevitable not only because of the way we define culture
but rather, and more importantly, because of the sort of questions
we want it to answer for us. Reification in Scheper-Hughes's analysis
comes from her whole approach – anthropological approach as she
claims – to the problem of schizophrenia in the west of Ireland,
because she wants to see schizophrenia as the consequence of
certain child-rearing practices, and she wants to see those practices
as the consequence of a particular cultural form. Culture acquires in
this explanatory model a coercive force akin to a coercive institution
such as the political system, or, more in line with her theoretical
inclinations, to an instinctual drive: i.e. something that can act
independently of the subject's will, even against the subject's will.
This is the power of culture. And this is, I repeat, a mistaken way of
looking at it.

As Sahlins has recently written, 'to say that a given sentence is
grammatical is not to say that the grammar determined what was
said' (2000a: 27). In other words, culture does not tell us what to do;
it simply gives meaning to whatever we do. Admittedly, this is a bit
of an understatement, because by 'merely' giving meaning to what
we do, culture is practically coercing us into doing something. But it
will be conceded that this form of coercion is substantially different
from the coercion exercised by, say, economic or political forces. So
much so that I doubt whether the term 'coercion' is appropriate
here. But this is actually a minor point. An approach to the power of
signification that stops at its coercive effects is really and truly

missing the point; it falls short of a genuinely anthropological approach. Stated otherwise, that culture coerces us into behaving in a particular way should be seen as the consequence, as the result – not a negligible result by any means, but a result all the same – of a more primordial and genuine capacity of culture: its semiotic capacity.

Notes

1. In his later writings, Foucault coined the expression 'governmentality' to supersede precisely the conventional opposition between coercion and consensus in political analysis (e.g. 1991). For Foucault the concept of governmentality, by linking the notion of 'government' with that of 'mentality', enables us to associate forms of power with processes of subjectification, or technologies of domination with technologies of the self. Foucault understood that power was not just a question of sovereignty (juridical notion of power) but rather of moulding other people's wills so as to achieve certain ends, that is, the 'art of government'. To this effect, power can no longer be seen as a singular transcendent entity (Machiavelli's Prince, the state) but as a plural immanent structure of practices and discourses. There is a fundamental continuity, Foucault maintained, between governing a state and governing a family or governing oneself: the concept of governmentality is thus what turns political domination into a technology of the self and vice versa. The way in which this concept differs from my own approach to the question of power is explained in note 2.
2. Further to note 1, it seems to me that Foucault's concept of governmentality is still anchored on a 'behaviourist' understanding of power, in terms of which the efficacy of power is shown in its capacity to make people behave in a certain way, to produce certain conducts, even if such capacity is dissociated from coercion understood in purely physical terms (cf. Foucault 1983a: 220–22). Power of signification, in contrast, is not the power to produce conducts but to signify them. The following chapter will show how crucial this distinction between conduct and meaning can be.
3. Like Herdt, Scheper-Hughes has also been self-critical of her initial assumptions in her later publications (1983: 155).

CHAPTER 9

Disciplinary Regimes in the History of Irish Sexuality

The power of culture manifests itself in its semiotic capacity. But how does that semiotic capacity operate? Is there any way in which we can appreciate this power of culture in concrete terms? I shall try to answer these questions by going back to the ethnographic information that has already been presented. We saw in chapter 7 that the modern ideology that informs current sexual morality draws heavily on notions about individual sovereignty and responsibility. But the apparently abstract character of these concepts should be qualified by their incorporation into local narratives that construct them in historical terms. Thus they become the final stage of an evolutionary process that sets modern values against the bygone morality of the past. In what follows I would like to think about this transition towards modern conceptions of sexuality in more theoretical terms. Through the analysis of the idioms of marriage and fertility carried out in chapter 7 we had a glimpse of a significant change in sexual mores, a change that divided the history of Irish sexuality into two fundamental periods. But what exactly do we mean when we talk about a change from 'a past' dominated by the Catholic Church towards 'a present' in which that dominance seems to be on the wane? My point is that this history of sexuality contains a change of disciplinary regime. Borrowing again from Foucault's insights concerning the nature of power, I think I will be able to demonstrate the effectiveness of the power of signification. But first let me introduce a last ethnographic snapshot.

On one occasion, when I was sitting in a van with a middle-aged couple, we saw a group of youngsters coming out of the local disco. It was early in the morning and the disco had just closed. There was plenty of joking and laughing as they walked towards one of the bridges in the village. 'There is going to be fun down the bridge tonight,' one of my friends remarked. It was obvious from their comments that those teenagers were going to have sex under that bridge. Needless to say, I did not go to check the veracity of my friends' suspicions. But I was naively surprised by the amused and humorous tone in which they made their observations. They did not seem to have any doubt as to the teenagers' intentions, and none of them seemed to place any importance on it.

I was surprised – somewhat ingenuously, I admit – because on another occasion these same people had lectured me on how important it is for young unmarried women not to let any man 'walk on them'. They insisted on the crucial meaning of virginity for any single woman who wants to establish honest and respectable relationships. You have to keep sex out of your mind if you want an Irish girlfriend, they repeated to me several times. Apparently, these rigid standards of sexual morality did not apply to teenagers going to discos. I do not take my friends to be moral hypocrites, but at the same time their attitude seemed to be, at first sight, hopelessly contradictory. Yet, as I will try to show, it was perfectly coherent.

In rural Ireland, discos and dancehalls are the customary places where single people meet and have a good time. The difference between the two has to do with the average age of the customers. Whereas it is understood that discos are essentially for teenagers, dancehalls draw mainly adults from twenty or twenty-one onwards. At the same time, these age differences are directly related to the sort of relationships one is supposed to engage in while there. You go to a disco 'to have fun', 'for the crack', to enjoy yourself with your friends, and sex seems to be part of this enjoyment. This is what teenagers do. It is different in dancehalls. As Bourdieu (2002: 229) observed among the Béarnais, dancing is here the visible form of the new logic of the marriage market. In a dancehall the main objective appears to be to find a boyfriend or girlfriend, that is, to meet someone with whom you may have a long stable relationship that normally leads to marriage. Sexual contacts would be improper in this context. Obviously, this distinction is far from rigid, but I could not fail to notice the divergent attitudes that prevail in one place or the other. Now the question is: on what grounds is the relatively free sexual activity enjoyed by youngsters in discos restricted and frowned upon as regards adults in dancehalls? Do these Irish teenagers enjoy a period of sexual licence similar to that reported by Malinowski for adolescent Trobrianders?

It all makes a bit more sense if we pay attention to the characteristics of the new disciplinary regime that prevails in rural Ireland now that the Catholic Church has lost its moral monopoly. I am certainly not trying to infer any deep ethnographic interpretation from what appears to be a rather shallow fieldwork anecdote; I merely want to use it as a springboard to introduce a brief conceptual excursus. In the history of sexuality in rural Ireland that has been depicted, we can see a transition from a sexual morality centred on the discipline of the body – which was essentially, for reasons we have already discussed, a female body – to a sexual morality centred on the discipline of the self as a knowledgeable and responsible subject. Traditional Catholic sexual morality has very little concern with the vicissitudes of the faithful self in its modern meaning. Quite the contrary: 'Christianity substituted the idea of a self which one had to renounce because clinging to the self was opposed to God's will for the idea of a self which had to be created as a work of art' (Foucault 1983b: 245). In fact, what traditional Catholicism required from its believers was the surrender of their bodies to the Church's dictates. This is why I define this moral regime as 'obedience-sexuality'.

Table 9.1. Obedience-Sexuality and Knowledge-Sexuality

Disciplinary regimes	Morally irregular sexual behaviour		Causes
Obedience-sexuality	Single mothers Small families		Disobedience
Knowledge-sexuality	Single mothers Large families	Past	Ignorance
	Single mothers Large families	Present	Irresponsibility

To have a moral sexual behaviour simply meant to obey the Church. But with the demise of Catholic morality an entirely different situation has arisen. It is no longer the body that is the object of the new disciplinary regime but the self, and it is not merely obedience that is required from the self but knowledge and responsibility. Thus sexual conduct will be morally evaluated according to the 'knowledge' attributed to the subject. 'One could not form oneself as an ethical subject in the use of pleasures without forming oneself at the same time as a subject of knowledge' (Foucault 1985: 86). I call this new disciplinary regime 'knowledge-sexuality'.[1]

Let me elaborate on this by going back to the cultural idioms that we saw which make sexual morality explicit: marriage and fertility. In the system of obedience-sexuality, morally irregular sexual behaviour is simply 'disobedient' behaviour. This is epitomised in single mothers and small families. People who practise contraception, and thus have few children, or unmarried women who have sex, and get pregnant, are merely not doing what the Church says; they are 'immoral' because they are disobedient. In the system of knowledge-sexuality, in contrast, morally irregular sexual behaviour is explained either in terms of 'ignorance' or in terms of 'irresponsibility'.[2] Single mothers and large families from the past are a clear instance of this 'ignorance'. In the past people had so many children because they were simply ignorant and blindly obeyed the dogmas of the Church. Similarly, this same ignorance also accounts for the existence of single mothers, in the past. They had no knowledge of their own bodies, of their sexuality, of contraception, so they got pregnant without actually knowing what they were doing. That was the ignorance of past times.

But this has changed now. A small family is no longer seen as indicative of morally irregular behaviour but, quite the contrary, it is the result of sexually responsible behaviour. Conversely, it is a large family that is defined nowadays as 'irregular', not so much because of ignorance but because of irresponsibility, since today people are no longer 'ignorant'. And the same applies to single mothers. They are no longer ignorant, they can't be – remember the case of the 'educated' 22–year–old girl mentioned in chapter 7. They are simply irresponsible. This is how a regime of knowledge-sexuality categorises current sexual behaviour that is morally irregular. But there is an exception to it. Not all single mothers can be or should be as knowledgeable as that girl.

An adult woman with irregular sexual behaviour will never be classed as 'knowing too much' since adults are supposed to be knowledgeable, but in the case of teenagers the judgement can be more qualified. A pregnant unmarried girl under twenty, for instance, can be accused of either 'knowing too much' or 'knowing too little'. In the first case, she will partake of the pejorative meanings associated with the adult woman but not for being irresponsible, since teenagers are not supposed to be responsible subjects (in the same way as adults are not supposed to be ignorant any more), but for being too knowledgeable. In the second case, in contrast, she will partake of the compassionate meanings associated with single mothers from the past and she will be seen as 'ignorant'. A teenager can never be accused of being irresponsible – 'they're only kids' – but conversely they can be accused of either knowing too much or knowing too little, precisely for the same reason – 'they are only kids'. As we saw earlier, in a knowledge-sexuality regime, irregular sexual behaviour originates in an imbalance between knowledge and responsibility, but the same imbalance is described from a different perspective according to whether it applies to teenagers or to adults. When knowledge and responsibility do not match in the case of adults, it is a problem of lack of responsibility; when they do not match in the case of teenagers, it can be a problem of excess of knowledge or, somewhat paradoxically, lack of knowledge. In the first case the judgement will be harsh and severe, since teenagers are in the same cognitive and moral situation as current adults: their knowledge goes beyond their responsibility. In the second case, in contrast, the judgement will be much more lenient precisely because they will be allocated to the same moral category as ignorant adults from the past. That would explain why my friends held those seemingly contradictory attitudes as regards young adults' and teenagers' hypothetical sexual relationships (especially those of women), that is, dancehall and disco-goers. In a dancehall one encounters only responsible adults, their sexual behaviour being, consequently, more strictly scrutinised since they are no longer 'ignorant'. In a disco, in contrast, one finds only immature youngsters who hardly know what they are up to.[3]

I am certainly not saying that there is a generalised acceptance, much less encouragement, of youngsters' sexual activity.[4] My contention is that, in a disciplinary regime of knowledge-sexuality, sexually active adolescents are likely to be judged in much the same way as single mothers in the past: they all deserve the same kind of compassionate reprimand, they are all ignorant. But how can we know whether teenagers' irregular sexual behaviour will be seen as resulting from ignorance or from surplus knowledge? We cannot. The actual sense of the final judgement will be situationally determined according to the specific circumstances and characteristics of each particular case. My cultural analysis can only go as far as identifying the specific meaning of a particular course of action, but I cannot predict this course of action. And very often I cannot even predict the actual moral sense that this particular course of action might take in each case. At any rate, this is the specific meaning provided by the disciplinary regimes I have analysed. The aim of this ethnographic investigation is not so much to slot adolescents' sexual behaviour into one or the other category, but rather to highlight the difference between those two disciplinary regimes that appear in the history of Irish sexuality and the way in which sexual behaviour acquires its meaning in each case.[5]

This is precisely the point on which I would like to anchor my reflection on the nature of cultural power or the power of signification. The actual conducts that can be understood as resulting from any of those disciplinary regimes might not be all that different, and the moral evaluation that these conducts deserve might also be the same. Take the case of single mothers: the same type of behaviour is considered morally irregular in both disciplinary regimes, but for different reasons. In other words, the history of people's actual conduct, as shaped by different forms of coercive instances, is not coterminous with the history of its meaning. If we look at power simply from a coercive perspective (power to make people behave in a certain way), we cannot differentiate between the two disciplinary regimes I have identified, because from this coercive perspective both disciplinary systems, obedience-sexuality and knowledge-sexuality, call for the same type of conduct. The inference that I am trying to work out from this is that systems of meaning can never be seen as the ultimate cause of actual behaviours, if only because similar or analogous behaviours can be wrapped up in different cultural formations, and vice versa.

What becomes clear, then, is the way in which the analysis of meaning differs from the analysis of conduct.[6] Here we are not so much interested in what women may actually be doing in their sexual lives, or in whether it is 'right' or 'wrong', but in the reasons that account for it; in other words, we want to know what it means to be doing whatever they do, say, not having sex or not getting pregnant before marrying. But some readers may argue that, even though we might not be interested in women's actual behaviour, there are some facts that can hardly be ignored. For instance, there is a higher percentage of non-marital pregnancies in the regime of knowledge-sexuality than in the other disciplinary regime; there is also a lower marital fertility rate in knowledge-sexuality than in obedience-sexuality. Can we explain these demographic facts by reference to this change of disciplinary regime? This takes us back to the same question that was being discussed in chapter 6: the importance of the cultural factor in explaining the peculiarities of Irish demographic history.

In demographic history sexual conduct and sexual meaning can be easily differentiated. Here we can clearly identify the effects of a particular sexual behaviour: marrying or remaining celibate, practising contraception or not and having more or fewer children, marital children or non-marital children, and so on. Notice that it is not sexual behaviour as such that is recorded in these demographic events, but only its effects, its external manifestations, so to say (properly speaking, marriage is not an 'effect' of sex, but it can be seen as its external manifestation: we presume that married people have sex in the same way as we infer that a pregnant woman also had sex, etc.). Now what about the meaning of this behaviour? How can we relate meaning with actual conduct in this particular case? In chapter 6 we concluded that, as far as the explanation of demographic events is concerned, cultural meanings only seemed to be relevant for demographers when they were confronted with 'irrational' behaviour. What made demographers call for a cultural explanation for Irish demographic behaviour, what made that behaviour meaningless in their eyes, were simply their taken-for-granted assumptions concerning rational human behaviour, particularly sexual behaviour. Thus, when people behave according to those rationality expectations, everything looks as if 'social and economic' conditions are enough to make sense of a particular course of action. But the distinction between rational and non-rational behaviour merely depends on the perspective from which we view that behaviour.

If all this is accepted, that is, if we accept that the difference between 'rationally determined' human conduct – i.e. the sort of conduct we would expect given certain social and economic conditions – and the conduct that can only be understood by reference to a particular set of cultural meanings – plus those social and economic conditions – depends on the observer's point of view rather than on the object being observed, then it cannot be denied that the 'coercive' power of meaning is not on a par with the coercion that those social and economic conditions exercise upon human behaviour. People who behave 'rationally' are as 'coerced' by cultural meanings as those who behave 'culturally'. The only difference is that in the first case we simply take for granted the cultural meanings that inform that particular behaviour: we take them for granted because we share them; they are invisible to us. Inversely, people who behave 'culturally' are as coerced by their social and economic conditions as those who behave rationally. But, precisely because the cultural meanings that inform this behaviour are unknown to us, its social and economic conditions become, in turn, invisible as such (as social and economic conditions); they become 'culture'.

In conclusion, to repeat the question that has led us to this enquiry: can we explain the current increase in non-marital pregnancies and the fall in marital fertility on the basis of this transition from one disciplinary regime to another, or should we look instead into the social and economic 'causes' behind these demographic events? We cannot answer this in absolute terms. It all depends on how much we decide should be taken for granted and how much we decide should not. If we consider, for instance, that the regime of knowledge-sexuality is perfectly rational, that it actually corresponds to what human individuals would do in any circumstance, then no culture will be involved in the explanation of all the behavioural consequences to be derived from it. Conversely, if we believe that obedience-sexuality does not correspond to any rational pattern of behaviour, then we should call upon culture for an explanation (this is more or less what happened to demographers looking at Irish demographic history, as we saw in chapter 6). In other words, knowledge-sexuality will appear as 'reason' whereas obedience-sexuality will appear as 'culture'. Thus, if no other explanation can be found for a low percentage of non-marital pregnancies coupled with high marital fertility, demographers will tend to see that as the result of cultural pressures and, subsequently, the inversion of such demographic trends will be accounted for by the disappearance of those pressures. But do not forget that it is explanations of events we are talking about now (the current increase in non-marital pregnancies and the fall in marital fertility).

If we concentrate our attention not on people's actual conduct but on the reasons that make it intelligible, on the motives people have for behaving the way they do, then culture can be equally valid, i.e. it can be equally informative of the characteristics of a particular way of life, irrespective of the events it may or may not account for.

After arguing that the rationality or irrationality of a particular conduct depends on the perspective we take rather than on the conduct itself, my next objective is to maintain that the very existence of sexual behaviour as an object of knowledge – not sex as an 'etic' act – also depends on the perspective we have on that behaviour and on social life in general. This is in fact one of the main theses of this book and it will reach its full development in the last chapter. But it is time now to provide some grounds for it. In several parts of this work I have referred to sexual behaviour as an 'imagined behaviour'. What does that mean, exactly? If we apply the distinction between structure and event to this particular type of conduct, we would have, on the one hand, people's actual sexual behaviour (events) and, on the other, the set of cultural values, disciplinary regimes, that give meaning to that behaviour (structures). My point is that sexual behaviour as an event is an imagined behaviour, not in the obviously absurd sense that people do not have real sex but in the, perhaps equally obvious, sense that we do not normally see it.[7] Human sexual behaviour is, from this perspective, a myth in its anthropological meaning and, as such, it can be viewed as paradigmatic of all human behaviour considered as structure, not as event. I shall attempt to elaborate a little on these somewhat bold statements.

All human behaviour, as soon as it ceases to be a set of bodily movements, becomes a meaningful fact, an imagined behaviour, a myth. In ethnography, the so-called etic interpretation of human behaviour is always a preliminary step, a mere description – what people do – towards the real, 'emic', understanding – the meaning of what they do. In our cognitive trajectory towards this emic understanding we will inevitably tend to lose sight (though we never do so completely) of the original etic basis in favour of the imagined behaviour. Consider someone who begins to learn a foreign language. At first, he or she will hear meaningless sounds (etic, phonetics), but eventually those sounds become meaningful in such a way that they are no longer sounds, but are turned into words, meanings. 'I can't hear you': this sentence does not mean that I cannot hear your sounds but that I cannot hear your meanings, i.e. I cannot understand you. Now, the extent to which ethnographers, as they begin to learn the meaning of what people do, lose sight of what they are actually doing varies. It essentially depends on what sort of human conduct they intend to analyse. In looking at work practices, for instance, the actual bodily movements involved in tending the cattle, or tilling a field, will normally appear in close association with the meanings that such-and-such a people confers upon them. So much so that, once the ethnographer has gained some mastery over the cultural meanings of that particular society, she will tend to see those activities through those cultural meanings as if she were seeing those meanings instead of mere bodily movements. At this stage, cultural meanings and actual behaviour become for our ethnographer practically indissoluble. But at any time, theoretically at least, she will be able to differentiate the etic perception of such-and-such an activity from the emic understanding of it. The significance that the ethnographer wishes to attribute to such a distinction is a different question altogether.

When dealing with sexual behaviour the situation is radically different. Think of an ethnographer in a society in which sexuality is easily verbalised – by no means the case in rural Ireland. He or she will end up by having detailed accounts of what people think about sex from whatever perspective, moral, aesthetic, erotic and so on. Problems are likely to arise, however, when we take into consideration the ways in which that information might be elicited. Remember our discussion in chapter 1 on the 'clinical interviews' done by Herdt among the Sambia. But, in any case, very rarely will the ethnographer be able to go beyond that: he will not be able to go from emic understanding to etic perception.[8] Suppose now that our ethnographer had been bold enough to peer into people's homes during their most intimate interactions, setting aside now the ethical questions that such an activity would raise. What would she see? I shall not discuss the even more complex ethical dilemmas involved in the ethnographer's actual sexual experiences during fieldwork (see Kulick 1995). Let us remain at the mere observational level – dubious enough in itself from the ethical point of view. What could be observed in those circumstances? What meaning should we attribute to what we have seen?

That is etic perception without emic understanding. We hear sounds, but we cannot hear words. Besides, in the case of rural

Ireland, as in many other Western and non-Western societies, it is not only the ethnographer who is debarred from the etic perception of sexual behaviour, but the locals themselves will very seldom know anything about the conduct of their neighbours. As has been argued throughout, sexuality is only socially visible, or imaginable, through certain symbolic evidence, the cultural discourses that stand for it.[9] In the area of culture and sexuality research, Suggs and Miracle (1999: 46) maintain, 'the "play of symbols" is virtually all to which we have access'. But how, they ask, can we 'understand ideation about something we cannot observe?' After having defined themselves as cultural materialists, this is a prospect that they find 'disconcerting' (Suggs and Miracle 1999: 46–47).

Let me return very briefly to what has been advanced in the above paragraphs. When a priest denounced the existence of a non-marital pregnancy in the parish, or reprimanded a married man or woman for not having enough children, he was not interested in the problems that a young woman might have in rearing a child on her own, or in raising the population's birth rate: it was their respective sexual habits, imagined sexual habits, that he was concerned with. What is the situation in the new disciplinary system of knowledge-sexuality? Things have changed but perhaps not as radically as one might suppose at first sight.[10] Unmarried pregnant women can be equally reprimanded now, not for having had sex, but for having had it in the 'wrong way'. And the same applies to large families. They also highlight and symbolise the existence of an irregular sexual activity. In this particular case, economic arguments might be utilised to reinforce their stigmatisation; as a man said to me once, 'nowadays a man with a lot of children is either very rich or very poor'. But my point is that implicit in that economic rationality argument is the idea that a 'proper' sexual conduct is missing. We can apply the economic rationality entailed in having a small family precisely because we know, as we all should in a regime of knowledge-sexuality, how sexual activity should be carried out. Stated otherwise, by means of the patent economic irrationality of a large family, we can imagine a latent and irregular sexual conduct. Yes, we can only imagine it, we will never see it, any more than priests of an earlier age could see the sexual misconduct that worried them so much. In sexual behaviour there is a discontinuity between the sexual norm, a cultural structure, and the sexual act, a historical event, much more salient, I believe, than in any other kind of human behaviour.

But what is the point of seeing as 'sexual discipline' what in local terms is likely to be phrased differently, either as religious morality or as economic rationality? In other words, what is the point of constructing sexuality as an object of knowledge for a society in which there is no such object? Am I not trying to reveal some sort of repressed sexual meaning behind cultural screens? If all my analysis is accepted, the alleged implicit sexual meanings that were conveyed by the explicit discourses of marriage and fertility, the invisible sexual disciplines hidden behind visible social institutions, have finally come to the open only in virtue of my own analysis. It is I, the ethnographer, who in the last instance has imagined, and made imaginable through my narrative, all the sexual ideologies, moralities, even behaviours, that lurked behind the scenes. This is an interestingly radical proposition, which I think obtains equally for all social behaviour but in the case of sexual behaviour is more clearly manifest precisely because sexual behaviour is, of all human social conduct, the most invisible and thus the most 'mythical' – at least as far as the society we have been studying is concerned. So now it is not just the problem of judging some human conduct as more or less cultural or more or less rational, depending on the observer's perspective; it is the very existence of that conduct as an object of knowledge that seemingly also depends on who is observing it. What looks like sexuality from one point of view looks like something else from another point of view.

Notes

1. Remember what was said in chapter 3 concerning Foucault's distinction between a 'code-oriented' and an 'ethics-oriented' sexual morality (1985: 29–30).
2. Disobedience, ignorance, irresponsibility: these are simply 'experience-distant' concepts (Geertz 1983: 57) that do not necessarily correspond to the terms used by informants. It is the meaning of certain attitudes that I am trying to make explicit with them, not the documentation of concrete linguistic usages.
3. Significantly, there has been in the Republic of Ireland a noticeable increase in the number of pregnancies among unmarried teenagers over the last twenty to thirty years. This increase, according to the Dublin physician Dr Brennan, is due to the gap between 'teenagers' knowledge of sexuality and the messages bombarding them from all sides to engage in sex' (Sweetman 1979: 63). These observations were made in the mid 1970s, but data coming from the latest surveys are even more revealing. According to Inglis, 'While the number of births to women under twenty years has not

changed significantly since 1972, the proportion of these which have
occurred outside marriage has increased from three per cent in 1972 to 89
per cent in 1992' (1998b: 11; see also Mahon et al. 1998: 23–24; Fahey and
Russell 2001: 20). Nevertheless, it is interesting to point out that, in the
government's education campaign of the late 1980s and early 1990s to
fight against the HIV threat, it was still considered, according to one
author, that young Irish people would not choose to have sex outside
marriage (Smyth 1998: 670).

4. Cf. the English father from a working-class background who went to the
   pub to celebrate his teenage daughter's pregnancy (Russell 2001: 230). See
   Tremayne (2001: 18–21) for cross-cultural data on teenage sexual activity.

5. In 1997 the Irish Department of Education commenced the
   implementation of the Relationships and Sexuality Education (RSE)
   programme, the aim of which was to develop sexual education in national
   schools. As was to be expected, this project aroused all sorts of criticisms
   from the most conservative sectors of Irish society. Among these criticisms,
   I think it is worth quoting one particular commentator:

   The ideology at the root of RSE-1 is a closed individualism that places
   God at the outer fringe rather than the centre of life. The word 'God'
   doesn't appear once in RSE-1, but there's lots and lots of talk about
   'self'. 'Self-esteem' and 'self-confidence' are mentioned about thirty
   times, not to mention self-awareness and self-worth as well. (cited by
   Inglis 1998b: 108)

   It couldn't be otherwise. As one of the participants in this programme,
   Irish sociologist Tom Inglis, admits: 'Perhaps the most important aspect …
   of the RSE programme for the teachers was that it concentrated on helping
   children and young people to develop a strong, independent sense of self
   which became the basis of forming good relationships' (1998b: 136). I
   believe that this transition from obedience-sexuality to knowledge-
   sexuality, that is, from a disciplinary system centred on the body – again,
   mostly the female body – to a disciplinary system centred on the self,
   constitutes the major turning-point in the history of Irish sexuality, and
   probably of sexuality in other European countries.

6. This is Ryle's distinction between winks and twitches, referred to and
   elaborated on by Geertz (1973: 6–7). Winks and twitches are identical
   physical movements but only winks can be said to convey some meaning;
   and identical winks, in turn, can produce very different meanings: 'it is
   possible, if not very common, for two or more overt actions done in quite
   dissimilar frames of mind to be photographically and gramophonically as
   similar as you please' (Ryle 1949: 134). Ryle is talking about 'actions'
   whereas in the main text I have used the word 'conduct'. Some might argue
   that the word 'conduct', when it refers to human conduct, points to an
   already meaningful event in such a way that the idea that we can
   differentiate between the history of meaning and the history of conduct,
   when conduct already implies meaning, becomes somehow blurred. But
   the difference between Ryle's and Geertz's thesis and mine is more

apparent than real. An already meaningful event, say, an unmarried woman bearing a child, can be re-signified in different moral terms in different historical periods, for different social groups, in different cultural traditions and so on. The fact that we start out from an already meaningful signifier does not prevent other signifieds from being cumulatively or alternatively attached to it.

7. 'When asked to define, on the basis of their professional experience, what a sexual act is for them, the anthropologist and the psychoanalyst apparently find themselves in distinct, but from a certain standpoint, similar, situations. Neither is in the habit of observing sexual acts *directly* in the course of their practice' (Godelier 2003: 179).

8. Godelier thinks that the only exceptions have been Captain Cook's and Bougainville's accounts of their voyages to Polynesia in the eighteenth century (Godelier 2003: 179, 197 n. 1). See Suggs and Miracle's interesting self-criticism (1999) concerning the limits of a cultural materialist analysis of sexuality.

9. It is true, on the other hand, that, if we consider, for instance, the dangers of the HIV/AIDS epidemic, it could be plausibly argued that it is far more important to find out what people are actually doing in their sexual life than whatever they say they do (see Herdt 1999b: 18–19). Again, setting aside the ethical dilemmas that so intrusive an ethnographic method might pose, I believe that, at least in anthropological terms, it is equally important to be able to differentiate between culturally meaningful and culturally meaningless, or less meaningful, acts. Even in this extreme case, it is certainly difficult to imagine how a culturally sensitive medical practice can succeed without taking into consideration what for some are merely 'cultural ideals' or 'cultural prejudices'.

10. 'Sexual constraints have changed from being external under the supervision of priests and doctors, to more internalised forms of self-restraint. But internalised self-restraint may be more repressive than liberating' (Inglis 1998c: 104).

PART III
Anthropological Remarks

CHAPTER 10

Clarifying the Culture Concept

To see sexual behaviour as a 'meaningful fact' is only the starting-point of the analytical process that leads to the production of anthropological knowledge. In this final part, I would like to discuss what is actually involved in this production process so that we can see more clearly what an anthropological perspective on sexual morality consists of. To this effect, I wish to engage the ethnographic information that has been provided in the foregoing chapters with key theoretical concerns in anthropology.

'Culture' is normally taken to be the object of anthropological knowledge *par excellence*. So many definitions have been provided of this controversial concept that it is not very sensible, it seems to me, to try to formulate a new concept for our present purposes. In this essay, we began to envisage the presence of a cultural object in terms of a theoretical empty space, an unexplained residue of human behaviour, something that could only be visualised when certain taken-for-granted assumptions concerning human behaviour stopped being taken for granted. Culture, if I may begin with a boutade, does not exist: it is not a reality, it is a fiction; it is not a thing but a perspective upon things; it is not an object but an optical illusion. Still, I believe it is a useful optical illusion. I am going to explore the possible contents and the epistemological implications of this non-existent entity by means of a discussion of three interrelated themes: the relationships between culture and language, the problem of intersubjectivity and the concept of interpretation. My purpose is not to put forward a fully-fledged anthropological theory (a meaningless term, in my view); more modestly, I simply wish to articulate the analysis of some theoretical questions in a minimally coherent argument, an argument to be developed not lineally but in a circular fashion (in the way that much of this book has been written). The same or very similar questions will be recurrently confronted from different perspectives. In so doing, a particular view of anthropological research will emerge germane to, or in correspondence with, the analysis of sexual morality furnished in the previous chapters. (Ideally, in anthropology – and perhaps this could be my first theoretical proposition – theory does not explain ethnographic experience but flows from it.)

At the beginning of this essay, I claimed that my anthropological perspective on sexual morality can be seen as a response of sorts to the psychoanalytic approach, so let us start off from one of its well-known principles: the 'repressive hypothesis'. If it is true that sexuality in rural Ireland is only socially visible through certain symbolic evidence – the cultural discourses that stand for it – why, one might wonder, should sexuality be 'hidden' to begin with? For all my initial criticism of Freudian thinking, as the end of the previous chapter has somehow suggested, the psychoanalytic perspective, or something close to it, seems to be coming back with a vengeance, as if a hidden sexual truth behind cultural symbols were in need of some sort of disclosure. One of the purposes of this and the following chapters is precisely to show the extent to which repression, the repressive hypothesis, cannot be held responsible for the 'hidden' nature of Irish sexuality.

The reader will remember that in chapter 3 I posited Freud's and Foucault's theories on human sexuality as two polar opposites. Sexuality as cultural arbitrariness, or historical contingency, and sexuality as a biological imperative: these were the two apparently irreconcilable views that were at stake. But I also advised the reader that Freud and Foucault share some common ground. Whereas it is true that from Foucault's perspective sexuality cannot be seen as anything but a cultural construct, my account of Freud's views as biologically deterministic deliberately left aside a crucial aspect of his work: his investigatory procedure. As is widely acknowledged, Freud's biological theory of human sexuality did not give rise to, or was not accompanied by, an equally biological research strategy. On the contrary, Freudian psychoanalysis grasps human sexuality through an interpretative approach. This is what Ricoeur (1970: 65 ff.) has described as the tension between the 'energetics' and the 'hermeneutics' in Freud's work. Whether this tension is just an unsolvable contradiction or if it should be regarded as a theoretically coherent option need not concern us here. What I wish to point out is that in Freudian thinking, for all its emphasis on the instinctual-biological origin of desire, human sexuality could only be analytically seized through a dialogic method, since it was only through the interpretation of the patient's utterances that the analyst could disclose the patient's sexual instincts.

True, Freud did not see 'culture' in his patients' narratives as an ethnographer may see it in those of his or her informants; yet he was equally confronted with a symbolic language of sorts. The sense in which the symbolic language of culture differs from the symbolic nature of a psychoanalytic patient's talk marks the difference between anthropological and psychoanalytic interpretation. This is what we shall try to investigate now.

Our first step will be some clarification concerning the concept of culture. An ethnographer searches for culture in his or her interpretative task. What can this possibly mean? Perhaps the most remarkable fact of the culture concept is the new meaning that it has acquired in the last few years. In the past, people spoke culture without knowing it – 'they were just living it' (Sahlins 2000b: 197) – but not any more. Culture emerges nowadays as a powerful intellectual weapon in all sort of political struggles, even though it is an intellectual weapon with an indefinite political meaning. For some, culture has been the dreadful alibi of imperial and colonial capitalism for the marginalisation and over-exploitation of non-Western societies. The intellectual legitimation of South African apartheid can be seen as a prominent example of this. For others, culture is the weapon of those colonised non-Western societies in their struggle against assimilation and globalisation. The new Mexican Zapatist movement epitomises this other meaning. In both cases, culture is self-consciously used to enhance particular political objectives. Anthropologists have been for more than a century documenting cultural difference in a context in which those differences 'were just lived', and suddenly they have become self-consciously asserted. There is no doubt that in the globalised multicultural atmosphere of the contemporary world the meaning of culture as used in Western or Westernised societies has been substantially altered (see Hannerz 1993).

A crucial point related to the notion of culture from an anthropological perspective is the taken-for-granted nature of its object. It is normally assumed that people live their cultures without thinking about them. Until recently, a form of expert knowledge was needed in order to turn the lived experience of culture into an object of self-awareness. After a painstaking research process, anthropologists were supposed to disclose the hidden culture behind their informants' apparently irrational beliefs or behaviours in the same way as psychoanalysts discovered repressed sex behind their patient's neurotic symptoms. But nowadays the word culture has become so common in ordinary language that it is difficult to imagine why we might need a form of specialised research in order to uncover it. Peoples all over the world have become, all of a sudden, culturally self-conscious. Does this make the anthropologist's job redundant? Does this mean that the ancient culture-as-lived has been fully replaced by the new politically self-conscious notion?

Culture has certainly acquired a new meaning, which, nevertheless, adds to the old one without substituting itself for it, if only because current cultural nationalism and multicultural ideologies are, themselves, cultural constructs (see Turner 1993). There is an interesting paradox in this process. Our cultural self-consciousness is culturally arbitrary. We can make a provisional analytical distinction between the two concepts of culture we have been implicitly using so far: culture 'as lived' and culture, let us say, 'as thought of'.[1] From an anthropological perspective, culture-as-lived is always previous to culture-as-thought-of, never the other way round. I cannot 'live' my culture as a consequence of some process of conscious self-awareness because that would involve that I am a thinking subject before being a cultural being. People do not discover their cultures, they are born into them. Or, rather, people do discover their cultures-as-thought-of but they are born into their cultures-as-lived. These two concepts of culture are different from but not independent of each other; they are obviously related in many ways. As I have said, my becoming conscious of my cultural identity, culture-as-thought-of, is subsequent to my own cultural being, culture-as-lived; but 'being subsequent to' does not mean 'being the same as'. That is why I believe that the distinction between the two concepts is apposite. Another way of putting this would be to draw the difference between 'cultural being' and 'cultural identity'. The first is the consequence of culture-as-lived and the latter of culture-as-thought-of.

People do not discover their cultures-as-lived, they simply live them: this means that cultures-as-lived are somehow opaque to the individual. Cultures-as-lived can only be made visible, can only be objectified, from a certain perspective. Here we have a preliminary definition of the anthropologist's interpretative task. And this is the important difference between the concept of culture as used by anthropologists and the concept of culture that we currently find in modern political and social-scientific (non-anthropological) discourse on multiculturalism. Culture-as-thought-of gives rise to cultural identity and eventually to all forms of identity politics with all its different, and sometimes contradictory, political meanings. But it is important to realise that this concept of culture is essentially distinct from culture-as-lived. People cannot turn their culture-as-lived into an object of political dispute and negotiation, into an object of political consciousness, because their culture-as-lived, their cultural being, is opaque to them. Only cross-cultural analysis (anthropological analysis) can erase this opacity because it has the virtue of placing the knowing subject in a different cultural space, or departing from a knowing subject that, by definition, belongs to a different culture (as lived). I can create, negotiate, manipulate, invent, fabricate, my cultural identity but not my cultural being because I cannot even see it. I can only see the cultural being of a particular subject if I have a different cultural being; otherwise it would be as opaque to me as it is to the subject I am looking at.

And yet the idea that there is some nuance in the word 'culture' that transcends the individual and is opaque to him or her (and thus somehow 'untouchable'), obvious as it may seem to some of us, is very likely to spur the accusation of cultural essentialism and primordialism (see Grillo 2003). Does this mean that individuals are totally enslaved by the culture in which they live? Where does human agency come into the picture? I will deal with the problem of human agency in a moment, but first I wish to state my point in an even more radical fashion. Culture-as-lived cannot be seen as the consequence of purposeful action. Worse still, it cannot even be seen as the consequence of any extracultural determinant, if we are to take a serious, philosophically coherent, anthropological perspective on it. I do not deny that culture-as-lived is the result of particular social, political and economic conditions (extracultural conditions). In the same way as, for instance, discoveries in chemistry or physics are also the product of certain extrascientific conditions: social, political, economic, etc. We could write a history of the social and political determinants of scientific discoveries in physics, for instance, but this history would have little to do with the science of physics. In other words, the verifiability of the physicist's statements is not contingent upon the extrascientific conditions of possibility of those statements. Could a similar point be argued in relation to culture in its anthropological sense? Certainly not in the radical way that natural scientists can. More about this later, but now let me remove any possible ambiguity. As should be clear from the ensuing argument, I am not defending here an objectified concept of culture on a par with the natural entities studied by physicists. I am simply saying that the use of the culture concept as an explanatory device of human conduct involves certain abstraction: certain aspects of human conduct are necessarily overlooked or downplayed whereas others must come to the foreground. Anthropological explanations are always partial explanations.

The anti-essentialist critic will see my preceding argument as a straightforward provocation. My distinction between culture-as-lived and culture-as-thought-of is just another device to celebrate a (new) form of cultural determinism that clearly transcends the power of our almighty and beloved free individual. Individuals create their cultures-as-thought-of but the poor fellows are at the mercy of their cultures-as-lived. We freely manipulate and negotiate our culture identities (and, if successful, manage to make them look like expressions of our 'cultural being') but, at the end of the day, we will always be under the power of our real cultural being. So free individuals have been erased once again. They naively imagine that they are creating their own culture but there will always be some sort of untouchable remnant, as it were, that not only can never be manipulated but, much worse, is somehow determinant of the individual's behaviour and thoughts. But this gloomy picture is decisively misleading in many respects. As happens very often, anti-essentialist critics are fighting a quixotic battle against an imaginary cultural essentialism that they themselves have produced.

Arguably, cultural essentialism is not always an imaginary foe. What I am saying is that a cultural essentialist position does not necessarily follow from the preceding argument. A cultural essentialist sees individuals as mere powerless puppets at the mercy of an overpowering structure called 'culture' that obliges them to behave, and even to think, in a particular way. That is what the time-honoured Durkheimian theory of social facts seems to be all about, or what seems to be at the basis of it all. Social facts are characterised by their compulsory nature, Durkheim contended. Now the mechanistic conception of social compulsion that underlies the critic's conception of cultural essentialism is far from Durkheim's views. It is only one of the numerous simplifications that his theories have gone through at the hands of his detractors. Compulsion for Durkheim was not at all mechanical, it was moral (Durkheim 1974: 35 ff.).[2] If social facts exercise a mere moral compulsion upon us, that implies, as its condition of possibility, that we are free individuals, able to choose whether or not we are going to follow their moral dictum. So we could translate Durkheim into modern anthropological jargon and say that culture (culture-as-lived) enforces upon us not a mechanical compulsion but a semantic compulsion. This is the sort of (unconscious, certainly) compulsion that culture produces. From this perspective, individuals are still free agents that can happily decide whether they will follow this or that course of action, but they cannot decide the meaning of that action: their culture (as lived) does it for them. The conclusions reached in the previous chapters concerning the anthropological understanding of power should be recalled now. We saw then that language provided a useful metaphor for culture. I can decide what to say in a particular language, I can even decide, if I have the required proficiency, which language I will use for saying what I want to say, but I cannot decide upon the grammar of that language: language itself does it for me. 'I encounter language as a facticity external to myself and it is coercive in its effect on me. Language forces me into its patterns' (Berger and Luckman 1966: 53).

Granted that culture-as-lived is a kind of language or grammar as far as its compulsory nature is concerned, we shall see how this linguistic understanding of culture raises important questions. What we call culture in anthropology has to do with the conditions, and the effects, of a communication process that takes place in an unfamiliar context. Both culture and language are means of communication and, as such, are inherently social. It is easy to see why language is a social phenomenon, for the idea of a private language is hopelessly contradictory. This means that we need more than one individual human being for language to exist. Culture is just an 'inter-societal' language of sorts. If there were only one form of social organisation all over the world and throughout all human history (call it one single 'way of life'), there would be only 'one culture', that is, there would be no culture at all. A single human society has no culture in the same way as a single human being cannot be said to have any language.

The analogy between culture and language prevents us from falling into a naively culturally deterministic conception of social action. It is true that, if we envision culture as a kind of language, and social action as a kind of speech (Sahlins 2000a: 286), we may claim that human behaviour can by no means be causally but can only be semiotically related to cultural structures. Grammar does not oblige us to say anything in particular; it only tells us how to say it. Similarly, culture does not oblige anyone to act in any particular way; it only gives meaning to one's actions. This has been a pervasive thesis throughout this book.

All children have to learn linguistic grammar at school. Children do not need grammar to be able to speak, or to understand those who speak in a particular language, but they need to know grammar in order to be able to speak and write properly. Now suppose that in some imaginary country children had to study not only the grammatical rules of their language but also the cultural grammar of their society. How would that sound? Without a doubt, such a teaching policy could only lead to a crude, and probably useless, essentialisation of that society's culture. Furthermore, if we remember what has been argued above as regards the concept of culture-as-lived, that teaching policy would be not only useless but also impossible. Culture-as-lived is opaque to the individuals: the teachers of that imaginary country could never see the object of their teaching.

Thus we begin to see how the linguistic definition of culture can be misleading. Think now of the following question: what should we include in the study of culture? According to Goodenough (1994), the concept of culture comprises all we need to know in order to behave as a native. If we define culture as a form of lived experience; this seems to agree, at first sight, with Goodenough's meaning. English children do not need to study English grammar to understand and speak English because they are born and grown into the language, but those rules need to be made explicit to foreigners if they wish to achieve the same degree of proficiency. Thus the students of culture seem to be confronted with an identical, or at least very similar, situation. As the foreign student of a language needs to know a great deal so as to be able to understand and to speak the language as a native, so the anthropologist also needs to know a great deal so as to be able not only to understand and to speak but also, and more importantly perhaps, to behave as a native.

Now I believe this approach is simply inadequate. First of all, I doubt that a standard ethnography can provide useful knowledge as to how to become, or behave like, a native of any particular culture. To comply with Goodenough's definition we would need not one or two but forty years at least of ethnographic fieldwork to know a people's culture. And even in that hypothetical case we would be hard put to it to communicate all our cultural knowledge in a standard ethnographic monograph (there would be endless practical appendixes with instructions as to how to perform this or that task). Clearly, we do not need to learn the cultural grammar of a particular society in the same way as we need to learn the linguistic grammar of a particular language. Culture is not what we need to know in order to behave or to perform acceptably in every kind of activity some particular people engage in (Goodenough 1994: 268); culture is what we need to know in order simply to understand them so that, in Geertz's (1973: 13) words, we may be able to converse with them. But, and this is the key point in the present discussion, understanding a culture is different from understanding a language.

Goodenough's misleading view of culture originates, to my mind, in the inadequacies of the analogy between culture and language. We cannot make an inventory of the structural principles of a particular culture in the way we can list the grammatical rules of a language. We can objectify a language syntax in a grammar book, we can even objectify the meaning of its words in a dictionary. True, such objectifications are always imperfect since nobody can expect to master a language only by studying a grammar book and learning a dictionary by rote. But, imperfect as they are, can we produce something even remotely similar with cultural grammar and cultural meanings? We cannot or, at least, I think we should not. Culture escapes objectification in the way in which language can be objectified.

Some people might share the same culture without sharing the same language and vice versa. To state the obvious: consider a group of urban middle-class university students coming from different European countries, say, France, Italy and Germany. They are likely to share a great deal of cultural knowledge even though they have reciprocally unintelligible languages. Some linguists may need to learn something of the culture of a particular linguistic community when they study their language, in the same way as most anthropologists need to learn a foreign language when they decide to study an alien culture but by no means all of them. But what exactly do those urban middle-class students share? A life-world, a state of mind, a set of beliefs, a form of life? And, more importantly, how can we see it?

I wish to put the distinction between culture and language in more theoretical terms, starting out from Saussure's theory of the arbitrariness of the linguistic sign. We will notice how the distinctions between signifier and signified, meaning and referent, sign and symbol, language and culture are all multiple sides of the same coin. Saussure (1966: 67–68) wrote:

> The idea of 'sister' is not linked by any inner relationship to the succession of sounds s-ö-r which serve as its signifier in French; that it could be represented equally by just any other sequence is proved by differences among languages and by the very existence of different languages: the signified 'ox' has as its signifier b-ö-f on one side of the border and o-k-s (Ochs) on the other.

He clearly took it for granted that the idea of 'sister', or that of 'ox', existed independently of the language that provided those ideas with signifiers. But how can I think of a sister without a language to name my idea? Was he confusing 'signified' with 'referent', as he has been recurrently accused of? Saussure decided to demonstrate his theory of the arbitrariness of the linguistic sign by showing how the same signified could be associated with different signifiers in different languages. But this demonstration is only possible if the chosen languages have the same life-world as their referent – i.e. they belong to the same 'culture', and therefore both 'sisters' and 'oxen' are meaningful concepts for their speakers. In this context, the distinction between signified and referent is simply redundant. The idea of 'sister' must correspond to the 'real' sister; otherwise that would be a meaningless idea. Signifieds and referents happily coincide. But if, along with the well-known linguistic relativity hypothesis (Whorf 1956), Saussure had taken two culturally distant languages he would have been hard put to it to find so neat a correspondence between their respective signifieds. If the word 'sister' cannot be translated into any other language, how could I demonstrate that there is no necessary relationship between that word and its signified? Now it is precisely the distinction between signified and signifier that becomes redundant, and it is not the linguistic sign but the world that becomes arbitrary.

The distinction between signified and referent is only visible when we envisage the possible existence of a different life-world from the one referred to by any one particular language. Following Frege's famous argument (1960), since the language of astronomy enables me to represent a life-world in which the object Venus exists, I can see that the expressions 'morning star' and 'evening star' refer to the same object despite their different meanings. But the difference between 'Venus' and 'morning star/ evening star' is not linguistic; it is, let me put it this way, a 'cultural' difference to the extent that those expressions refer to different life-worlds. Venus is only visible when we look at the morning star and the evening star from a different point of view; Venus is only a meaningful concept when we talk about it in a different language from the one we use when we talk about the morning star or the evening star, and vice versa.

It is from this vantage point that native languages appear as 'symbolic' languages since their signifieds do not seem to correspond to the real world as we see it. So we reach the conclusion that those signifieds are only apparent; the real ones must be somehow behind them. Symbolic languages are therefore cultural languages. Durkheim (1915) saw 'society' where the Australian aborigines saw their totemic gods. Society was the 'real' thing whereas the totemic god was merely a cultural construct, a symbol; but this was simply because Durkheim did not believe in the existence of those gods, and thus their religious language became symbolic for him: it became culture.

> The god of the clan, the totemic principle, can therefore be nothing else than the clan itself, personified and represented to the imagination under the visible form of the animal or vegetable which serves as totem …

> Now the totem is the flag of the clan. It is therefore natural that the impressions aroused by the clan in individual minds – impressions of dependence and of increased vitality – should fix themselves to the idea of the totem rather than that of the clan: for the clan is too complex a reality to be represented clearly in all its complex unity by such rudimentary intelligences. (Durkheim 1915: 206, 220)

It is a wonder that so mundane a concept as that of clan could not be represented by the 'rudimentary intelligences' of the aborigines who, in contrast, understood without difficulty the complex relationship between the totem and the totemic principle or god of the clan. But it could plausibly be argued that Durkheim's 'society' is as symbolic a construct as the aborigines' gods. The split between signified and referent, god and society, language and culture is no more than a visual effect: the result of looking at the aborigines' religious beliefs through Western eyes. Cultural meanings or symbols do not exist in themselves; it was Durkheim's unbelief which turned totemic gods into symbols. In other words, it was Durkheim's perspective which turned totemic gods into a theoretical 'empty space', into an irrational belief which had to be accounted for by some other means, in the same way as it was demographers' understanding of what rational behaviour consists of that turned certain events in Irish demographic history into a cultural object. So we might conclude that cultural objects are relative, but perhaps more in Einstein's sense of the term, as derived from the concept of relativity, than in terms of what is normally understood by cultural or anthropological relativism. What I mean by this is that the existence of a relative object depends in a very fundamental sense on who is looking at it. Relative objects are intersubjective objects, which is just another way of restating the by now familiar notion of perspectivism.

Notes

1. I am borrowing these concepts from Schneider (1980: 129ff) and Sahlins (2000a: 286–87), but I am not sure I am using them in the same way; besides, both authors use the expression 'culture-as-constituted' for my 'culture-as-thought-of'.
2. It should be noted that Durkheim's concept of social constraint or compulsion was not devoid of ambiguities. See Giddens (1995: 124–25) and Lukes (1985: 11–14, 412 ff.) for further discussion.

CHAPTER 11

Intersubjectivity Revisited

Both language and culture are intersubjective phenomena: it has been said that we need two individuals for language to exist in the same way as we need two societies, or two life-worlds, for culture to exist. But the intersubjectivity of culture poses some deep intricate and specific problems. My claim is that the difference between understanding a language and understanding a culture originates in the different kinds of intersubjectivity we find in language and culture respectively. As a provisional thesis we could affirm that the intersubjectivity of culture is a much more radical one; it is more radical because it comes from the dialogical nature of anthropological knowledge. In this chapter, I would like to explore cultural intersubjectivity as a natural property derived from the relativity of cultural objects.

'Attempts to hide the subject in anthropological discourse too often result in epistemological hypocrisy' (Fabian 2002: 90). In Gilbert Herdt's book *Intimate Communications*, written together with the psychoanalyst Robert J. Stoller, we have a prominent instance of a form of analysis in which the subject of anthropological discourse comes fully into the open. Right from the beginning, the authors stress that their main concern is with 'erotics and the study of culture'. This is not what I have been studying in the present essay. I was interested in the social layers that shape a particular form of sexual behaviour rather than in the explicitly sexual content of that behaviour as such. Furthermore, I have my doubts concerning the status of erotism as a cross-cultural object of analysis. With Elliston, I believe that 'erotics and sexuality certainly merit anthropological investigation. The problem, however, is how to investigate these

domains without assuming we already know what it is we seek'
(Elliston 1995: 861). This is certainly far removed from the
perspective adopted by Herdt and Stoller in their work. But my
intention now is not to deal directly with the problem of the cross-
cultural validity of erotism. Instead, I would like to take an indirect
path that starts specifically with the question of intersubjectivity.

Herdt argues at some length against the traditional way of looking
at ethnographic knowledge as the product of an objective
description of a state of affairs that exists irrespective of who is
providing the description. For him, this way of understanding
ethnography overlooks the important role played by the
ethnographer himself or herself in the production of ethnographic
knowledge. Hence, his stress on the analysis of subjectivity and his
borrowing of a great deal of psychoanalytic concepts and
methodology. It is not very clear, however, to what extent Herdt's
emphasis on subjectivity can be taken as synonymous for what I
understand as the dialogical nature of anthropological knowledge
and the intersubjectivity of ethnography – if only because he never
uses explicitly the word intersubjectivity. But let us assume that this
is precisely what he means, in which case I fully endorse his
criticisms. It could be said that different ethnographers produce
different ethnographies on the same people, in the same way as,
and for the same reason that, one single ethnographer produces
different ethnographies on different peoples. For some this might be
the proof of the arbitrary, unscientific and subjective character of
ethnography. For others, in contrast, this should be taken as a proof
neither of the objectivity nor of the subjectivity but of the
intersubjectivity of ethnography. Should we still call the final
outcome scientific knowledge, or should we say that it is halfway
between science and artistic creation? I will leave it to analytic
philosophers to answer this nominalistic puzzle.

My purpose is somewhat more far-reaching. I would like to pursue
the idea of the intersubjectivity of ethnography towards what I take
to be its natural extension: the intersubjectivity of the very concept
of culture. Not only are ethnographic descriptions inevitably
intersubjective, but so is the culture that they are meant to throw
into relief. In other words, if we take seriously the intersubjectivity of
ethnography we must draw the conclusion, I believe, that cultures
have no objective existence either, but are only the product of the
specific communicative process between the anthropologist and his

or her informants. García Düttmann (2000: 12, 73) has recently stated that culture always means between cultures and every in-between withdraws from attempts to objectify it.[1] '[T]o try to escape from one's own concepts in interpretation', wrote Gadamer (1989: 397), 'is not only impossible but manifestly absurd. To interpret means precisely to bring one's own preconceptions into play so that the text's meaning can really be made to speak for us.' Notice, incidentally, how different this kind of intersubjectivity is from the intersubjectivity of language. When I study a foreign language, I might need to use my own 'linguistic preconceptions' at the beginning, but the sooner I can get rid of them, the sooner I am able to speak this foreign language paying little or no heed to my own mother tongue, the better. Gadamer defined cross-cultural research as 'fusion of horizons' (1989: 306–7). How inappropriate this concept would be to the study of a foreign language!

The conclusion I am trying to reach is that what we understand in anthropology as culture is always the product of an interpretative process that originates in the intersubjective experience of ethnographic research. But neither the intersubjectivity of ethnographic fieldwork nor, notably, the act of interpreting ethnographic facts is an ordinary event or activity in social life. As Searle (1995: 134) has observed, 'we normally just see an object or understand a sentence, without any *act* of interpreting. It is a very special intellectual performance to produce an act of interpretation.' Thus, if the interpretation of ethnographic facts is in this sense specific to the intersubjectivity of ethnographic experience, culture, the genuine product of this kind of interpretation, cannot be dissociated from that intersubjectivity. In other words, societies or human beings do not have cultures: only societies and human beings in interaction with anthropologists do. A different question is, as we will see, the problem of the validation of the anthropological knowledge thus produced, for the culture that anthropologists describe can be an 'erroneous' culture. Something in the interpretative process that gives rise to it can go wrong; the anthropologist might misunderstand his or her informants. But the fact that an interpretation can be wrong does not make it any less intersubjective. I will come back to this.

Consider now the imagined nature of sexual behaviour as has been postulated in different parts of this essay. Because the moral norms that we have been looking at have such an elusive object, it

would be practically impossible to see the extent to which a
particular moral principle, or disciplinary regime, is actually obeyed
in some specific circumstances. It would be impossible unless we
infer the existence of such an elusive object from the visible effects,
the 'symbolic evidence' as we have called it, that enable us to
imagine that object – a particular sexual behaviour. Now it is clear
that this process of inference (which by rights should be called
'abduction') has been arbitrarily posited as a result of my own
analytical perspective in interaction with the data on which that
perspective has been focused, i.e. my informants' narratives. But
sexual morality does not exist, any more than sexual behaviour, as an
object of knowledge, as an object of social and cultural significance,
outside the limits of this particular encounter.

The intersubjectivity of anthropological knowledge I defend is
not, in my view, a new paradigm. It is certainly fashionable nowadays
to define anthropology as a form of intersubjective knowledge. Yet
my point is that there is no need to call upon any sophisticated
philosophical metanarrative to bring it forward: intersubjectivity has
been inherent in anthropological knowledge right from its inception,
and I shall try to demonstrate this by looking at such time-honoured
anthropological dichotomies as nature/culture and primitives/
moderns. Those dated and much criticised (and rightly so, to some
extent) oppositions are, in actual fact, indicative of intersubjectivity
– what many would define as a trendy perspective in anthropology.

I shall begin with the opposition between nature and culture. It is
not the same thing to set out to study natural entities, in the way
natural scientists do, as to study natural scientists studying natural
entities, for instance, as anthropologists might do, even though the
two intellectual activities are undoubtedly related. Let us think of sex
as a natural entity, and let us think of a biologist or a physician
studying this natural entity. Imagine now an anthropologist studying
Sambia sexual beliefs. What is the difference between these two
types of research? A biologist might be interested in what her
colleagues have said about sex, in the way they have produced their
theories, perhaps even in the social and cultural context in which
those theories have emerged and so on. But, in the end, the biologist
will have to deal with the truth claims of the different theories she is
looking at. That is what the biologist's job as a natural scientist is all
about. She will have to deal with the truth of sex, and all the theories
she looks at will only be interesting to her in so far as they are means

to reach that truth. Conversely, the anthropologist studying Sambia sexual beliefs does not need to be an expert in the biology of human sexual reproduction, he does not need to know the whole truth about sex, but it will do no harm to know a little bit of the basics of human biology. Sambia believe that boys need semen in order to grow into men, and that women need their husbands' semen to fill up their breasts. Is that really necessary? Certainly not, and not much Western biological knowledge is needed to reach this conclusion. But the truth or falsity of Sambia beliefs is not what makes those beliefs interesting to the anthropologist, it is precisely the existence of those beliefs that makes Sambia behaviour meaningful. Still, the fact that a particular belief can be true or false seems to make a difference when it comes to interpreting it. But does it really?

The case of false or irrational beliefs is an old anthropological problem: how do we make sense of them? Culture is our magic tool, culture as a web of meanings, a way of life, etc. But culture – let me insist on this fundamental principle – in whatever way we wish to define it, is not an invisible cloud hovering over people's heads that gives meaning to what they do and what they say, and that only clever anthropologists can make visible after painful ethnographic fieldwork. This is a misleading metaphor for several reasons. Specifically, because it makes us think about culture as something that exists irrespective of the anthropologist's existence and activity, in such a way that the anthropologist only has to discover it, as the natural scientist discovers a new natural entity that obviously existed before he or she discovered it. The anthropologist has to discover a particular culture of sexuality in the same way as a physician discovers a particular sexual disease or a biologist discovers a new element or characteristic of the human reproductive apparatus. And in this sense sexuality as a cultural construct can be opposed to sex as a natural entity as two different kinds of objects that exist side by side. But can we think of culture and nature as two 'objects'? I believe we cannot. There is a way in which it could be said that anthropologists 'discover' cultures, but this, I want to repeat, has nothing to do with the way in which natural scientists discover natural entities.

I shall use the word sexuality to refer to the set of attitudes, dispositions, theories and beliefs (explicit or implicit, true or false) entertained by a particular people – physicians, biologists, Irish priests or the Sambia – concerning sex and I shall use the word sex to refer to a natural entity, say, human biological reproductive behaviour. Sexuality in this context (i.e. sexuality as a cultural entity as it becomes explicit in the anthropologist's text) is merely a concept produced by the anthropologist in interaction with a particular people in order to make sense of those people's behaviour. It is an intellectual artefact that exists neither before the existence of the anthropologist who is its creator nor, quite obviously perhaps, before the existence of the particular people whose behaviour it is meant to make intelligible. The Sambia might have their beliefs concerning sex, erotism, human reproduction but these do not need to correspond to the anthropologist's concept of sexuality; perhaps they do not even have such beliefs. Or maybe they do have some theories in the back of their minds but never talk about them (or never talk to the anthropologist about them, which amounts to the same thing). Yet they must have sex in one way or another, in whatever way they wish to talk or not to talk about it. The anthropologist's concept of sexuality can be useful to make sense of these people's behaviour not only because sex, as a natural entity, is universal and therefore all humans must have some form of sexual behaviour but also, and perhaps more importantly, because it so happens that people all over the world tend to attribute some cultural significance to this type of activity. 'All societies have to make arrangements for the organization of erotic life' (Weeks 2003: 28), in such a way that we can posit the existence of a family resemblance between the cultural forms that it has given rise to. I insist, this cultural significance does not need to be a set of explicit theories on sexual behaviour, or on desire, eroticism, sexual morality, etc. Whatever it is, only ethnography can eventually tell.

But how do we produce sexuality as an anthropological object? Even though it does not need to correspond to explicit indigenous conceptions, it cannot be an entirely arbitrary intellectual construct made by the anthropologist with no relation whatsoever to the way in which those native people see and understand their behaviour. To repeat: we produce sexuality as an anthropological object by interacting with the natives; sexuality in that sense is merely the product of a particular kind of intersubjective experience. We (anthropologists, not the natives) produce sexuality, a particular culture of sexuality (in interaction with the natives) in a way entirely different from the way in which a physician or a biologist can be said to produce sex – i.e. a natural scientist can be said to 'produce' nature. It is impossible to export this model to natural scientists' intellectual activity. Admittedly, an idealist philosopher could argue that sex is a concept too, an intellectual construct, but in no way could he or she claim that it has its origin in the interaction – intersubjective interaction – between the natural scientist and sex as a natural entity. Hence the incommensurability of culture and nature.

But notice that the distinction between nature and culture is not an absolute distinction. Because we have defined sexuality as what these or those particular people think about sex, it is perfectly conceivable that I, as an anthropologist, might wish to study the sexual beliefs and theories of a biologist or a physician. That is, I might wish to study what in all appearances look very much like true or perfectly rational beliefs and theories. But even in that case those sexual beliefs become, by definition, cultural beliefs, to be accounted for in the same way as any other kind of cultural beliefs. When anthropologists decide to make sense of someone's beliefs by means of culture, that is, considering them as cultural beliefs, they make no claims as to the truth value of those beliefs. It is simply a particular way of making them intelligible. Obviously, if those beliefs happen to be right, the anthropologist's attempt at making them intelligible by means of the culture concept might look a bit redundant. But it does not have to be always redundant. It all depends on what sort of explanation we are looking for. Imagine a physician treating a patient for a sexual disorder. Do we need an anthropologist to make sense of his behaviour? Not if what we are interested in are the truth claims of his diagnosis and treatment: what we need is simply another physician, preferably a more experienced one, to check on the first one's activity. But maybe we are interested in something different. Physicians do not work in an empty space. They probably belong to some institution, or their research has been funded by another institution, etc.; in a word, they work in a social and cultural context. And so we may be interested in analysing this context, this extrascientific context, because science, the science our physician is using in his clinic, may have all sorts of different effects on the society he belongs to irrespective of its truth value. To give a very obvious example: the majority of us rely in our day-to-day life on a myriad of scientific theories about the world that surrounds us simply because we believe in them, not because we have personally checked their veracity (we would not be able to do so even if we wanted to). We believe in science even if we do not understand a word of it, so our belief cannot be explained by the truth value of science (you might say it is explained because science is effective, but that is a different thing). We believe in science because of the meaning science has in our way of life, in our culture.

So, if science is only part of our culture, of a particular culture, where do we find nature then? How can we see it? Nature is merely the absence of culture, i.e. that which does not need to be studied by anthropologists because it does not pose problems for cross-cultural communication. Nature is another word for 'reason'. We could say that once upon a time nature/reason used to be identified with Western society, with science, whereas culture was what primitives have, those deprived of science and who, therefore, cannot see things the way they are (thus they do not have knowledge, they have 'beliefs', they have 'culture'). But now we merely have to identify it with the anthropologist's beliefs, i.e. whatever it is that we decide to take for granted. They cannot be 'culture' for very obvious, analytical reasons because in that case we would need another anthropologist to explain the first anthropologist's cultural beliefs (since, do not forget, anthropologists' culture is also opaque to themselves), and so ad infinitum.[2]

Sex and sexuality have provided us with a superb example because sex and sexuality are exactly the same thing but seen from different perspectives, or from different intersubjectivities. We realise now how ambivalent the distinction we made at the beginning is: sex as a natural entity and sexuality as a cultural construct. Sex as a natural entity can only be apprehended by means of some sort of natural-scientific activity, but as soon as this natural-scientific activity becomes the object of anthropological research it is metamorphosed into a cultural practice that produces cultural beliefs concerning sex, i.e. it produces sexuality. And yet, for all its ambivalence, this does not mean that we should get rid of this distinction, precisely because, in order to analyse anyone's beliefs or attitudes concerning sexual activity, be they priests', biologists', physicians' or lay people's beliefs, I should entertain some ideas as to what sexual activity amounts to, irrespective of anyone's beliefs – not so much because I need to know whether they are right or wrong, true or false, but rather because in order to understand those beliefs I need to know,

first of all, their object: what they are about.[3] Hence the nature/
culture opposition cannot be disregarded.

A similar line of argument could be followed if we concentrate our
attention on the dichotomy between primitives and moderns. In
fact, Latour (1993: 97 ff.) has postulated a correlation between the
nature/culture and primitive/modern dichotomies, which I fully
endorse. But I cannot see how we can dispose of these dichotomies,
at least not in the radical way Latour proposes. Arguably, the
primitive/modern dichotomy as it was used in conventional
evolutionist anthropology no longer holds water. But some form of
distinction between 'us' and 'them' has to be in force for
anthropological knowledge to be produced in any way. The problem
with this dichotomy is that it has been used, by Latour and others,
as an ontological dichotomy: there are people out there who are
native-born primitives and others who are moderns, and so the
moderns, some of them, study the primitives. That might have been
the case for the old colonial times, but those times are over – at least,
theoretically speaking, colonial anthropology is defunct. Hence, the
distinction between primitives and modern has been fully
abandoned in current anthropological discourse. In fact, it was
theoretically abandoned quite a long time ago, with the time-
honoured Malinowskian revolution, even though terminologically
(and somehow ideologically) it lasted for another few decades. We
should talk simply about anthropologists and indigenous peoples.
Years back, anthropologists were identified with modernity, with
Western society, and indigenous peoples with primitiveness,
backwardness, etc. Not so any more. But we still need some form of
distinction between 'us' and 'them' if anthropology as a form of
cross-cultural communication has to make any sense. Clearly, this
distinction is not an ontological distinction; it is merely what we
might call an epistemological distinction (an epistemological fiction,
it could even be called), which can be applied, so to speak, to any
kind of two given subjects, provided that there is some form of
cultural distance between the two. I would prefer to define it as a
perspective distinction: those who look like 'moderns' from one
point of view become 'primitives' from another point of view. In the
same way as a natural scientist's theories can become cultural beliefs
if they happen to be studied by an anthropologist, irrespective of
their truth claims, it could be said that this natural scientist becomes
a 'primitive', irrespective of how modern his practice and attitudes

happen to be, as soon as an anthropologist gets interested in his activity.

Because the conceptual distinction between primitives and moderns and that between nature and culture do not emanate from some objective reality out there, we cannot separate 'things belonging to culture' on the one side and 'things belonging to nature' on the other as if we were sorting out books on poetry from books on geology. Exactly in the same way, and for the same reason, we cannot classify human beings into 'primitive' and 'modern' categories as we would classify them according to their nationality. Those distinctions are not objective distinctions; they are merely the product of the intersubjectivity of anthropological knowledge. Since anthropological knowledge is intersubjective, we need to differentiate the two subjects that intervene in its production, in the same way as we need to differentiate the theories that will help us to produce that knowledge from the theories that are going to be studied and made intelligible by it or, which amounts to the same thing, we should be able to differentiate between beliefs and their objects. Perhaps this is so because those two subjects and their respective theories and beliefs do not participate on an equal basis in the production process of anthropological knowledge. Intersubjectivity does not mean co-authorship. Whether this inequality is fair or unfair is a different question and I shall not pursue it now.[4]

Be that as it may, intersubjectivity as we have defined it, for all its acceptance in current anthropological discourse, leads us to an important predicament. It can turn ethnography into a series of individual ('inter-individual'), idiosyncratic and, therefore, incommensurate experiences. If ethnography – and anthropological knowledge – originates solely in the experience of fieldwork interactions, there is no way I can cognitively compare my fieldwork experience, my ethnography, with anyone else's. But why should this be a 'danger' to begin with? I am deliberately avoiding the notion of 'scientific knowledge' in this discussion. This is not because I maintain that anthropological knowledge cannot be defined as scientific in any way; it is simply because I do not wish to make of this a nominalistic question of scientific versus non-scientific kinds of knowledge.

Obeyesekere (1990: 217 ff.) wrote about three kinds of intersubjectivity in anthropology. There is first the intersubjectivity of fieldwork practice. Anthropologists gather their data by means of an indisputably intersubjective activity. Secondly, there is the intersubjective nature of the object of anthropological knowledge. Culture (or 'social structure' for that matter) is an inherently intersubjective entity. And, finally, we have the intersubjectivity of the academic or intellectual community that will eventually receive, evaluate and profit from anthropological knowledge. It should be clear that these are different kinds of intersubjectivity with different effects upon the nature of anthropological knowledge. What some phenomenological approaches seem to be suggesting is a reduction of the three forms of intersubjectivity to the first one, as if everything in anthropology hinged on the nature of the encounter between the anthropologist and his or her informants and the conditions of possibility of this encounter. This is certainly not the case.

The first kind of intersubjectivity serves to define what sort of ethnography is being produced and why. But it cannot by itself determine the quality of the anthropological knowledge that will emerge from this ethnography in the end. This can only be ascertained to the extent that a particular set of ethnographic data are able to 'converse' with other ethnographic data. Because my ethnography can 'say something' to other ethnographies, from both culturally distant and culturally nearby societies, and vice versa, some sort of anthropological knowledge will eventually emerge out of it. In other words, this can only be ascertained by the third type of intersubjectivity according to Obeyesekere, or something definitely included in it, if I understood him well. Otherwise we would be reducing the value of anthropological knowledge to the conditions of its production, that is, notably the conditions of possibility of ethnographic fieldwork. Since these are always different depending on the particular life experiences of the anthropologist and the particular group of people he or she is doing research with, the sort of knowledge produced by every single anthropologist would turn out to be idiosyncratic and incommensurate, as idiosyncratic and incommensurate as the context and the conditions under which his or her research was carried out. This, to my mind, is a *reductio ad absurdum* of the anthropological project.

Incommensurate anthropological knowledge would be impossible to validate. There must be a way in which a particular ethnographic account or anthropological interpretation can be, or can be shown to be, wrong. But how is that possible, taking into account our intersubjective point of departure? Under what circumstances can we say that a particular piece of anthropological knowledge is right or wrong, true or false? Despite the risk of taking the reader too far afield from the main purpose of this essay, let us have a quick look at the way in which knowledge is validated in the so-called hard or natural sciences, following a very simple theory: the so-called correspondence theory of truth. According to John Searle (1995: 9–13), an eminent advocate of this theory, objectivity and subjectivity can have both an epistemic and an ontological sense. In the epistemic sense, they are predicates of judgements: judgements can be epistemically objective when their truth does not depend on anyone's opinion, and epistemically subjective when their truth is relative to someone's opinion. In the ontological sense, they refer to worldly objects and their properties. Facts of nature are ontologically objective, because they exist even if people do not believe in them. Facts of society are ontologically subjective, because they only exist if people believe in them – they correspond to a certain 'state of mind'. The point is that we can make epistemically objective judgements about both nature and society (and, similarly, we can also make epistemically subjective judgements about them). But their objectivity would be different in the two cases. When we make epistemically objective judgements about nature (i.e. about ontologically objective entities) their truth does not depend on anyone's opinion. If I say 'fertilisation occurs when the sperm meets the ovum', fertilisation will occur when the sperm meets the ovum even if nobody believes in that. The truth or falsity of that statement does not depend on one's beliefs but on the non-cultural (i.e. natural) fact that fertilisation actually takes place in those circumstances. In contrast, we can only make epistemically objective judgements about society (i.e. about ontologically subjective entities) if enough people believe in them (Searle 1995: 190). If everybody – or most people anyway – believes that priests used to have a very severe attitude with unmarried mothers, this judgement is epistemically objective.

Searle's thesis epitomises what later I shall define as 'objectifying social science' (see below). And yet the outcome of the anthropological project I defend in this essay is almost the opposite. When I say that culture is intersubjective, I mean, paraphrasing Searle, epistemically intersubjective, since that intersubjectivity originates in the process of production of anthropological knowledge rather than in the intersubjectivity of the beliefs and meanings that constitute the object of culture; notably because these beliefs and meanings do not exist as cultural objects outside the process of production of anthropological knowledge. What I have previously defined as culture-as-lived can be perfectly objective for those who 'live' in that culture. In fact, culture-as-lived is not culture for those who live in it, it is just 'nature'. This is because the object of a belief can be objective, ontologically objective, for the person who actually believes in it, whereas a belief in itself is a state of mind which can only be intersubjectively apprehended. Now statements, anthropological statements, about this belief are always epistemically intersubjective because they originate in the intersubjective interaction between anthropologists and informants. There is no 'correspondence theory' to be applied here in the way we can apply that theory for the validation of statements about natural entities. How do I know my informants' beliefs? I know that my informants held those opinions concerning priests because I asked them, because I talked to them and interacted with them. I do not know that fertilisation occurs when the sperm meets the ovum because I asked the sperm. Probably I know it because somebody told me, but this is irrelevant to the truth value of that assertion because it is not an assertion about anyone's beliefs; it is an assertion about a natural fact. But can I say 'so-and-so believes in God' even if he or she denies it? Would that make any sense?

Compare the following statements: 'priests used to be very strict with unmarried mothers', 'fertilisation occurs when the sperm meets the ovum', 'my informants believe that priests used to be very strict with unmarried mothers' and 'Western biologists believe that fertilisation occurs when the sperm meets the ovum'. They refer to two ontologically different realities.

The first two sentences are assertions about an objective reality. To those who actually believe in them, it does not make much difference whether the first refers to a social fact whereas the second refers to a natural fact. It is clear that social institutions and the objects of cultural beliefs are, or can be, perfectly objective realities, ontologically objective, for the people who live in those institutions and have those beliefs (see Berger and Luckmann 1966: 77). The object of Sambia belief in the nutritious power of semen – i.e. the nutritious power of semen – is, from the Sambia's perspective, as objective a reality as Western biologists' theories on human reproduction are from those biologists' perspective. But note that this does not contradict my intersubjective definition of culture, for the intersubjectivity I am postulating originates in the process of production of anthropological knowledge, not in the way in which institutions or beliefs come to be constituted in a particular society.

The last two of the statements to be compared, in contrast, are assertions about a state of mind, they are not assertions about a *res extensa*, so neither my informants' nor Western biologists' beliefs are an objective reality (even though they refer to an objective reality), they are not ontologically objective: I do not 'observe' those beliefs because beliefs do not have an objective existence like physical entities – they only exist in people's minds.[5] Someone might contend that I can infer people's beliefs from their conduct in the same way as I infer natural laws from the observation of natural phenomena. But this is wrong for at least two reasons: first, because the relationship between people's conduct and their beliefs is always arbitrary and, secondly, beliefs cannot be inferred from conduct because conduct is not a physical entity either. Take, for example, people worshipping a particular god. I do not observe this fact in the same way as I observe water evaporating at 100 degrees Celsius. The only thing I observe is people moving in a certain way, they are on their knees, they put their hands together and make certain sounds with their mouths. I put forward a hypothesis: they are praying. Why? Because Europeans do something very similar when they pray. But this is only a hypothesis. I should learn more about their culture (talk to them, etc.) before I can validate that hypothesis. (Hundreds of anthropological theories have turned out to be wrong precisely because they were based on superficial analogies of this sort between 'their' behaviour and 'ours'.)

So the statements concerning my informants' beliefs can never be epistemically objective even if those beliefs refer to an ontologically objective reality, for my access to those beliefs is not contingent on their correspondence with their object but on the interaction between myself and my informants. In other words, I need to know what my informants are talking about in order to understand them, whereas a natural scientist, for instance, might want to understand his or her colleagues in order to know what they are talking about. Thus statements concerning my informants' beliefs are epistemically intersubjective, and this is the only way I can validate my initial hypothesis. The final intersubjectivity is only reached when I have managed to learn more about my informants' culture, I have talked to them and interacted with them, and I have compared their statements with what other anthropologists say about other people's beliefs, etc.: that is, ethnographic research and anthropological analysis.

This is only a preliminary approach to the sort of questions that we should try to answer when we think about the object of anthropological knowledge from an intersubjective viewpoint. The discussion about the problem of validation should be taken as an introduction to the central concept in interpretative social science, the concept of interpretation. In the following chapter I will explore the theoretical and political dimensions of this essential and disputed concept in the light of what we have seen so far.

Notes

1. There is a very clear example in the history of the anthropology of sexuality that supports very explicitly my point about the intersubjective nature of culture. I am thinking of the well-known 'Samoan controversy' between Mead and Freeman concerning the character of Samoa sexual culture (Mead 1928; Freeman 1983). I will not enter into a discussion of Freeman's critique of Mead's data nor in the particularities of his theoretical approach; I only wish to remark on a rather obvious detail: how different two ethnographies can be when done by two very different authors. It might well be the case that Samoan sexuality corresponds neither to Mead's nor to Freeman's account and at the same time partakes of both viewpoints. If we take Samoan sexuality as being part of Samoan culture and, as I have just argued, cultures do not exist objectively but only intersubjectively, it is clear that the specific intersubjective events in which Mead and Freeman participated while doing their fieldwork were remarkably different. They were different not only because these authors probably did not probably come across the same native informants, but also because Mead and Freeman were two very different sorts of individuals who, consequently, were engaged in very different interpersonal relationships with their informants; hence the differences in the sort of 'cultures' that emerged from their respective intersubjectivities.

2. Pálsson (1993: 32–33) has rightly criticised the idea according to which 'the "natives" are depicted as being imprisoned by culture, while the anthropologist is presented as culture-free'. But I wonder to what extent, with all due qualifications, this should not be regarded as a necessary fiction of ethnographic research: we are all cultural beings, or culture-free individuals, but only some of us are 'anthropologised' while the others become anthropologists. How shall we account for this distinction?

3. I understand the statement 'so-and-so believes in God' only to the extent that I know what the concept of God is, irrespective of so-and-so's belief – which does not mean that I need to believe in God myself. The word 'God' must have some meaning for me; otherwise I would find the statement 'so-and-so believes in God' totally unintelligible. If we call this meaning the object of so-and-so's belief, then understanding that belief presupposes the knowledge of its object.

4. With care, we can try again the analogy with language. Suppose I can translate into Greek any statement uttered by an English-speaking individual who does not understand Greek. My English-speaking interlocutor is totally unaware of what I say when I translate her words, the Greek text into which her statements are translated is opaque to her, and yet my translation has to correspond to what she says. But this correspondence does not mean that she is in any way co-author of that translation; I am the sole author and the only person responsible for the accuracy of that translation.

5. According to Needham, there are no criteria to identify belief, there is no particular facial expression, no particular action, no particular utterance that can make us infer without the shadow of a doubt that someone believes in something. 'Where, then, do we get the notion of belief from? From the verb "believe", and its inflected forms, in everyday English usage. Statements of belief are the only evidence for the phenomenon; but the phenomenon itself appears to be no more than the custom of making such statements' (1972: 108).

CHAPTER 12

Subjectification and
Interpretation

We have seen that the validation of any anthropological statement, such as so-and-so believes in God or the Irish believe that priests were strict with unmarried mothers, is contingent upon a genuinely dialogical activity. We should ask the natives and interact with them to find out about their beliefs (i.e. carry out ethnographic research), but what exactly are we looking for in this type of research? It is not 'truth', or, at least, it is not the truth that the natural scientist wishes to find in his or her investigatory procedure. The natural scientist's search for truth corresponds to the intersubjective social scientist's quest for meaning. But what sort of meaning is this? Where does it come from? How do we get at it? These are the issues I will try to explore in the following paragraphs.

Suppose, now, that intersubjectivity is not a necessary condition of anthropological knowledge. Admittedly, despite the popularity enjoyed by intersubjectivistic approaches in anthropology and in the social sciences in general, the opposite perspective, the so-called objectivistic point of view, is by no means absent from current social-scientific thinking. To understand the implications of intersubjectivity, a cursory approach to the problems raised by objectivistic social sciences is now in order. We shall be able to identify the specific predicament that besets any social scientists that endorses this viewpoint and, specifically, the particular way in which social anthropology can confront it.

According to Dreyfus and Rabinow (1983: 163), the objectifying human sciences (i.e. those that treat the human individual as an object) have to face the following dilemma: 'if the human sciences claim to study human activities, then the human sciences, unlike the natural sciences, must take account of those human activities which make possible their own discipline'. Will this not lead us to an endless regression? If the human sciences study human activity, it is true then that the practice of the human sciences, to the extent that it is obviously a human activity, can be studied by the human sciences as well. I can imagine a particular social-scientific discipline, let us call it 'sociology of knowledge', whose practitioners produce the background practices of a particular social-scientific activity (or just scientific activity *tout court*) as a theoretical object of knowledge. But I cannot imagine those same practitioners producing as a theoretical object of knowledge the background practices that make possible their own activity without falling into a sort of vicious endless regression.

'The important point for the natural sciences is that natural science is successful precisely to the extent that these background practices which make science possible can be taken for granted and ignored by the scientists' (Dreyfus and Rabinow 1983: 163). Apparently, this is equally true for the objectifying social scientist, since the fact that the social scientist's practice is itself a human activity does not necessarily imply that the social-scientific account of this practice is a condition of possibility of all social-scientific knowledge. (For we could say there is no such a thing as 'human activity' outside the definitions of a particular social-scientific discipline. Human society, human social behaviour, etc. do not exist irrespective of the theoretical activity of social scientists who produce them as an object of knowledge.) As for the reflection on the conditions of possibility of a particular social-scientific practice – which can by no means include the reflection on the conditions of possibility of such reflection – this sort of reflection should not lead to an endless regression as long as it is carried out within the limits of a particular social-scientific activity and avoids falling into some bottomless philosophical pit. In other words, using Strathern's metaphor (1996), the 'network' has to be cut somewhere if we want to produce some form of 'objective' sociological knowledge.

But the problem for the objectifying social sciences has only started. There is no way this network cutting can be seen as an objective requirement of the research process. Its inevitable arbitrariness casts very corrosive doubts on the very objectivity of social-scientific research. Objectifying social scientists always seem to have a hidden political agenda of sorts. They adamantly disapprove of the moralistic and political rhetoric of their subjectifying colleagues, which they see as unscientific. But they cannot confer intelligibility on the social practices that make them possible without falling into some sort of endless regression. So they have to 'cut the network', but this very act of network cutting cannot be objectively accounted for. And it is never an innocuous act of epistemological hygiene. So at the end they are bound to fall into a sort of subjectifying betrayal; they end up being political when they most wholeheartedly tried to avoid it.

Subjectifying social sciences, in contrast, do not have to face this problem. Dreyfus and Rabinow have cogently argued that, for those social sciences that treat the human individual as a subject, the problem of accounting for the background practices that make scientific activity possible does not emerge. Objectifying social science could not account for the scientist's practices because it could not account for the existence of the subject. This does not pose a problem for subjectifying social sciences since they treat human individuals as subjects. Their field of knowledge is inhabited by subjects, so there is no problem in accounting for the very practice of the scientist, who is just another 'subject'.

So what problem do the subjectifying social sciences have? To treat human individuals as subjects means that we cannot analyse their behaviour in causal terms, as we do with any natural entity, any object, but we should consider them as meaning-producing entities. Therefore, the problem for the subjectifying social sciences is obviously the problem of meaning. What sort of meaning are we looking for? Surface meaning? Why do we need a scientific practice to uncover surface meaning? Every able member of any society must know this surface meaning, so what can social-scientific practice add to what is already common knowledge? What about 'deep meaning'? A meaning unknown to the actors? This is what the hermeneutics of suspicion are meant to find out. But why should there be any deep meaning in the first place? Because some form of power prevents us from grasping this deep meaning, i.e. the 'repressive hypothesis'?

The subjectifying social scientist does not need to furnish an objective account of the background practices that make her scientific activity possible because she has no interest in 'objective' accounts of anything to begin with – she is not interested in the 'truth'. Far from it, her own subjectivity is the condition of the possibility of her own research activity, in the same way as anyone's subjectivity is the condition of the possibility of conducting meaningful social interaction. Because she is a subject of such-and-such characteristics, interests, values, etc., she is producing this kind of research in such a way that her own subjective characteristics are not potential or actual biases to the validity of her findings, as was the case with the objectifying social scientist, but the very foundations of her cognitive activity. But the unbridled happiness of our subjectifying social scientist will not last long: she is bound to suffer from a terrible epistemological disease. If objectivity has been discarded *ex hypothesi*, on what grounds are we going to validate her findings? The answer is very simple: on the very same grounds on which we judge and evaluate the practice of any other subject, to wit, on moral grounds. Thus the strait-jacket of political ideology makes its unwelcome appearance once again. The only difference is that now it is not a hidden political agenda but an open and explicit viewpoint. Subjectifying social science is openly political right from its inception. This is a conclusion with numerous supporters in current social-scientific thinking.

Let me try to show the way in which I believe it is not a necessary conclusion. First of all, it is predicated upon a gross simplification as to the nature of intersubjective interaction in ordinary social life. Once 'objective truth' has been discarded, it is simply not correct to conclude that in our dealings with other subjects we can only judge the validity of their assertions according to their political or moral value. There is a bit more in human communication than simply political staging. As a matter of fact, there is something much more primordial going on in social interaction that must take place before any judgement – a value judgement (moral, political) or a fact judgement – can be in any way uttered, so primordial that we normally take if for granted: understanding. Surely before judging so-and-so's behaviour or mode of thought we must understand it.

Granted that the problem of understanding lies at the very foundations of human communication, we still have to demonstrate what role can be accorded to the subjectifying social scientist in this new context. By definition, she cannot provide any objective picture of the social world we live in. True, she can certainly offer a subjective, yet highly sophisticated, political or moral judgement upon this wretched world. But there is something else she can do that is not, at first sight, directly correlated with the moral or political correctness of her viewpoint. She might give us a hand while we try to understand our fellow subjects. She cannot tell us about the truth of what they do, say or think (unlike her objectifying colleague, she does not believe in such a thing), but she might tell us something about what they mean. Apparently, she is not doing anything qualitatively different from what we all do in our day-to-day interaction. So much so that we might as well wonder whether we really need her at all. It was nice to hear her sophisticated political rhetoric, but now she says that somehow we should forget her political views and that she will simply help us in a seemingly more modest endeavour: to understand the meaning of these or those people's acts. But we already understand them, don't we? No, she authoritatively asserts. You think you do but you are wrong. You only understand the surface meaning of social life, but there is a deeper, hidden, 'truer' meaning that only a well-trained social scientist can bring to the open.

The 'repressive hypothesis' seemed to offer a plausible explanation of why social life needs to have those mysterious hidden meanings that only the clever social scientist can grasp. Power prevents ordinary people from seeing through, so to speak; power represses the real meanings of our social life and throws them back into our collective unconscious. But the interpretative social scientist will come to our rescue, she will help us to gain consciousness of all that repressed material,[1] very much like a psychoanalyst helping his patient become conscious of her repressions and thus enabling her to rid herself of her neurosis. The subjectifying social scientists has become something more than a mere political propagandist. She is not only the one who knows better, but she has a real therapeutic job to carry out: to liberate mankind by showing the real meaning of social life (my excuses for this somewhat pompous language). The social scientist's job continues to be a political job through and through, a liberating job. But this is simply because of the way we have chosen to account for the existence of those hidden meanings.

I believe there is another way in which interpretation in the social sciences can have a politically much humbler and, simultaneously, intellectually more creative task. Suppose that culture is a set of implicit meanings that can only be made explicit through anthropological investigation; we then have to tell why anyone should be interested in making those meanings explicit. If we stick to our initial approach to the culture concept as a form of lived experience, there does not seem to emanate any necessary hermeneutical consequence from it. In other words, why does this lived experience have to be understood by means of specialised research? In normal circumstances, people have no unsolvable problems in understanding each other on the basis of their reciprocal behaviour. In certain circumstances, however, this might not be case for the very simple reason that the rules that regulate human interaction among certain people are unknown to us. In Wittgenstein's terms, we cannot find our feet with them (1958: 223). Note that no necessary repression or distortion carried out by an external, presumably oppressive, power is needed to account for that ignorance. Repression is not the only reason that might explain why there are hidden meanings in social life. Cultural distance is another one. And this might give us a clue as to why interpretation in anthropology is somewhat different from interpretation in sociology and psychoanalysis. There is no need to invoke any repressive hypothesis if our assumption is that it is merely a problem of cultural distance that prevents us from grasping the meaning of social life.[2]

It is time to say a few words about the concept of 'understanding' in cross-cultural research. The problem of understanding is closely related to the problem of meaning and that of interpretation. I will devote the following paragraphs to discussing the concept of interpretation. But now we should focus our attention on what 'understanding' can possibly mean in anthropological terms. Philosophers have been struggling for quite a long time with this concept. It is normally assumed, even though there are several contradictory theories on this issue, that understanding a human being means something like grasping his or her intentions. But apparently this only leads us to the even more complicated problem of intentionality. How do we understand 'intentions'? How do we differentiate between intentional and unintentional acts? What do we mean when we say that we did not mean what we did? These are well-known riddles of analytic philosophy that should not detain us here.

I shall try to tackle this question from the point of view of the constraints that operate upon any individual's activity. The reader will remember what we said in chapter 8 as regards the characteristics of semantic constraints. Consider now a more elementary type, such as logical constraints: I cannot speak and remain silent at the same time.

There are also physical constraints: I cannot fly, I cannot climb mount Everest in a couple of hours. I cannot take off my clothes in the middle of the classroom: what sort of constraint is that? Let us call it 'social constraint'. Some authors may add what they call 'existential constraints', i.e. those derived from the particularities of each specific situation. There are lots of things I might not do in a classroom apart from not taking off my clothes. For instance, I should not give an outdated reading list to my students, and so on. Now on top of all these constraints, there is the intention of a particular individual to act in a certain way or to do a certain thing. But it should be clear that this intention, what the subject decides to do or not to do, cannot be understood (its meaning cannot be grasped) without taking into consideration all the constraints within which anyone's activity necessarily occurs. Now in ordinary communication (i.e. intra-cultural communication) all those constraints – perhaps with the exception of the existential ones – are simply taken for granted, so that we can concentrate exclusively on the subject's intentions to understand the meaning of his or her actions. But think of what happens in non-ordinary circumstances such as ethnographic fieldwork. It is clear that in this context understanding the natives' behaviour involves a bit more than grasping their intentions, specifically because the existential, social and perhaps even physical constraints that operate upon that behaviour are simply unknown to us. Thus we see that, in whatever way we wish to define intentionality, understanding and interpretation in a cross-cultural context are substantially different. Ethnographers can still claim that to understand the meaning of an individual's action they need to know his or her intentions, but it is clear that these 'intentions' include much more than what is involved in ordinary communication.

Thus we come face to face with the key concept in the present discussion: the concept of interpretation. Interpretation is the method that will enable us to grasp the meaning of social life. We have just seen that meanings can be opaque because of two reasons: repression and cultural distance. Does this mean that we have not one but two concepts of interpretation? Yes, two different concepts of interpretation should be distinguished, two different conceptions of interpretation which I believe cannot be easily reconciled. On the one hand, there is the conception stemming from what we might call the phenomenological hermeneutic tradition. From this point of view, the purpose of interpretation is always, essentially if not exclusively, intellectual: 'to learn different possibilities of making sense of human life' (Winch 1970: 106). In contradistinction to this approach is interpretation as originating in critical theory or critical hermeneutics. Interpretation has for critical theorists a political aim, it is an emancipatory activity. This distinction is far from rigid and clear-cut, but still I believe it can be defended with some plausibility. In my view, anthropological interpretation falls closer to the first pole, that of phenomenological hermeneutics, than to the second pole. I shall try to demonstrate why I believe this should be the case.

Psychoanalysis shows us the way in which we can link interpretation in critical hermeneutics with an emancipatory activity. The end of analytic practice does not consist in uncovering the hidden meanings repressed in the subject's unconscious. That would be equivalent to a naively positivistic understanding of psychoanalysis. In Freud's view, psychoanalysis is not merely concerned with the disclosure of some hidden truth deeply buried in the patient's unconscious but with the patient's understanding of that truth, in other words, with the patient's self-understanding: that is the purpose of psychoanalytic therapy. In Habermas's terms: 'The subject cannot obtain knowledge of the object unless it becomes knowledge for the object – and unless the latter thereby emancipates itself by becoming a subject' (1987: 262). The validation of psychoanalytic knowledge, in Habermas's interpretation of Freud's theory, cannot be severed from its final therapeutic objective (see also Ricoeur 1981: 247 ff.). But the interesting thing is that therapy is achieved by the patient's self-knowledge resulting from the analytic treatment. From this we can see that the intersubjectivity of psychoanalytic investigatory procedure manifests itself in two different, and complementary, ways. First, a hermeneutic investigation is needed to reach the patient's unconscious. But this is only the first stage. Why do we need hermeneutics to get at the unconscious? Could hypnosis not be equally valid? No, precisely because hypnosis is not based on the patient's self-knowledge, which is the second purpose of psychoanalytic intersubjectivity. That is the reason why Freud abandoned the hypnotic method after *Studies on Hysteria* (Habermas 1987: 250–51). The unconscious has to become conscious as a result of a process of self-reflection.

Now, the need to transform the unconscious into the conscious can only be explained by the therapeutic objective of psychoanalytic treatment. It is because the patient's ignorance of him- or herself is defined as pathological that the overcoming of that ignorance appears as therapeutic. In other words, the therapeutic effect of psychoanalytic hermeneutics presupposes a pathological condition. Neurosis, and the repressive instance that produces it, is the pathological state that results from the analysand's lack of self-understanding. Neurosis is the illness to be countered by analytic therapy, it is the pathological condition to be eliminated by self-knowledge.

What happens when we apply this model to the social and cultural sciences? The transposition of the psychoanalytic model onto the cultural sciences – which is what Habermas has done in his critical hermeneutics – transforms psychological therapy into social emancipation. Enlightenment makes people free in the same way as the analysand's self-knowledge puts an end to his or her neurosis. But notice that it necessarily involves the constitution of a similarly pathological state as the starting-point of social-scientific investigatory procedure. Interpretation for the critical-hermeneutic tradition originates in a situation of systematically distorted language communication, which is the sociological counterpart to the psychopathological state of neurosis. The illegitimate and repressive power responsible for this failed intersubjectivity will find its antidote in the process of self-reflection induced by critical hermeneutics. The point I wish to stress is that the need for interpretation originates in this context, as in Freudian psychoanalysis, in a pathological condition, a situation that has to be therapeutically superseded by means of the critical-hermeneutic practice.

Here we can find the reason why, I believe, the concept of interpretation in critical theory cannot be utilised in anthropological research. The need for anthropological interpretation does not spring from any pathological condition: it originates, as we have seen, in cultural distance. The application of the critical-hermeneutic perspective to the interpretation of ethnographic facts would inevitably result in making cultural distance pathological. I do not see how this can be considered a legitimate end for anthropology. (Remember what we said in chapter 8 concerning Scheper-Hughes's cultural analysis of schizophrenia.) It is true that cultural distance, and cultural homogeneity, can be politically and ideologically manipulated in a thousand different ways. But should we not consider the dangers (and benefits as well) of this political manoeuvring as, somehow, external to the anthropological endeavour? Furthermore, cultural distance should not be taken as an undisputed premise of anthropological research for the simple reason that it might as well be totally inexistent. But the existence or inexistence of cultural distance (an anthropological premise, certainly, but never unquestionable) should be ascertained by ethnographic research, not by the disclosure of some illegitimate or perverse 'knowledge-constitutive' interest. Stated otherwise, the effects of those manipulative political and ideological interests are external to, and (relatively at least) independent from, the existence of cultural distance as an ethnographic fact. Cultural distance can be pathological – I am not too sure about the meaning of this statement – but this does not mean that cultural distance as a pathological condition should be taken as a premise of anthropological interpretation in the same way as neurosis, a psychologically pathological state, and distorted language communication, a sociological pathology in Habermas's theorising, can be taken as the premises of psychoanalysis and critical hermeneutics, respectively. I do not think that the history of anthropological thought and research can in any way be understood with this assumption as a starting-point.

We could make these abstract theoretical assertions more concrete by returning to the ethnographic fact that we have been looking at throughout, that is, sexual morality in Ireland. The repressive character that has been traditionally, and almost unanimously, attributed to the historical sexual morality in Ireland would apparently call for an interpretation, anthropological or otherwise, very close to the psychoanalytic-critical-hermeneutic model. In fact, much of what has been said in the previous chapters would seemingly confirm this conclusion. Have we not reached sexuality, or sexual norms, by means of the hermeneutic analysis of some sort of symbolic evidence? To what extent can my disclosure of sexual meanings behind certain social discourses be seen as fulfilling some socially emancipatory purpose? I think it would be utterly mistaken to interpret my analysis from this point of view, as leading to the disclosure of a repressed sexual truth by means of a critical-hermeneutical investigation. It is true that sexual meanings have become apparent behind certain discourses and institutions, not always explicitly concerned with the verbalisation and regulation of sexual behaviour. But the non-thematised character of sexuality in rural Ireland does not originate in repression in the same way as its explicit articulation in my own analysis has no emancipatory purpose or function.

Let us go back, once again, to the distinction between structure and event, sexuality as a cultural form and sexuality as an activity. This distinction can be recast as the dichotomy between observer and observed in the following way. The cultural forms from which the sexual act acquires a particular moral significance are the disciplinary regimes of obedience and knowledge. But those disciplinary regimes are just perspectives upon human conduct, watch-towers from which behaviour can be observed; depending on which tower we carry out our observations from, different things become visible. For instance, from the watch-tower of obedience-sexuality, we could see how small families fall onto the wrong side of the moral divide. But these same small families shift their moral location as we move to the watch-tower of knowledge-sexuality, and so on. Besides, it has been from this new observatory that the first watch-tower, the disciplinary regime of obedience-sexuality, itself became visible.[3]

The reader may have noticed that there was some asymmetry in the way those watch-towers have been analytically constructed. We inferred the existence of obedience-sexuality not so much from historical research into the period in which it was supposed to prevail, but rather from the narratives of those who were actually looking at and thinking about their past from the perspective of the new disciplinary regime, from the watch-tower of knowledge-sexuality. Obedience-sexuality appears both as a structure from which certain events can be observed, and thus signified, and as an event, a historical event to be observed and signified from another structure, from the structure of knowledge-sexuality. Think now of anthropology as another watch-tower. What can we see from it?

The 'view from afar' that anthropology provides enables us to see, we could argue, sexuality in itself as an object of cultural and moral significance. This is not sexuality, or sexual behaviour, as an etic act. I have already explained why etic sexual behaviour is not visible. More importantly, as the etic concept indicates, it is meaningless. We saw sexuality as an imagined behaviour, as a myth. But notice that this type of sexuality is not a hidden truth in need of disclosure by some form of critical-hermeneutic investigation; it is (merely) a structure of intelligibility that helps us, or helped me, make sense of certain social and cultural institutions. The cultural invisibility of Irish sexuality, its non-thematised character, is not so much the consequence of a repressive instance but is rather because sexuality should be seen in this context as a life experience and not the product of some sort of explicit cognitive practice. Remember the distinction between culture-as-lived and culture-as-thought-of that we drew in chapter 10. Paraphrasing Sahlins, we could say that for ages people have been speaking sex without knowing it: they were just living it. It is true, on the other hand, that from the point of view of knowledge-sexuality, the disciplinary regime of obedience-sexuality could be, and has been, plausibly defined as 'repressive'. But this repression, and this is the point I must stress, comes to light simply because we have shifted our perspective, we (my Irish friends) looked at sexual conduct in the past from the vantage point, from the watch-tower, of knowledge-sexuality, and thus they saw 'repression'. (I would dare to say that something similar happened to Freud when he assessed the sexual lives of his contemporaries.) Neither repression nor sexuality exist – or can be seen – except for those who can climb the appropriate watch-tower. Whether this type of analysis is socially emancipatory or not is, in my opinion, totally beside the point.

And the same applies to culture, or cultural distance. Culture can be seen as a pre-condition of the practice of ethnography, or it can equally be considered as its final product. But neither culture, in its anthropological meaning, nor cultural distance is an objective fact. They are what in current jargon we would call, fictions, anthropological fictions. How would we define the culture concept from a critical-hermeneutical approach? As a set of hidden meanings kept under cover by a pernicious power structure? Or perhaps we should see in it the objectification of that power structure as it conceals some sort of extracultural truth? Neither of these definitions seems to fall anywhere near to what culture is from an anthropological point of view. Culture, let us repeat, is not a thing but a perspective; it is a matter of shifting perspectives.[4]

Notes

1. It could be argued that the repressive hypothesis works equally well for the objectifying social sciences. In this case it is the truth of social life that is repressed, not its meaning. The difference is that an objectifying social scientist does not need the repressive hypothesis in the way in which the subjectifying social scientist apparently does. Truth can be invisible for the lay public simply because ordinary people lack the required training. I do not see the truth of quantum mechanics simply because I have no

knowledge of physics; there is no need for any power to repress or to hide that truth. This observation is perhaps particularly relevant as regards the oscillations of Freudian psychoanalysis between the objectifying and subjectifying views (see below).

2. For some this is simply the recipe for a conservative social science, a social science that gives no trouble to the establishment. The mere celebration of cultural diversity, even if it is done in aseptic academic terms, can by itself have highly problematic political repercussions for any established power system. But this is simply not the point. To what extent can sociological knowledge (i.e. the scientific knowledge of one's own society, in whatever way we define it) have any strictly theoretical utility, irrespective of its political, extratheoretical, meaning? Can anyone indulge in studying his or her own society without having a political end in mind? I have no straightforward answer to this question. But, interestingly, this does not seem to be applicable to anthropological knowledge (i.e. the scientific knowledge of an alien society, in whatever way we define it). The problem of intelligibility does not seem to be reducible to any particular political intention, no matter how many additional political meanings may go with it in specific historical circumstances.

3. I would like to thank my friend and colleague Heonik Kwon for helping me to clarify the ideas developed in these paragraphs.

4. Or shifting contexts, as Strathern (1995: 8) has argued: 'It is salutary to frame whatever claims anthropologists might make for their paradigm shifts, and indeed for their knowledge at large, by reference to the diverse ways in which people (including them) shift the contexts of perception and thus make knowledge for themselves.'

CONCLUSION

By attempting to distil general anthropological knowledge from a particular set of ethnographic data we do not try to enlarge its sphere of applicability, we do not want to make if 'more representative'. We are only trying to make it a bit more meaningful, that is, to enlarge its dialogical capacities beyond the restricted fields of regional or thematic specialists. This also implies that the sort of general knowledge that has hopefully emanated from my Irish ethnography is only contingently related to it. Very probably, the same kind of general ideas could have been produced on the basis of a different set of ethnographic information. I in no wise take that as a shortcoming, precisely because it is not the production of particular ethnographic knowledge that I am aiming at. That similar theoretical ideas can be reached from different ethnographic experiences can only prove the validity of those ideas as general anthropological knowledge.

In the same way as I define good ethnographies as dialogical ethnographies, that is, ethnographies able to converse with other ethnographies, I believe that good general anthropological knowledge should also manifest some form of dialogical capabilities. These are to be found without a doubt in the very ethnographic material from which that general knowledge has emerged. But also, and perhaps more importantly, general anthropological knowledge must be able to entertain a dialogue with the sort of social-scientific knowledge produced by cognate disciplines. The ultimate aim of any scientific investigation, or of any intellectual endeavour for that matter, is to be useful to those who are not members of the academic clique that has engendered it. This means that some sort of interdisciplinary rhetoric is always unavoidable in theoretical or 'general knowledge' researches. To this effect, the final utopia that general anthropological knowledge seeks to achieve manifests itself in a dialectically contradictory fashion. By making anthropological knowledge more meaningful to non-anthropologists, more 'interdisciplinary', we are simultaneously trying to find out what makes it 'anthropological'. Something very close, incidentally, to what ethnographers do when they attempt to understand cultural otherness: it is also the self's cultural identity that gradually becomes more visible and comprehensible.

We may call general anthropological knowledge theoretical knowledge, but the relationship between social anthropology and theory is a complex one, and somewhat peculiar. I believe it can be cogently argued that anthropology is a theoretical discipline but I have yet to come across a definitive publication on 'anthropological theory' commensurate with the 'social theory', 'economic theory' or 'political theory' that we find in these neighbouring fields of social research. Take, for instance, the well-known handbook by Marvin Harris *The Rise of Anthropological Theory* (1968). Despite its explicit title, what we find in the contents of this book is a well-documented history of the different theoretical paradigms that have influenced or dominated anthropological research since its very beginnings. But I do not see any anthropological theory 'rising' from there, but only a collection of different theoretical styles, most of them not even specifically anthropological styles, that have inspired social and cultural anthropologists in the interpretation of their data. I know that Harris's book is somewhat dated by now, but take any of the more recent publications in this line and the result is much the same (see Layton 1998; Moore 1999; Barnard 2000). There might be more theoretical schools included in the analysis, critical judgements might be more qualified and better balanced, but a systematic anthropological theory (i.e. a set of commonly accepted programmatic principles and conceptual tools to be used by anthropologists in their field researches) is conspicuously absent.

I believe that this absence should not be seen as some form of impeding deformity that would prevent anthropologists from producing the sort of general knowledge that other social scientists are so proud of. Far from it, I think it has to do with the elusive character of anthropology's object of research, what we normally call 'culture', and its inherently dialogical nature. It would be inimical to my objectives here were I to conclude with an (always tortuous) attempt to formulate a definition of culture as an object of anthropological investigation. But I hope that in the previous pages an approximation to that definition has gradually unfolded, not in the guise of a well-structured set of theoretical propositions, but in the form of a prolonged reflection upon a particular ethnographic experience.

Let me try to pull together some of the threads of this reflection. At different points throughout this essay I have been following Rylean philosophical behaviourism (Ryle 1949), which I believe is perfectly coherent with my own approach. Ryle attacked what he called the Cartesian myth, the belief according to which we can differentiate between two different entities: mind and matter, soul and body, etc. The interesting thing about Ryle's theory is that he criticised Cartesian dualism without falling into either a materialist or an idealist reductionism. A person's mind is not a secret compartment inside his or her head, a person's mind is simply a disposition, a propensity to behave in a certain way (see also Tanney 1998). In other words, we can talk about human minds, we can see human minds simply by looking at and interpreting human behaviour. If we substitute the concept of culture for that of mind, we can link my understanding of the anthropological project to Ryle's position.

I have used the culture concept in this book as a critique of essentialist definitions. By an essentialist definition of culture I understand something close to Cartesian dualism in Ryle's theory. Similar to minds, cultures have often been defined as ghostly essences that causally determine human behaviour, just as the behaviour of non-human animals seems to be determined by their instincts, by their genetic endowment. This is clearly inadequate, and I hope that my essay has contributed to demonstrating why it is so. The dichotomy between mind and body is coextensive with the dichotomy between culture and nature and, as we saw in chapter 11, between sexuality and sex. Sexuality is merely sex that is being looked at through culture's looking-glass and, conversely, sex is merely sexuality looked at through nature's looking-glass.

One of the main ideas I have developed in the former account is that the specificity of the culture concept in anthropology arises from the intersubjectivity of anthropological research. This is what 'produces' culture and this is the origin of the perspectivist view on culture I defend. 'A "culture" can materialize itself only in counterdistinction to another culture' (Boon 1982: ix). Quite naturally, anthropological accounts, descriptions of particular cultures, are always accounts from a particular point of view, for the culture they describe is only visible from this point of view. I would like to relate this perspectivist concept with the notion of epistemological autonomy as it emerged in chapters 4 and 5. We saw then that the culture of sexual morality allegedly characteristic of Irish rural society from the second half of the nineteenth century was not reducible to a set of social and economic conditions; it was not reducible in the sense that it could not be thought of as a necessary consequence of those conditions. There was some sort of unexplained residue or theoretical empty space in the ingenious functionalist arguments that we examined. The origins of this unexplained residue were the taken-for-granted assumptions concerning sexual behaviour embedded in those arguments. In other words, functionalist explanations worked only as long as we assumed that individuals had to behave in a certain way under certain conditions. That is why, apparently, no culture was needed to account for the emergence of a particular sexual morality, since sexual morality was taken almost as a 'natural' fact.

A similar line of thought was pursued in chapter 6 and following chapters, but this time in regard to the history of Irish demography. In a way, we were simply looking at the same thing but from a different angle. If we understand that a particularly repressive or inhibitive sexual morality is the necessary consequence, in functional terms, of the SFS – because the SFS gives rise to high celibacy rates and, for the proper working of the system, it is believed that the unmarried should not have children – then the specific demographic events that can be put down to the existence of that repressive sexual morality, such as a low rate of non-marital births, become the effect not of that sexual morality but of the SFS itself and its social and economic context (inheritance system, land tenure, etc.). People do not have children outside marriage because that would impair the proper performance of the SFS, and sexual repression only comes in to reinforce the functional need of the SFS to prevent people from having sex, and children, outside marriage. In other words, the SFS is the real cause of everything, whereas sexual morality is merely the 'superstructure', the ideological legitimation of certain social and economic needs. But, if we do not consider that a repressive sexual morality is the necessary consequence, or the functional need, of the SFS, then the explanation of the same demographic events looks rather different. A low rate of non-marital fertility can no longer be seen as the result of the SFS because, as argued in chapter 5, the SFS may work perfectly well with high illegitimacy rates. Thus the fact, the demographic fact, that those rates were actually low can only be made intelligible in terms of a particular sexual morality – call it repressive, inhibitive or whatever you wish.

The purpose of that argumentation was to highlight the epistemological autonomy of cultural forms. By postulating that cultural forms cannot be explained as the result of certain social and economic conditions, we are actually arguing that cultural forms are unexplainable as cultural forms, i.e. they are 'irrational' (needless to say, not in a pathological or psychopathological sense), and they can only be, as the philosophical motto has it, described. But do not forget that 'culture' and what we have called 'social and economic conditions' are not two different entities or mysterious energies (Rylean ghosts) lurking behind human beings and at odds with each other, so to speak, for the determination of those human beings' behaviour. We are all equally, or alternatively, depending on our perspective, determined in our behaviour by culture and by social and economic conditions. It all depends on what we take as rational or irrational behaviour. And this is always, in the last instance, a totally arbitrary choice. Remember that rational behaviour is simply that which proceeds in accordance with certain underlying assumptions that we take for granted because we share them and, conversely, irrational behaviour is that whose underlying assumptions are unknown to us. As Tremayne (2001: 6) has argued, '"Irrational" reproductive behaviour, both in a historical perspective and in contemporary societies, can only be understood in the light of the priorities people have over what might be considered "logical" behaviour.' But it is we, the observers, who define this 'logical' behaviour, who make a particular human behaviour look rational or irrational, or, rather, it is the specific intersubjective relationship between observer and observed that creates the objective appearance of rationality or irrationality.

That is why culture and social and economic conditions are incommensurable. They are incommensurable because by postulating such commensurability we are committing a 'category mistake', in Ryle's words, equivalent to saying, for instance, that thoughts are the cause of human behaviour. In chapter 6 we saw that most events in Irish demography seemed to accord with the requirements of a particular social and economic context. But, then, a somewhat anomalous 'cultural factor' had to be called upon at certain points. Some of those events did not seem to agree with what was to be expected from the behaviour of a 'rational man'. That is what made demographers appeal to the cultural factor. It is our expectations, or the demographers' expectations, as to what should and what should not be rational that cause the appearance of the cultural factor in the explanation of human conduct. It could be argued that the irrationality that demographers have identified in Irish population history confirms the epistemological autonomy of cultural forms that I have postulated. But the capacity of a cultural form to make intelligible certain demographic facts is directly correlated to the demographers' incapacity to provide a fully 'rational' account of these facts. In other words, when I talk about the autonomy of cultural forms it is precisely the alleged power of culture to 'cause' things that I am questioning. Once again, we can envisage the possibility of committing the same category mistake in the demographers' use of culture as an explanatory factor of demographic events: in so far as we put culture on a par with social and economic forces, as if under certain circumstances individuals' behaviour was the result of some mysterious cultural pressures whereas under other circumstances it was merely the consequence of social and economic forces. Whatever credit we might attribute to the notion that social and economic forces cause people to behave in a certain way, this notion should certainly not be extrapolated to culture.

Now what is this cultural factor and how can we relate it to actual conducts? The answer to this question came in chapters 7 and 9, and the impossibility of taking culture as the cause of any human conduct was theoretically argued in chapter 8. In chapter 7 we saw that cultural understandings of sexual morality, of the proper way of conducting one's sexual life, originated in a certain view of history. I do not think that all cultural forms include historical knowledge in their configuration, but it is clear that at least in Western societies people tend to think about their present condition in historical terms, as a result of what has happened to them, to their society or their community in the past. Now, what can we make of this historical knowledge and the sort of cultural structures into which it crystallises? In chapter 7 I drew a distinction between objective and subjective histories, even though I pointed out that the boundaries between the two are always fuzzy. Objective and subjective histories are dialectically related in a double sense. First, subjective histories can be seen as the product of objective histories. People's understanding of their own past is based on their own personal experience, on oral narratives and on written histories learned at school, from the media, from history books, etc. In other words, the objective history written by historians is, to some extent at least, filtered down to ordinary people's understanding of their own past and turned into a form of historical consciousness, into subjective history. But because this model of history is also used as a model for history, i.e. people's actual behaviour, what in the last instance gives rise to historical facts is moulded, is signified, by their own historical consciousness. Then we can say that objective histories are equally the product of subjective histories.

But 'to be signified by' does not mean 'to be a consequence of'. Historical events are contingent because human action is unpredictable, and no amount of social science can challenge such an elementary truth. The fact that in our day-to-day life we can normally guess what other people will do does not contradict this statement. Our guesses are not based on knowledge of certain laws, like the weather forecast, for instance, but on the meaningfulness of our interlocutor's activity. I can imagine that my students will not jump out of the window in the middle of a lecture, not because I have come to know the neurophysiological law that regulates their bodily movements in the classroom, but simply because such conduct would be entirely meaningless in that context. It is the potential meaningfulness or meaninglessness of an individual's behaviour that enables us to have guesses as regards what he or she will do. This is the 'coercion' of meaning that we have analysed in chapters 8 and 9.

Culture is what enables us to confer meaning upon social action, thus culture can never determine, or 'cause', human behaviour. Knowing a particular culture does not involve knowing what this or that people will do; the relationship between culture and history is not causal but semiotic, as I have argued in different parts of this essay. Now how do we discover culture? At some point I contended that the discovery of culture is different from the discovery of natural entities. Perhaps a distinction between meaning and culture is in order now: meaning is simply culture 'as lived', it is culture from the native's point of view, whereas culture is meaning from the anthropologist's point of view, or meaning 'as thought of'. Again, it is all a matter of perspectives. But I believe this distinction is necessary in order to account for the discovery of culture through a research process: ethnographic research. We do not discover the meanings that rule over our social life, we simply live them, we are born and grown into them, they are 'natural' to us. That is why we tend to believe that we – Westerners, anthropologists – do not have culture: only the others – primitives, natives – do. We have reason in its stead. This is the optical illusion, so to speak, provoked by ethnographic research. But it is a necessary optical illusion, even though we need to be aware of its illusory nature. Remember the distinction between sexuality-obedience and sexuality-knowledge that I discussed in chapter 9. From my point of view – and (hopefully) from the reader's point of view too – both disciplinary regimes can be seen as cultural structures that confer meaning upon specific sexual events or sexual acts. And as such they are both equally arbitrary. But, from my informants' point of view, only sexuality-obedience, the disciplinary regime of the past, could be considered as arbitrary; only sexuality-obedience was 'culture' whereas sexuality-knowledge was simply 'reason'. Sexual acts done under the regime of sexuality-knowledge did not need any culture to be accounted for, they were simply rational acts. A demographer working under a sexuality-knowledge regime would not need any culture to account for the demographic events subsequent to those rational acts. But an anthropologist can disclose the cultural structures underlying that rational behaviour, simply by a change in perspective.

And what do we gain from this different viewpoint?

This book ends with a perspectivist concept of culture: we see culture when we look at human behaviour form a certain standpoint but we no longer see it if we shift our location. The existence of culture, or, rather, its visibility, depends on the observer's point of view and not on the thing being observed. What happens when we see culture? We simply make our experience intelligible in a certain way. By means of this perspectivist notion we can define the sexual meanings that have been disclosed in the previous analysis as a structure of intelligibility.[1] No pernicious power, no repressive instance, precludes us from reaching those sexual meanings. No emancipatory effect can be achieved by that disclosure (or not necessarily). The effect is merely intellectual: by seeing a particular form of sexual morality behind certain discourses and institutions we do not become 'freer'. We simply learn to look at things in a different way. Now the purpose of this shifting of perspectives can be commensurability, which is another way of talking about intelligibility. Commensurability does not lead to emancipation, the sociological counterpart to psychological therapy, because we do not start with a pathological condition brought about by repression. The 'distorted communication' that gives rise to an ethnographic enquiry is not the result of any pathological state but of cultural distance. Anthropology can be seen as a way of bridging that cultural distance without obliterating it, because anthropology, unlike psychoanalysis or critical hermeneutics, let me put it this way, 'leaves everything as it is'.

Note

1. '[L]'effort proprement scientifique consiste à décomposer, puis à recomposer suivant un autre plan' [The properly scientific endeavour consists of decomposing and then recomposing according to a different plan] (Lévi-Strauss 1962: 331).

BIBLIOGRAPHY

Arensberg, C.M. 1937. *The Irish Countryman*. London: Macmillan.

Arensberg, C.M. and S.T. Kimball. 2001 (1940, 1968). *Family and Community in Ireland*. 3rd edition. Ennis: Clasp Press.

Barnard, A. 2000. *History and Theory in Anthropology*. Cambridge: Cambridge University Press.

Barrett, S.R., S. Stokholm and J. Burke. 2001. 'The Idea of Power and the Power of Ideas: A Review Essay'. *American Anthropologist*, vol. 103, no. 2: 468–80.

Bauman, Z. 1999 (1973). *Culture as Praxis*. 2nd edition. London: Sage.

Berger, P. and T. Luckmann. 1966. *The Social Construction of Reality. A Treatise in the Sociology of Knowledge*. Harmondsworth: Penguin Books.

Birdwell-Pheasant, D. 1992. 'The Early Twentieth-Century Irish Stem Family: A Case Study from County Kerry'. In M. Silverman and P.H. Gulliver, eds. *Approaching the Past. Historical Anthropology through Irish Case Studies*. New York: Columbia University Press.

Black, J. 1997. 'Taking the Sex out of Sexuality: Foucault's Failed History'. In D.H.J. Larmour, P.A. Miller and C. Platter, eds. *Rethinking Sexuality. Foucault and Classical Antiquity*. Princeton: Princeton University Press.

Bolin, A. and P. Whelehan. 1999. *Perspectives on Human Sexuality*. Albany: State University of New York Press.

Boon, J.A. 1982. *Other Tribes, Other Scribes. Symbolic Anthropology in the Comparative Study of Cultures, Histories, Religions, and Texts*. Cambridge: Cambridge University Press.

Bourdieu, P. 2002. *Le Bal des célibataires. Crise de la société paysanne en Béarn*. Paris: Éditions du Seuil.

Breen, R. 1984. 'Dowry Payments and the Irish Case'. *Comparative Studies in Society and History*, vol. 26, no. 2: 280–96.

Brody, H. 1973. *Inishkillane. Change and Decline in the West of Ireland*. London and Boston: Faber and Faber.

Brown, P. 1988. *The Body and Society. Men, Women and Sexual Renunciation in Early Christianity*. New York: Columbia University Press.

Buckley, A. 1989. '"We're Trying to Find our Identity": Uses of History among Ulster Protestants'. In E. Tonkin and M. McDonald, eds. *History and Ethnicity*. London: Routledge.

Caplan, P. 1987. Introduction to P. Caplan, ed. *The Cultural Construction of Sexuality*. London: Routledge.

Clancy, P. 1992. 'Continuity and Change in Irish Demographic Patterns'. In P. Clancy, M. Kelly, J. Wiatr and R. Zoltaniecki, eds. *Ireland and Poland: Comparative Perspectives*. Dublin: University College of Dublin.

Coale, A.J. and S.C. Watkins, eds. 1986. *The Decline of Fertility in Europe*. Princeton: Princeton University Press.

Coleman, D.A. 1992. 'The Demographic Transition in Ireland in International Context'. *Proceedings of the British Academy*, no. 79: 53–77.

Collard, A. 1989. 'Investigating "Social Memory" in a Greek Context'. In E. Tonkin and M. McDonald, eds. *History and Ethnicity*. London: Routledge.

Collier, J.F. 1997. *From Duty to Desire. Remaking Families in a Spanish Village*. Princeton, N.J.: Princeton University Press.

Compton, P.A. 1982. 'Fertility, Nationality and Religion in Northern Ireland'. In D.A. Coleman, ed. *Demography of Immigrants and Minority Groups in the United Kingdom*. London: Academic Press.

Connell, K.H. 1957. 'Peasant Marriage in Ireland after the Great Famine'. *Past and Present*, no. 12: 76–91.

————. 1962. 'Peasant Marriage in Ireland: the Structure and Development since the Famine'. *The Economic History Review*. Second Series. vol. 14, no. 3: 502–23.

————. 1965. 'Land and Population in Ireland. 1780–1845'. In D.V. Glass and D.E.C. Eversley, eds. *Population in History*. London: Edward Arnold.

————. 1968. *Irish Peasant Society. Four Historical Essays*. Oxford: Clarendon Press.

Connolly, S.J. 1979. 'Illegitimacy and Pre-Nuptial Pregnancy in Ireland before 1864: the Evidence of some Catholic Parish Registers'. *Irish Economic and Social History*, vol. 6: 5–23.

————. 1985. 'Marriage in Pre-Famine Ireland'. In A. Cosgrove, ed. *Marriage in Ireland*. Dublin: College Press.

————. 2001 (1982). *Priests and People in Pre-Famine Ireland, 1780–1845*. 2nd edition. Dublin: Four Courts Press.

Coulter, C. 1997. '"Hello Divorce, Goodbye Daddy": Women, Gender, and the Divorce Debate'. In A. Bradley and M.G. Valiulis, eds. *Gender and Sexuality in Modern Ireland*. Amherst: University of Massachusetts Press.

Coward, J. 1980. 'Recent Characteristics of Roman Catholic Fertility in Northern and Southern Ireland'. *Population Studies*, vol. 34, no. 1: 31–44.

Davis, D.L. and R.G. Whitten. 1987. 'The Cross-Cultural Study of Human Sexuality'. *Annual Review of Anthropology*, vol. 16: 69–98.

Dreyfus, H.L. and P. Rabinow. 1983. *Michel Foucault. Beyond Structuralism and Hermeneutics*. Chicago: University of Chicago Press.

Durkheim, E. 1915. *The Elementary Forms of the Religious Life*. London: George Allen and Unwin.

Durkheim, E. 1974. *Sociology and Philosophy*. New York: The Free Press.

Elliston, D.A. 1995. 'Erotic Anthropology: "Ritualized Homosexuality" in Melanesia and Beyond'. *American Ethnologist*, vol. 22, no. 4: 848–67.

Evans-Pritchard, E.E. 1956. *Nuer Religion*. Oxford: Oxford University Press.

————. 1962. *Essays in Social Anthropology*. London: Faber and Faber.

Fabian, J. 2002 (1983). *Time and the Other. How Anthropology Makes its Object.* 2nd edition. New York: Columbia University Press.

Fahey, T. and H. Russell. 2001. *Family Formation in Ireland. Trends, Data Needs and Implications.* Dublin: The Economic and Social Research Institute.

Fitzpatrick, D. 1983. 'Irish Farming Families before the First World War'. *Comparative Studies in Society and History*, no. 25: 339–74.

————. 1985. 'Marriage in Post-Famine Ireland'. In A. Cosgrove, ed. *Marriage in Ireland.* Dublin: College Press.

Flandrin, J-L. 1983. *Un Temps pour embrasser. Aux origines de la morale sexuelle occidentale (VI–XI siècle).* Paris: Seuil.

Foucault, M. 1972. *The Archaeology of Knowledge.* London: Tavistock Publications.

————. 1977. *Discipline and Punish. The Birth of the Prison.* Harmondsworth: Penguin Books.

————. 1978. *The History of Sexuality. An Introduction.* Harmondsworth: Penguin Books.

————. 1980. 'The Confession of the Flesh'. In *Power/Knowledge. Selected Interviews and Other Writings, 1972–1977.* London: Harvester.

————. 1983a. 'The Subject and Power'. In H.L. Dreyfus and P. Rabinow, *Michel Foucault: Beyond Structuralism and Hermeneutics.* Chicago: University of Chicago Press.

————. 1983b. 'On the Genealogy of Ethics: An Overview of Work in Progress'. In H.L. Dreyfus and P. Rabinow, *Michel Foucault: Beyond Structuralism and Hermeneutics.* Chicago: University of Chicago Press.

————. 1985. *The Use of Pleasure. History of Sexuality, vol. II.* Harmondsworth: Penguin Books.

————. 1986. *The Care of the Self. History of Sexuality, vol. III.* Harmondsworth: Penguin Books.

————. 1991. 'Governmentality'. In G. Burchell, C. Gordon and P. Miller, eds. *The Foucault Effect. Studies in Governmentality.* Chicago: University of Chicago Press.

Fox, R.G. and B.J. King, eds. 2002. *Anthropology beyond Culture.* Oxford: Berg.

Frayser, S.G. 1999. 'Human Sexuality: The Whole Is More than the Sum of Its Parts'. In D.N. Suggs and A.W. Miracle, eds. *Culture, Biology, and Sexuality.* Athens and London: University of Georgia Press.

Freeman, D. 1983. *Margaret Mead and Samoa. The Making and Unmaking of an Anthropological Myth.* Cambridge, Mass.: Harvard University Press.

Frege, G. 1960. 'On Sense and Reference'. In P. Leach and M. Black, eds. *Translations from the Philosophical Writings of Gottlob Frege.* Oxford: Basil Blackwell.

Freud, S. 1953. 'Three Essays on the Theory of Sexuality'. In *The Standard Edition of the Complete Psychological Works of Sigmund Freud.* Vol. VII. London: Hogarth Press and the Institute of Psycho-Analysis.

————. 1959. '"Civilized" Sexual Morality and Modern Nervous Illness'. In *The Standard Edition of the Complete Psychological Works of Sigmund Freud.* Vol. IX. London: Hogarth Press and the Institute of Psycho-Analysis.

————. 1961. 'Civilization and its Discontents'. In *The Standard Edition of the Complete Psychological Works of Sigmund Freud*. Vol. XXI. London: Hogarth Press and the Institute of Psycho-Analysis.

————. 1963. 'Introductory Lectures on Psycho-Analysis'. In *The Standard Edition of the Complete Psychological Works of Sigmund Freud*. Vol. XVI. London: Hogarth Press and the Institute of Psycho-Analysis.

————. 1964. 'New Introductory Lectures on Psycho-Analysis'. In *The Standard Edition of the Complete Psychological Works of Sigmund Freud*. Vol. XXII. London: Hogarth Press and the Institute of Psycho-Analysis.

Friedl, E. 1994. 'Sex the Invisible'. *American Anthropologist*, vol. 96: 833–44.

Frigolé, J. 1998. 'Procreation and its Implications for Gender, Marriage, and Family in European Rural Ethnography'. *Anthropological Quarterly*, vol. 71, no. 1: 32–40.

Gadamer, H.G. 1989. *Truth and Method*. London: Sheed and Ward.

García Düttmann, A. 2000. *Between Cultures. Tensions in the Struggle for Recognition*. London: Verso.

Geertz, C. 1973. *The Interpretation of Cultures*. New York: Basic Books.

————. 1983. *Local Knowledge. Further Essays in Interpretative Anthropology*. New York: Basic Books.

Gellner, E. 1957. 'Ideal Language and Kinship Structure'. *Philosophy of Science*, vol. 24: 235–42.

————. 1973. *Cause and Meaning in the Social Sciences*. London: Routledge and Kegan Paul.

————. 1979. *Spectacles and Predicaments. Essays in Social Theory*. Cambridge: Cambridge University Press.

————. 1995. *Anthropology and Politics. Revolutions in the Sacred Grove*. Oxford: Basil Blackwell.

Gibbon, P. 1973. 'Arensberg and Kimball Revisited'. *Economy and Society*, vol. 2, no. 4: 479–98.

Gibbon, P. and C. Curtin. 1978. 'The Stem Family in Ireland'. *Comparative Studies in Society and History*, no. 20: 429–53.

Gibbon, P. and C. Curtin. 1983. 'Irish Farm Families: Facts and Fantasies'. *Comparative Studies in Society and History*, no. 25: 375–80.

Giddens, A. 1995. *Politics, Sociology and Social Theory. Encounters with Classical and Contemporary Social Thought*. Cambridge: Polity Press.

Goddard, V.A. 1996. *Gender, Family and Work in Naples*. Oxford: Berg.

Godelier, M. 2003. 'What is a Sexual Act?' *Anthropological Theory*, vol. 3, no. 2: 179–98.

Good, B.J. 1994. *Medicine, Rationality, and Experience. An Anthropological Perspective*. Cambridge: Cambridge University Press.

Goodenough, W.H. 1994. 'Toward a Working Theory of Culture'. In R. Borofski, ed. *Assessing Cultural Anthropology*. New York: McGraw Hill.

————. 1973. 'Bridewealth and Dowry in Africa and Eurasia'. In J. Goody and S.J. Tambiah, eds. *Bridewealth and Dowry*. Cambridge: Cambridge University Press.

Goody, J. 1983. *The Development of the Family and Marriage in Europe*. Cambridge: Cambridge University Press.

Greenhalgh, S. 1995. 'Anthropology Theorizes Reproduction: Integrating Practice, Political Economy, and Feminist Perspectives'. In S. Greenhalgh ed. *Situating Fertility. Anthropology and Demographic Inquiry*. Cambridge: Cambridge University Press.

Grillo, R.D. 2003. 'Cultural Essentialism and Cultural Anxiety'. *Anthropological Theory*, vol. 3, no. 2: 157–73.

Guinnane, T.W. 1997. *The Vanishing Irish. Household, Migration, and the Rural Economy in Ireland, 1850–1914*. Princeton, N.J.: Princeton University Press.

Habermas, J. 1987. *Knowledge and Human Interests*. Cambridge: Polity Press.

Hajnal, J. 1965. 'European Marriage Patterns in Perspective'. In D.V. Glass and D.E.C. Eversley, eds. *Population in History*. London: Edward Arnold.

Handwerker, W.P. ed. 1986. *Culture and Reproduction. An Anthropological Critique of Demographic Transition Theory*. Boulder and London: Westview Press.

Hannerz, U. 1993. 'When Culture is Everywhere. Reflections on a Favourite Concept'. *Ethnos*, vol. 1–2: 95–111.

Harris, M. 1968. *The Rise of Anthropological Theory*. New York: Thomas Y. Crowell.

Harris, M. and E.B. Ross. 1987. *Death, Sex, and Fertility. Population Regulation in Preindustrial and Developing Societies*. New York: Columbia University Press.

Harris, R. 1988. 'Theory and Evidence: The "Irish Stem Family" and Field Data'. *Man* (N.S.), vol. 23, no. 3: 417–34.

Herdt, G.H. 1984a. 'Ritualized Homosexual Behavior in Male Cults of Melanesia, 1862–1983: An Introduction'. In G. Herdt, ed. *Ritualized Homosexuality in Melanesia*. Berkeley and Los Angeles: University of California Press.

———. 1984b. 'Semen Transactions in Sambia Culture'. In G.H. Herdt, ed. *Ritualized Homosexuality in Melanesia*. Berkeley and Los Angeles: University of California Press.

———. 1993. 'Sexual Repression, Social Control, and Gender Hierarchy in Sambia Culture'. In B.D. Miller, ed. *Sex and Gender Hierarchies*. Cambridge: Cambridge University Press.

———. 1994. *Guardians of the Flutes. Idioms of Masculinity*. Chicago: University of Chicago Press.

———. 1999a. *Sambia Sexual Culture. Essays from the Field*. Chicago: University of Chicago Press.

———. 1999b. 'Sexing Anthropology: Rethinking Sexual Culture, Subjectivity, and the Method of Anthropological Participant Observation'. In D.N. Suggs and A.W. Miracle, eds. *Culture, Biology, and Sexuality*. Athens and London: University of Georgia Press.

Herdt, G.H. and R.J. Stoller. 1990. *Intimate Communications. Erotics and the Study of Culture*. New York: Columbia University Press.

Hug, C. 1999. *The Politics of Sexual Morality in Ireland*. London: Macmillan Press.

Humphreys, A.J. 1966. *New Dubliners. Urbanization and the Irish Family*. London: Routledge.

Inglis, T. 1997. 'Foucault, Bourdieu and the Field of Irish Sexuality'. *Irish Journal of Sociology*, vol. 7: 5–28.

———. 1998a (1987). *Moral Monopoly. The Rise and Fall of the Catholic Church in Modern Ireland*. 2nd edition. Dublin: University College Press.

———. 1998b. *Lessons in Irish Sexuality*. Dublin: University College Press.

———. 1998c. 'From Sexual Repression to Sexual Liberation'. In M. Peillon and E. Slater, eds. *Encounters with Modern Ireland. A Sociological Chronicle 1995–1996*. Dublin: Institute of Public Administration.

Jarvie, I.C. 1967. *The Revolution in Anthropology*. London: Routledge and Kegan Paul.

Kennedy, F. 2001. *Cottage to Crèche. Family Change in Ireland*. Dublin: Institute of Public Administration.

Kennedy, R.E. 1973a. *The Irish. Emigration, Marriage, and Fertility*. Berkeley: University of California Press.

———. 1973b. 'Minority Group Status and Fertility: the Irish'. *American Sociological Review*, vol. 38, no. 1: 85–96.

Kertzer, D.I. 1995. 'Political-Economic and Cultural Explanations of Demographic Behavior'. In S. Greenhalgh, ed. *Situating Fertility. Anthropology and Demographic Inquiry*. Cambridge: Cambridge University Press.

Kulick, D. 1995. 'The Sexual Life of Anthropologists: Erotic Subjectivity and Ethnographic Fieldwork'. In D. Kulick and M. Willson, eds. *Taboo. Sex, Identity and Erotic Subjectivity in Anthropological Fieldwork*. London: Routledge.

Lacqueur, T. 1990. *Making Sex. Body and Gender from the Greeks to Freud*. Cambridge, Mass.: Harvard University Press.

Latour, B. 1993. *We Have Never Been Moderns*. New York: Harvester Wheatsheaf.

Layton, R. 1998. *An Introduction to Theory in Anthropology*. Cambridge: Cambridge University Press.

Leach, E.R. 1964. *Political Systems of High-Land Burma. A Study of Kachin Social Structure*. London: Athlone Press.

Lee, J. 1973. *The Modernisation of Irish Society 1848–1918*. Dublin: Gill and Macmillan.

Lévi-Strauss, C. 1962. *La Pensée sauvage*. Paris: Plon.

———. 1963. *Structural Anthropology 1*. Harmondsworth: Penguin Books.

———. 1969. *The Elementary Structures of Kinship*. Boston: Beacon Press.

Lewis, I.M. ed. 1968. *History and Social Anthropology*. London: Tavistock Publications.

Leyton, E.H. 1975. 'The One Blood. Kinship and Class in an Irish Village'. *Newfoundland Social and Economic Studies*, no. 15.

Lukes, S. 1985. *Durkheim. His Life and his Work. A Historical and Critical Study*. Stanford: Stanford University Press.

McCourt, F. 1996. *Angela's Ashes. A Memoir of a Childhood*. London: Flamingo.

Macfarlane, A. 1986. *Marriage and Love in England. Modes of Reproduction 1300–1400*. Oxford: Basil Blackwell.

McLaren, A. 1990. *A History of Contraception from Antiquity to the Present Day*. Oxford: Basil Blackwell.

McLoughlin, D. 1994. 'Women and Sexuality in Nineteenth-Century Ireland'. *Irish Journal of Psychology*, vol. 15, no. 2–3: 266–75.

Mahon, E., C. Conlon and L. Dillon. 1998. *Women and Crisis Pregnancy. A Report Presented to the Department of Health and Children*. Dublin: Stationery Office.

Malinowski, B. 1929. *The Sexual Life of Savages in North Western Melanesia*. New York: Harcourt, Brace and World.

———. 2001 (1927) *Sex and Repression in Savage Society*. London: Routledge.

Marcuse, H. 1987 (1956). *Eros and Civilisation. A Philosophical Inquiry into Freud*. London: ARK Paperbacks.

Martínez-Hernáez, A. 2000. *What's Behind the Symptom? On Psychiatric Observation and Anthropological Understanding*. Singapore: Harwood Academic Press.

Mead, M. 1928. *Coming of Age in Samoa*. New York: William Morrow.

Messenger, J.C. 1969. *Inis Beag, Isle of Ireland*. New York: Holt, Rinehart, and Winston.

———. 1971. 'Sex and Repression in an Irish Folk Community'. In D.S. Marshall and R.C. Suggs, eds. *Human Sexual Behavior*. New Jersey: Prentice-Hall.

Mokyr, J. 1980. 'Malthusian Models and Irish History'. *Journal of Economic History*, vol. 40, no. 1: 159–66.

Moore, H.L. ed. 1999. *Anthropological Theory Today*. Cambridge: Polity Press.

Morgan, L.H. 1868. 'A Conjectural Solution of the Origin of the Classificatory System of Relationships'. *Proceedings of the American Academy of Arts and Sciences*, vol. VII: 436–77.

Needham, R. 1971. 'Remarks on the Analysis of Kinship and Marriage'. In R. Needham, ed. *Rethinking Kinship and Marriage*. London: Tavistock Publications.

———. 1972. *Belief, Language, and Experience*. Chicago: University of Chicago Press.

Nugent, D. 1985. 'Anthropology, Handmaiden of History'. *Critique of Anthropology*, vol. 15, no. 2: 71–86.

Obeyesekere, G. 1990. *The Work of Culture. Symbolic Transformation in Psychoanalysis and Anthropology*. Chicago: University of Chicago Press.

Ó Gráda, C. 1985. 'Did Ulster Catholics Always Have Larger Families?' *Irish Economic and Social History*, no. XII: 79–88.

———. 1991. 'New Evidence on the Fertility Transition in Ireland 1880–1911'. *Demography*, vol. 28, no. 4: 535–48.

———. 1994. *Ireland: a New Economic History 1780–1939*. Oxford: Clarendon Press.

Ó Gráda, C. and N. Duffy. 1995. 'Fertility Control Early in Marriage in Ireland a Century Ago'. *Journal of Population Economics*, no. 8: 423–31.

Ó Gráda, C. and B. Walsh. 1995. 'Fertility and Population in Ireland, North and South'. *Population Studies*, no. 49: 259–79.

O'Neill, B.J. 1987. *Social Inequality in a Portuguese Hamlet*. Cambridge: Cambridge University Press.

O'Neill, K. 1984. *Family and Farm in Pre-Famine Ireland.* Madison, Wisconsin: University of Wisconsin Press.

Ortner, S.B. and H. Whitehead. 1981. 'Accounting for Sexual Meanings'. In S.B. Ortner and H. Whitehead, eds. *Sexual Meanings. The Cultural Construction of Gender and Sexuality.* Cambridge: Cambridge University Press.

Pálsson, G. 1993. Introduction to G. Pálsson, ed. *Beyond Boundaries. Understanding, Translation and Anthropological Discourse.* Oxford: Berg.

Peristiany, J.G. ed. 1965. *Honour and Shame: the Values of Mediterranean Society.* London: Weidenfeld and Nicolson.

Plummer, K. 1995. *Telling Sexual Stories: Power, Change, and Social Worlds.* London: Routledge.

Radcliffe-Brown, A.R. 1952. *Structure and Function in Primitive Society.* London and Henley: Routledge and Kegan Paul.

Ricoeur, P. 1970. *Freud and Philosophy. An Essay on Interpretation.* London: Yale University Press.

———. 1981. *Hermeneutics and the Human Sciences.* Cambridge: Cambridge University Press.

Roseberry, W. 1982. 'Balinese Cockfights and the Seduction of Anthropology'. *Social Research*, vol. 49, no. 4: 1013–28.

Ross, E.B. 1986. 'Potatoes, Population, and the Irish Famine: The Political Economy of Demographic Change'. In W.P. Handwerker, ed. *Culture and Reproduction. An Anthropological Critique of Demographic Transition Theory.* Boulder and London: Westview Press.

Ross, E. and R. Rapp. 1981. 'Sex and Society: a Research Note from Social History and Anthropology'. *Comparative Studies in Society and History*, vol. 23, no. 1: 51–72.

Russell, A. 2001. 'Teenage Pregnancy and the Moral Geography of Teesside, UK'. In S. Tremayne, ed. *Managing Reproductive Life. Cross-Cultural Themes in Sexuality and Fertility.* Oxford: Berghahn Books.

Russell, A. and M.S. Thompson. 2000. Introduction to A. Russell, E.J. Sobo and M.S. Thompson, eds. *Contraception across Cultures.* Oxford: Berg.

Ryle, G. 1949. *The Concept of Mind.* London: Penguin Books.

Sahlins, M. 1985. *Islands of History.* Chicago: University of Chicago Press.

———. 2000a. *Culture in Practice. Selected Essays.* New York: Zone Books.

———. 2000b. '"Sentimental Pessimism" and Ethnographic Experience. Or Why Culture is not a Disappearing "Object"'. In L. Daston, ed. *Biographies of Scientific Objects.* Chicago: University of Chicago Press.

Salazar, C. 1996. *A Sentimental Economy. Commodity and Community in Rural Ireland.* Oxford: Berghahn.

———. 1998. 'Identities in Ireland. History, Ethnicity and the Nation-State'. *European Journal of Cultural Studies*, vol. 1, no. 3: 369–85.

———. 1999. 'On Blood and its Alternatives. An Irish History'. *Social Anthropology*, vol. 7, no. 2: 155–67.

Santow, G. 1995. '*Coitus Interruptus* and the Control of Natural Fertility'. *Population Studies*, no. 49: 19–43.

Saussure, F. 1966. *Course in General Linguistics.* New York: McGraw Hill.

Scheper-Hughes, N. 1983. 'From Anxiety to Analysis: Rethinking Irish Sexuality and Sex Roles'. *Women's Studies*, vol. 10: 147–60.

———. 2001 (1977). *Saints, Scholars and Schizophrenics. Mental Illness in Rural Ireland*. Y2000 edition. Berkeley: University of California Press.

Schneider, D.M. 1980 (1968). *American Kinship. A Cultural Account*. 2nd edition. Chicago and London: University of Chicago Press.

Schneider, J. 1971. 'Of Vigilance and Virgins: Honor, Shame and Access to Resources in Mediterranean Societies'. *Ethnology*, vol. 10, no. 1: 1–24.

Schneider, J., and P. Schneider. 1984. 'Demographic Transitions in a Sicilian Rural Town'. *Journal of Family History*, vol. 9: 245–72.

Schneider, J. and P. Schneider. 1991. 'Sex and Respectability in an Age of Fertility Decline: A Sicilian Case Study'. *Social Science Medicine*, vol. 33, no. 8: 885–95.

Searle, J.R. 1995. *The Construction of Social Reality*. London: Penguin Books.

Sewell, W.H. 1999. 'Geertz, Cultural Systems, and History'. In S.B. Ortner, ed. *The Fate of 'Culture'. Geertz and Beyond*. Berkeley: University of California Press.

Shanklin, E. 1985. *Donegal's Changing Traditions. An Ethnographic Study*. New York: Gordon and Breach Science Publishers.

Shorter, E. 1977. *The Making of the Modern Family*. New York: Basic Books.

Simon, W. 1996. *Postmodern Sexualities*. London: Routledge.

Smyth, F. 1998. 'Cultural Constraints on the Delivery of HIV/AIDS Prevention in Ireland'. *Social Science Medicine*, no. 6: 661–72.

Stewart, C. 2002. 'Erotic Dreams and Nightmares from Antiquity to the Present'. *Journal of the Royal Anthropological Institute* (N.S.), vol. 8: 279–309.

Stone, L. 1977. *The Family, Sex and Marriage in England 1500–1800*. London: Weidenfeld and Nicolson.

Strathern, M. 1995. 'Foreword: Shifting Contexts'. In M. Strathern, ed. *Shifting Contexts. Transformations in Anthropological Knowledge*. London: Routledge.

———. 1996. 'Cutting the Network', *Journal of the Royal Anthropological Institute* (N.S.), vol. 2, no. 3: 517–35.

Suggs, D.N. and A.W. Miracle. 1999. 'Theory and the Anthropology of Sexuality: Toward a Holistic Approach in Practice'. In D.N. Suggs and A.W. Miracle, eds. *Culture, Biology, and Sexuality*. Athens and London: University of Georgia Press.

Sweetman, R. 1979. *On Our Backs. Sexual Attitudes in a Changing Ireland*. London: Pan Books.

Synge, J.M. 1979. *The Aran Islands*. Oxford: Oxford University Press.

Tanney, J. 1998. 'Investigating Cultures: A Critique of Cognitive Anthropology'. *Journal of the Royal Anthropological Institute* (N.S.), vol. 4, no. 4: 669–88.

Taylor, L.J. 1995. *Occasions of Faith. An Anthropology of Irish Catholics*. Dublin: Lilliput Press.

Tremayne, S. 2001. Introduction to S. Tremayne, ed. *Managing Reproductive Life. Cross-Cultural Themes in Sexuality and Fertility*. Oxford: Berghahn Books.

Turner, T. 1993. 'Anthropology and Multiculturalism: What is Anthropology that Multiculturalists should be Mindful of it?'. *Cultural Anthropology*, vol. 8, no. 4: 411–29.

Vance, C.S. 1991. 'Anthropology Rediscovers Sexuality: A Theoretical Comment'. *Social Science Medicine*, vol. 33, no. 8: 875–84.

Varley, T. 1983. '"The Stem Family in Ireland" Reconsidered'. *Comparative Studies in Society and History*, no. 25: 381–92.

Walsh, B.M. 1985. 'Marriage in Ireland in the Twentieth Century'. In A. Cosgrove, ed. *Marriage in Ireland*. Dublin: College Press.

Weeks, J. 1989. *Sex, Politics and Society. The Regulation of Sexuality since 1800*. London and New York: Longman.

———. 2003 (1986). *Sexuality*. 2nd edition. London: Routledge.

Whorf, B.L. 1956. *Language, Thought and Reality*. Cambridge, Mass.: MIT Press.

Whyte, J.H. 1980. *Church and State in Modern Ireland 1923–1979*. 2nd edition. Dublin: Gill and Macmillan.

Winch, P. 1970. 'Understanding a Primitive Society'. In B.R. Wilson, ed. *Rationality*. Oxford: Basil Blackwell.

Wittgenstein, L. 1958. *Philosophical Investigations*. Oxford: Basil Blackwell.

———. 1969. *The Blue and the Brown Books. Preliminary Studies for the 'Philosophical Investigations'*. Oxford: Basil Blackwell.

Wolf, E.R. 1999. *Envisioning Power. Ideologies of Dominance and Crisis*. Berkeley: University of California Press.

INDEX